Judith Arcana is pr...
Studies in The Grad...
Institute in the United States. She is the author of
Our Mothers' Daughters (The Women's Press,
1981).

Also by Judith Arcana from The Women's Press:

Our Mothers' Daughters (1981)

Judith Arcana
Every Mother's Son

The rôle of mothers in the making of men

The Women's Press

Published in Great Britain by The Women's Press Ltd, 1983
A member of the Namara Group
34 Great Sutton Street, London EC1V 0DX

Reprinted 1984, 1992, 1996

First published in the United States of America by
Anchor Press/Doubleday, 1983

British Library Cataloguing-in-Publication Data
Arcana, Judith
    Every mother's son.
    1. Mothers and sons
    1. Title
    306.8'743 HQ755.85

ISBN 0 7043 3916 1

Printed and bound in Great Britain
by BPC Paperbacks Ltd

*This book is for my son Daniel, who is
both the question and answer*

Contents

Preface

This book has been hard to write. The main reason for that is the subject, which, no matter how much I am talking about other people, even people in books or movies or legends, is my relationship with my son, Daniel. This book is about what it means to mothers to raise male children, especially now, during this wave of the women's movement, and the fact is that I am writing it because I am one of those mothers. Daniel understood this all along; he consistently referred to the book as "the one about *me*."

So a constant irony was that when, like any mother, my motherhood interfered with my work, the work was about the child who was interrupting the work. Raising my son was keeping me from writing this book about raising sons. But that was one of my sources of strength too, for I was always seeing the book's progress through the filter of my day-by-day struggle with Daniel, and I came to see that struggle through the insight and knowledge gained by writing the book.

I experienced a lot of fear and a sense of helplessness in trying to write both my feelings and the politics of the situation into a book. I worried about the impact on Daniel; I had to censor and guard myself, to protect his young privacy. Writing about mothers and daughters in my first book, two years into it I found myself swept along by a huge wave, a movement within a movement, of women who were studying, remembering, working on their relations with their mothers. We were all doing it at once; it was time. But with this book, no such wave has lifted and carried me. Instead, I feel something like Yossarian, in *Catch-22*, when all the secret supporters popped out to wish him well, to tell him they were on his side, and then disappeared. Everywhere I go to speak and teach, women ask me, "What about the boys?" But we are just beginning to confront the fear and anger that comprise the predicament of mothers of sons.

Mothers and sons? Do they go together? Isn't it supposed to be *fathers* and sons, mothers and *daughters?* The idea of a mother and son reunion makes people uncomfortable; somehow it doesn't seem right. I've learned that we mothers of sons are afraid, afraid to try to influence male character, afraid of being blamed. We are hesitant to make too big an impact, or to be too visible in our sons' lives—at the same time that we are desperate to do so, longing to build bridges between ourselves and our male children.

I interviewed sixty mothers and sixty sons in the first year of working on this book. The book contains the words of slightly more than half that number. They are of various races, ages, religions, and classes. Some of them are mother-and-son pairs; some of the men are brothers. Though most of the people, most of the time, told me the truth—that is, told me what they tell themselves—some did not. Some told me the lies they use for the public; some told me what they thought I wanted to hear, or what they thought I ought to be hearing. Their words make up a good part of this book, and much of my work here is inspired by what I learned from them; I am grateful to them all, as I owe a great debt to the women and men whose work has come before mine, inspiring and teaching me.

Over the last three years, several friends have encouraged me, making suggestions, giving criticism, lending materials, helping me to see more and more clearly what I wanted to do in this book: Susan Korn, Barbara Emrys, Mimi Lewin, Nancy Finke, Carol Kleiman, Jennifer Stone, the women of the first Chicago women's acting workshops, and the women and boys of the mother-and-son acting workshops in 1981. I am grateful for the care and criticism of my dear friend Omie Daniels.

Alice Ryerson, Joan Chase, and the Ragdale Foundation provided me with seven weeks of quiet and solitude in the spring and fall of 1981.

Linda Turner's careful and skillful typing once again assisted me.

I am hopelessly devoted to my agent, Jean V. Naggar, who has given me years of enthusiastic support and advice. And I am grateful for the interest of my editor, Loretta Barrett, who helped this book begin, and continue, to be written. My thanks to Paul Aron, who helped and educated me.

I am indebted to my Chicago group of readers, who clarified and strengthened the book: Jonathan Arlook, Flora Faraci, Pat Murray, and Lois Nowicki read every chapter as I finished it, and met with me for hours to question, argue and encourage.

Judith Arcana
Chicago
March 1982

Prologue

As the mother of a son, I recognize the frustration and pain of knowing that my child is at once of my body and alien to it; I live with the anxious understanding that my boy's life is not in my hands, that all I want for him must be wrested from the patriarchy that claims him. Though I made and fed him out of my flesh, I am now "other" than he.

Because I am writing this book in search of answers and solutions, I must begin by asking questions and posing problems. When I wrote *Our Mothers' Daughters*, a study of the mother/daughter relationship, I was impelled by a passion to know and understand my own mother, to overcome the grief and pain of our bond, and to strengthen the true, deep connection between us as women. With equal passion I now assert that my relationship with my son must be informed by my consciousness as a woman—and that consciousness must be informed by the reality of my son's life.

There is always conflict between the newly emerging behavior and attitudes of individuals and the larger, slowly changing institutions of society. As mothers in this time, we are faced with a dilemma: we see that the old ways are not good; we wish to raise our boys differently—but we fear they'll suffer ostracism, alienation, and loneliness in a society that has by no means given up its old definitions and restrictions. Mothers of little girls can say with breezy facility to their three- and four-year-olds, "Sure, you can wear pants as well as skirts. Why not?" But the reverse becomes a nightmare in our attempts to explain to small boys why long gowns are acceptable only for priests, short skirts for dead Egyptians. They may choose to wear the costumes of both sexes, but they must be warned about the humiliating, frightening and violent reception that awaits them if they do. As their mothers, we juggle to attain a balance between supporting the strength of their spirits and undermining the power of male supremacy.

I do not wish to make an argument here for recognition of the existence of male supremacy. I write from the premise that, whether we choose to challenge the power structure or not, we all can see it. Mothers and sons live in a culture in which sexual designation and distinction have become so important that some people actually submit to surgery that restructures their bodies so they may better suit the social definitions of "female" and "male." We live in a culture in which there is not only a sharp distinction between the sexes, but a hierarchy. We live in the culture of male supremacy: contemporary human society is designed and dominated by men.

What does it mean to mothers that we are primarily responsible for raising male children in such a world? To what extent are we the source of the ideas and attitudes our boys hold and display? What does it mean to both mother and son that men are expected to oppress and degrade women—or suffer for their refusal to do so? At the most basic level, for instance, what happens between mother and son when a six-year-old boy comes home from the first week of first grade at a new school, as my son did, and says, "I hate recess, Mom. And you're gonna hate it too. We don't play games or anything. All the big kids get the swings. And the girls won't talk to me and all the boys do is run around the playground, swooping their arms and yelling like monsters, chasing the girls. And the girls run away and scream, but the teachers don't do anything." Hearing again in memory that hysterical shriek, I asked, "What happens if the boys catch the girls?" "They knock 'em down or push 'em around and say they're gonna look at their underpants." "So the boys run after the girls and yell, and the girls run away and scream. What do you do, Daniel?" "I run with the boys. I know it's wrong; I don't even like it. I *hate* it, Mom. But if I don't run with them, they do it to *me*—and call me GIRL! They yell GIRL, GIRL, GIRL, and chase *me!*" These last words echo the playground hysteria, wailing into tears and hiccups.

What can this little boy do? What can the mother do? What to make of the sharp understanding they've both just gained—that the girls are the accepted prey of the boys, and that any boy who won't take his place in the pack is attacked, and vilified with the worst insult these male children have learned in their six years: he's called a *girl*—and treated as girls are treated. Given the choice Daniel was given, how many small boys, even the most gentle and nonsexist, would have chosen to martyr themselves, to become one of the despised ones? My horror at the recitation of the playground scene was equaled by my consternation at being faced with an unhappy little boy for whom I could not intercede, to whom I could offer no support beyond pep talks and cuddles, no solutions beyond strategies he'd have to carry out all alone. His task was to *make friends* and find a place for himself in male culture.

As mothers, we understand that men continue to be formed and prepared, to be socialized, much as they have been for centuries of patriarchal* culture. It is true that through the pressure of the women's movement, sex roles have begun to change—but the focus of this change has been on women. It is not enough to change only women—especially when the faulty goal of that change is "equality" with men. Mothers of daughters struggle mightily to combat sex-role stereotyping, recognizing it as a grave danger to their children. In the same way, mothers of sons cannot afford to simply let them be, for that, too, is dangerous—in view of *what* they may be, when left to this culture's direction for males of all ages.

Mothers who are raising male children need to confront and examine, as does the society at large, the pattern which has produced nonnurturant, emotionally unresponsive, highly competitive, and materially oriented males who are generally given to verbal and physical violence, to the domination and frequent abuse of children and women. Even among themselves, most men have great difficulty expressing their emotions and needs—especially in sorrow or fear—and giving or receiving love, comfort, and trust. Most of the men—both gay and straight—interviewed for this book told me that they'd rather confide in, or "be open to," a woman than a man.

Mothers need to understand that we are creating and nurturing the agents of our own oppression; once we make them, their education as men in this misogynist society will pull them from our arms, set them above us, and make them the source of our degradation. We would prevent this if we could, and to do so we must enter into conscious struggle with our sons, actively seeking to change what is

---

* "Patriarchy," as used by contemporary feminist scholars, generally refers to a social system run by "the fathers," male power holders in families, tribes, governments, etc.

currently defined as male and female behavior. Daring to defy the sociopsychological canons that label us emasculating or seductive mothers, we must raise our sons to feel their needs, to truthfully express them. They must be sensitized; they must develop the capacity to nurture; and they will come to understand that to live thus is to embody and be surrounded by contradictions.

The words of interviewed men and women appear throughout this book. They are of many ages, cities, professions; they come from all classes and races. The ideas these people hold and speak about almost always cross those lines, and obscure those labels. In any case, this book is not a sociological study, and I am not a scientist. My hope is that the reader will hear the voices of these mothers and sons as I have.

1

The Book of Daniel

> All that I try to save him from
> Is what he dreams about:
> Abandonment, abandonment.
> I watch his face
> Each night emerging clearer,
> Stern son who reads my dreams:
>
> He dreams I want to leave him,
> Roams through night-forests, desolate.
> And I dream I've abandoned him,
> Feel waxy pleasure of that sin,
> Its subsequent atonement.
> Next morning both our faces
> Mark the change:
> Mine with the guilty look of those
> Who knowingly succumb to dreams,
> And his the speculative gaze
> Of someone learning.

—RUTH FAINLIGHT[1]

Daniel was born October 27, 1971. On that day I was the wife of his father, Michael, whom I had met at fifteen and married at twenty-one. Four days after Daniel's second birthday, on Halloween, Michael and I were divorced. By Daniel's third birthday, he and I were living with Jonathan; Michael was living with Susan, whom he married a few years later. By Daniel's fourth birthday, he and I were living in what, for the first time in my life, was my own home—a three-and-a-half-room apartment on the north side of Chicago.

As my son grew, I grew. As I had nursed him, so I was nursed. Though I was nearly thirty at his birth, we were born at the same time; we came to consciousness together. Having just begun to understand that I'd been functionally unconscious for much of the first twenty-five years of my life, I was rising to my own surface when Daniel came—he, too, gasping and splashing to be *out*.

When he was about four, I began to keep a diary about our relationship. This journal is taken from those notes and the memories they recall. In the first couple of years of the journal, from 1976 to 1978, I recorded what seemed to me extraordinary incidents. Often I was encouraged to do so; someone said to me, "Write that down, Judith." But in the years since then, and especially in 1981, working on this book, the notes became a continuous series of journal entries. Growing more conscious of our struggle as mother and son, I decided to make it the center of my work.

February 1976

Having Daniel—a son—in my life, in my house, has made me acknowledge the humanity of men. The beauty and possibility of good in him, as a baby, as a boy, make it impossible for me to leave off with men, to count them out. I have to see that they all were once this, this tender little person, this graceful little body—innocent of its phallic destiny, symbol of guns and hammers, rapes and beatings.

May 1976

What should I say about having a male child when I sit down on a wet toilet seat in a dark bathroom at two o'clock in the morning?

November 17, 1976

Last night I was singing to Daniel before he went to sleep. I was singing "On Top of Old Smokey," which I've been singing to him since he was born; I had gotten to the line about how "they'll hug you and kiss you and tell you more lies than cross ties on a railroad or stars in the skies," when he stopped me, saying, "I don't want to hear that song. You hate men. You hate me. I'm a boy, and I'll be a man when I grow up. You hate what I'm going to be when I grow up." Shocked into silence, I recovered and began to talk. I explained why I "hated" most men—as briefly and simply as I could lay out male supremacy to a five-year-old, using examples from our lives that he already understood, like men who cruise by and call out to women on the street.

He seemed to be understanding, but what he wanted was reassurance, not politics. I told him that there were some good men, and that *he* was good. We hugged and kissed, and I thought I'd done pretty well. He asked me, "What about my dad?" Luckily, I was able to say honestly that his dad was better than many, that while I didn't love him, or want to live with him, I could see that he was basically a decent person. Daniel said, "What about this? Michael insults Susan; he makes her feel bad. I can hear him yelling through the door, shouting at her, and I can hear the drops from her eyes falling down, and the water comes under the door she's so unhappy."

I said nothing for a long time, stunned again by the clarity and depth with which he saw, in a rather ordinary argument, one of billions taking place every day between women and men, exactly the power dynamic I had described, exactly the inequity I had defined. He pressed me for more explanation, and soon, to my surprise, I found myself trying to define rape. Anxious to the point of halting speech, I slowly groped for the words that could give him a sense of it, without that full charge of horror and pain no five-year-old needs. And no adult either. I was fearful; should I be saying all this? Is this right?

This is what comes, I thought, of the principle of honesty, truth between mothers and children. How could I make him understand any of this? I had always assumed that we'd have these serious conversations when he was twelve. Laboring along, I was saying something like "the man forces his penis into the woman's vagina, forces her into sexual intercourse," when he interrupted. "But I thought sex felt *good,* how could he hurt her by having sex with her?" (My sweet boy—I'm so glad you don't know, can't understand, that human sexuality can become a weapon, a source of pain and shame, that it serves as the primary ground upon which men's hatred of women is displayed, worked out, violently consummated. I have to tell you, I have to put this vileness into words that will make it comprehensible to you, to make you see and feel what, in a better world, you would never have to know.)

Daniel sat up in his bed next to me, leaning forward on one arm, looking into my face as I spoke. I leaned forward too, and stroked his arm gently. "Doesn't that feel good?" I asked him. As he nodded yes, I struck out, hitting his arm and knocking it aside, pushing him over sideways. "You see, your arm is the same arm, and my hand is the same hand, but I can use my hand to hurt you as well as to make you feel good. That's how a man can use his penis to hurt a woman in what isn't really sex, but rape." I know that he understood; I had seen the understanding move from me to him —through his body to his mind.

April 3, 1977

Tonight as I sat in the rocking chair reading *Call of the Wild* to Daniel, he got up and came over to me. He said, "You're very special to me, Mom, very special." He leaned on me and nuzzled and stroked me. After saying that Mr. Rogers-special sort of thing for a while, he said, "I hope no men ever try to rape you when I'm not with you. And if they try when I'm with you, I'll beat them until I break their legs or something, and yell at them and call the police." He talked about how maybe I could get together a bunch of women to "take care of those men." And then, as his musing took him further into the world of sexual politics and twisted his loyalties till they hurt, he said, "If my dad was attacked by a bunch of women, you should help him, and not be on their side just because they're women. If you did help them, I'd have to get a knife and stick it in your foot. When the cops came, they'd let me go; because, they'd say, the boy had a right to do it; he was trying to save his dad." Well, there I was, Mom in the rocking chair, reading to her little boy.

April 27, 1977

Daniel said, upon returning to me after spending some days with his father: "I love you so much, Mom, that if I had a palace and all the riches in the world I'd give it all to you." Can this child have been listening to the singer in a piano bar?

Early May 1977

Daniel and I went shopping to buy him an umbrella. I knew, and he didn't, that there are people who say boys shouldn't carry umbrellas, but I didn't tell him that. It turned out that the child-sized umbrellas were all in the girls' section. But they were with hats and gloves and stuffed animals, so he didn't notice. This was fortunate because Daniel's become careful about publicly using anything that is designated "for girls": even in a shoe store where the sneakers are all the same except for the color of the boxes (!), he can be turned aside by some fool of a salesman's saying, "Hey, tiger, those are *girls'*

shoes; c'mon over here," pointing to the inevitably dark-blue some-
thing-or-other. So he looked through the umbrellas. Just as he chose
the most beautiful one—it had a curved wooden handle and was
made of thick poplin cloth in wide yellow, blue, pink, and green
stripes that blurred into a rainbow as he spun it on its point in the
aisle—a saleswoman walked toward us wearing a disapproving face,
but aiming it only at me. I hoped she would be decent about telling
him not to spin the merchandise, but she sidled up to me and stage-
whispered, "You know, that's a girl's—" Taken aback, but by now
experienced, I cut her off: "We don't think umbrellas have any sex,
and we're going to buy this one. He'll wear it home; thank you."
Perhaps a bit too clipped, but I just can't be good about it anymore.

June 13, 1977

The honeymoon is over. Daniel said today, "When I'm grown up, I
won't have you and my dad around anymore." Thinking he might be
worried about being left alone, I asked, "Do you think we'll be dead
when you're grown up?" "No," he answered, "I mean I'll be free."

September 21, 1977

Daniel told me that when I die he'll bury me in a glass coffin with
dolphins beside me and roses on top of me. And when he dies, he
wants to be buried with a costume on, a belt to hold up his pants,
and his school papers in an envelope "for serious work." Inspired by
Disney's necrophiliac dwarfs, his own style is nonetheless indelible.

End of October 1977

Well, this is it for public school. This is not the worst, not the
lowest, not the most fearful or ugly incident—but it's the last.
Daniel came home unhappy—as usual. I asked if I could see the
papers he'd brought with him. Among them was one with a story
printed on it—which they had all copied from the blackboard.
Across the top was an illustration; the teacher likes them to decorate
their papers. It was sweet; it was adorable. There were three little
ducks in a pond. Two ducks were purple and one was maroon. I
told him I loved the little ducks; they were so cute. He was *very* surprised and interested to hear that, and asked me, "Which duck do
you like the best?" I told him I liked the smaller purple one. He
gasped, "You do? You really *do*? Is that the truth, Mom, do you really?" "Well, sure, why not?" "Miss Limness said it was no good;

she said it was no good to be purple. She said ducks couldn't be purple. Here's what she did, Mom. She walked by my desk while I was doing my work, and she picked up my paper. She said the ducks shouldn't be purple; they should be brown; but I said I wanted them to be purple. She held my paper up to the class and said, 'Boys and girls—are ducks *purple?*'" (Jesus H. Christ!) "What did they say, Daniel?" "They all said, *'No,* Miss Limness.' She said, 'Boys and girls, are ducks *brown?'* And they all shouted, *'Yes,* Miss Limness.' So *this* duck"—he pointed to the maroon one—"I tried to cover over with brown. But when I was done, I decided to make the last one purple again. I *like* them purple—and my paper was no good anyway. . . . Oh, Mom, I'm so glad you like them purple." Hugging tightly. "Do you really think it's okay for them to be purple?" Do I? Do I think it's okay for them to be purple? Do I want to kill that woman? Do I hate those little creeps—traitors to their class? "Yes, Miss Limness. No, Miss Limness." Oh, my baby, let us run away together, down the Mississippi on a raft, across the ocean in a red balloon, far, far in a forest cottage, among the trees and the faery folk—anywhere, for the ducks to be okay to be purple.

December 16, 1977

Because I've used the Tarot for several years now, I sometimes take it for granted. Here's this deck of magic cards—lovely, evocative fairytale pictures and they help us visualize and grasp the influences and actions in our lives. But when Daniel uses the cards, I see again how powerful this visualization can be, how expressive. In choosing a significator for his reading, Daniel held up the Knight of Swords, saying, "This is revenge. That's how I feel about all my old friends. I'm angry because I feel like I haven't got any friends." He chose it over the eight of swords, which he said was a close second; "I feel like I'm left out, too." He also considered the three of swords and the Devil. The reading was full of emotions he's experienced coming back to his old school, the Parents' School, after starting first grade for two months at Wrightwood Public School. Not only was he miserable there, but since he's returned, after having been with this group of children since he was three, they've been treating him like the new kid, having already re-formed their allegiances for this year. It seems to have something to do with aligning by sex; his female friends no longer play with boys in the large group, while his male friends are attaching themselves to the older boys, to whom he is a stranger.

Spring 1978

Daniel says that he "won't listen to the bad men" who don't respect women. He says he "won't play with them." But he has already told me that he's afraid to talk back, tell off, or hit "a great big man," including his own father. Ever since he was a baby, strangers have spoken to him on the street and, almost as often, touched him. Men will pat his head or give him a mock punch on the shoulder or back, but never hear or try to hear what he actually says in response to them. It is true that women also touch him without permission, though they do not hit him or call him Butch or Tough Guy. We have spent a lot of time talking about what he can say or do when people use his body this way, and he seems to understand the correlation between his experience and men's use of women's bodies, the connection between women and children in a man's world. But he says that he just can't say anything to a man who uses him that way. "When it's a great big *man*, I'm too scared, Mom." I know the feeling well, honey, but we've got to be able to *do* something in these situations. One irony here is that some of these people—the ones who don't call him Butch—think he's a girl, anyway. They're still saying, "But such curly blond hair!" and "such pretty blue eyes!" as if they'd never seen a man or boy who didn't look like Edward G. Robinson. But whatever sex they think he is, they think he's fair game. They start conversations with him, and walk away or ignore him when he responds to their empty questions—"Would you like to come and live with me?"; "Hey kiddo, do ya like to play ball?"

Note: Reading over that last entry called up the memory of one such blatant trick played on Daniel. There was an elderly woman next to us on a crowded bus. She may have been the one who kept giving him pennies to make him smile; maybe not. At any rate, after gazing at him for several minutes, she spoke to me. "What a beautiful little girl; so sweet!" Daniel looked up at her. "I'm not a little girl; I'm a little boy." "Ohhh! How lucky! That's much better!" she replied. Now, maybe she was trying to be polite, thinking she had insulted him, knowing what an insult it is to call a boy a girl. For she was absolutely sincere. She really believed that it was "much better" to be a boy, and though in many ways, especially from her point of view, she may have been right, in more ways, especially from my point of view, she was sadly wrong. What a puzzle for the little boy to figure out. *Was* it better to be a boy? How? What made it better? And how did that woman feel, then, since she was obviously not a boy? And how did I feel, also not a boy? Well, I just couldn't take on that lady on the bus. I take on most of them, especially the men of course, but I was tired and she was more than twice my age, and we were getting off soon, and I just didn't do it that time. Later, of course, because I couldn't help myself, I talked to Daniel about it. He wasn't interested enough for me to make any positive impact, and I gave up. I wondered about his response, though. Did he say "I'm not a girl" because he *was* insulted? Or was he just trying to state his case, make his identity clear?

Later Spring 1978

Daniel brought up again the issue of the "big men," including his father, and how hard it is to talk to them, to state his case or argue, or be angry to them. We worked on ways to do it, and I stressed how important it was for him to work on it with his father. I hate to keep the burden on the child, but I'm hardly in a position to be a heavy influence with Michael. I can only support Daniel, and trust to Michael's love for him to make him listen. Daniel's gotten a lot of experience in arguing and working things through in his play group and at school, and god knows we can beat any issue to death around here, so I think he's getting good training. He told me that he doesn't want to be like the people "on the bad side" (life is a movie, a cowboy movie) but that he doesn't want to be "one of the ones who get beat up" either. He wants to know what to do about that. So do I.

June 1978

Daniel is going to that day camp up in Old Town. A few of his classmates will be in the same group. This is the first formally sex-segregated group he's been in, except for those two months of public school. This is also the first time he'll be with an adult who wasn't handpicked by me and the other mothers who search the city for people with high consciousness who are willing to take care of and teach our kids. But I'm the one who's scared; he doesn't realize this. Although he did know that the public-school teacher was different.

He said once in that September, "I had a terrible day today. I did everything wrong; the teacher yelled at me. She acts like she doesn't want me to come to this school. She acts like she doesn't want to be a teacher. She yells at me and then pretends to like me, and talks with a fakey accent on her voice. She says 'sweetheart,' but she doesn't mean it, she's just pretending; it's not real."

End of June 1978

That camp has begun. With Daniel's counselor, consciousness isn't the question; he's not even perceptive or friendly—and I mean to the parents, let alone to the kids. But—I will steel myself. Daniel has friends there; this will not kill him; this is the first of many such situations, etc., etc., etc. But I already see a difference in him. The sweetness and tenderness seem to have disappeared. He's too old to be my baby. (This must be normal motherhood withdrawal.) But he's more and more male, and further from me. How much is about being male, how much about being nearly seven years old, how much about his being more out in the world and exposed to this culture? And why does it matter where it comes from? Because I need to know if it comes by nature, *because* he is male. I need to know this. I want to know what is possible, or what might have been possible in another world. Then I will know what we can see in our minds' eyes, what we can hold before us as an ideal, what we have the right to expect of each other.

July 1978

Today Daniel referred to my vagina as "you-know-what." I asked him if he had forgotten the word vagina. He replied that he was embarrassed to say it. I asked if he felt the same way about penis. He said yes.

August 9, 1978

Today Daniel came home from camp and began to tell me a joke about a farmer's daughter whose father "stuffs razor blades up her pussy to hurt these three guys when they do it with her. The three guys are American, Indian, and Polish." I hardly knew where to begin. Fortunately, this happens on a day when I am so exhausted that I haven't the energy to get hysterical, so I behave calmly while I explain what I think of the joke, and why. This takes a long time, covering—as it must—not only women, sex, fathers and daughters, racism, profane/pornographic language, and the telling and hearing of such jokes by men and boys, but also an explanation of why, really, this "joke" isn't funny, even to him. Which he took in readily, having *wondered* why it was funny, all the while laughing with a bunch of other little boys. I realize that that may be why he rushed right off the camp bus and began to tell it to me, almost before saying hello. Maybe he was mystified by the story, by the experience. Am I always going to be there afterward? Will I continue to be willing to explain? At some point, certainly when he's older, I'm going to really resent this. I'm going to want him to be able to smell it coming like I do, to sense what's wrong, and not to laugh—even at cost to himself. I'm going to want him to *do* something about it, and maybe crack the glue of his male bond in the process.

September 1978

Daniel, worried, asked me, "If you stuck a knife into someone's dick, would he die?" And, "Why does it hurt so much to be hit in the penis? Is that the most painful hit a person could have?" Well, it certainly isn't the most painful hit *I* could have; but I soft-pedaled the criticism of his language, and got to the subject. This was the first time I'd ever heard anyone male question the pain-in-the-penis business. All my life, I've heard boys and men carry on about how bad it hurts,* but maybe they're exaggerating. Is he in the process of *learning to believe* that an injury to his penis is devastating? Granted, it must hurt, but it's no life-and-death matter. How much of that pain they talk about is psychosomatic, the result of treasuring and worshiping and investing the penis with all their psychic energy?

October 1978

Today Daniel really gave me something to think about. He showed me his erect penis, and called it Willie. If this is not classic, I don't know what is. To give his penis a personality—a name! (Though I must say that giving it a name is pretty typical of us both; I personify everything, i.e., "Mom, why did you move that table?" "It wanted to be able to see out the window.") He showed me that erection as if it were an accomplishment—and he said this while we were reading, snuggled up together on the big pillows. I feel like I found a stranger in my house, or ants in my bed.

---

* But then, they are often speaking of the scrotum and testicles, more sensitive than the penis itself.

The experience made me remember, years ago, visiting Diana and seeing five-year-old Colin, who was naked, come up behind her and rub his penis against her shoulder as we sat talking on the floor. She shrugged her acceptance of the gesture, laughed a little, and told me he'd been doing that kind of thing since he was three. And *that* reminds me of Sandy, talking about Joseph asking, "Do you think I love you more than my daddy? Well, I do. You know how much? About the size of my penis." Freud would have a good time in this neighborhood. *Is* all this about the sexual use of mothers by small sons who are trying to work out their sexuality? It would seem so, at least to some extent. We are women, we love them, we are sensual with them, we are naked together, and we are all, sons and mothers, surrounded by constant waves of outrageously sexist usage of women's bodies and the exploitation of sexuality and affection by the advertising and entertainment media.

November 16, 1978

Today Daniel brought Larry home from school with him—at my suggestion. It was an idea born of three sources: an impulse to have him accept the new children (remembering last year when it happened to him), some of that old guilty sense that he "should" have more kids over to play, and the really insane notion that if he had a friend over, I'd be able to work. Well, I can hardly stand it. They began with Daniel introducing Larry to his room and his stuff, including his current stash of five dollars, which was presented with pride and the underlying assumption that Larry would be impressed by the money. Which he was. They went on to a board game, which floundered because Daniel never explained the rules or the goal, just "played" it, and of course tried to control both the game and Larry with his knowledge. Larry quickly gave it over, and initiated war. This almost turned to good when Daniel added costumes and makeup, but Larry wouldn't paint himself or wear anything but a monster mask or hat, so the violence and noise continued. I had promised myself that I would not intervene, that I would let it go wherever it went—barring damage to the house or to them—but I cracked. I carried on about the mindless mess and noise and violence, so they switched into a hideous false giggling, with Larry shrieking about which girl loved Daniel, or which loved him. Add to this the fact that they fall all over each other, wrestling to the floor, and Larry says that Daniel is "gay," which he uses as a goading insult. Driven to it, I interrupted again, but got nowhere. The hysterical quality of their interaction has abated somewhat, maybe because now *I've* picked it up. I am disgusted and appalled. I see why people sedate their kids with TV. What's amazing is that so many mothers give sugar—which can only make this worse. Now they are ripping up the get-well cards Daniel got last week. Those cards were important to him. Will he regret this? It appears that Larry may like Daniel; he giggles incessantly at his words and actions. The constraints are obvious: no real touching, Larry's constant sexual allusions, mandatory noise and violence, almost no actual exchange, certainly no conversation. What a horror show—and I was dullwitted enough to let myself get roped into six hours of this. Never again for such a long time. On the good side: both are willing to do cleanup, in parlor and kitchen. Larry responds to me with a mask of a face, with obedience. I've found no way to break through the high-pitched, taut emotional wall they've made. I cannot actually be a person with them, only an outside authority. Now I hear Daniel making creepy squealing noises while Larry is the voice of reason whom he ignores. Because we've never known this boy before and because Daniel almost never brings kids home from school, I don't know if this is typical of our times, of our school, of children, of boys, of Chicago; I just know I hate it.

Very early 1979

It grows harder and harder to have him be real with me; we move further apart. What if we do have to separate? What if he has to live with his father, wants to live with his father because he is male, because of this gulf between us that seems to be made of sex? Maybe for a while. Maybe that will come before adolescence. So many divorced kids decide to go live with whomever they're not living with when they're fifteen or seventeen; I'm anticipating that. But this is too soon. Maybe we only need it for a short time? Maybe I'm not sure if we can sustain that intimacy of understanding that we've always had. Oh, how much of this *is* about his sex? How much about my own need for freedom and work time? Am I just less patient? Is the difference as great as I'm making it out to be? He seems less distinct, more like "a boy" than like Daniel.

March 1979

I have chosen a new order, design, way of living, that is in opposition to the one that Daniel, being male, is an automatic member of

—the patriarchy. I raise him toward what I perceive to be the good —but he may align himself with male culture; he has a life membership, conferred at birth. Since I see male culture as corrupt and oppressive, I work against that alignment in his life. The issue of the mother-father-son triangle comes in here, and the common theme of mothers acting as agents between fathers and sons, like Linda in *Death of a Salesman*. But that kind of triangle is active where mother and father live together with their son. There are traces of it when we're with Jonathan. They—the two of them—get along better without me than they do when all three of us are together. And Daniel and I do better alone, too. When I am with them both, I feel pulled by both; I haven't enough of whatever it is to give Daniel, give Jonathan, and work on their relationship as well—which I feel compelled to do; I get drawn into it—though I know that they'd do better if I didn't. In fact, they've told me so.

Spring 1979

Omie and I took the kids to Cocina Mexicana for dinner when we picked them up. They were full of excitement and information about their day, both eager to tell us about it. As they talked, I saw this happen: Daniel interrupted Nelly—talked right over her to finish most of the explanations she started, and she let him do it; she subsided when he took it away. At one point, she picked up a fork to illustrate her talk; they were explaining "the purpose of observation in the scientific method." He took the fork right out of her hands, finished her sentence, and went right on. She let him do it. I was in that bad position of not knowing what Omie thought about all this. Did she see it and choose to let it go by? Did she not want to remonstrate with *my* child? Could I take it upon myself to stop them both and run it down? I was too unsure, and let it go by. Later, at home, I reconstructed the scene with Daniel, explained what I'd seen and told him what was wrong. I was careful to explain it as a dynamic, so that he didn't think I was only blaming *him* for doing something to Nell. He understood, but, again, at least half the impact is lost when I don't do it *in the moment*. Whatever interplay there could have been between him and Nelly is impossible to construct, and she alone could have really told him what it meant to her to be interrupted, to have the fork taken out of her hands—and why she was *willing* to do that, to be that way.

Note: Talked to Omie about the Mexican restaurant episode;

she recognized it when I described what I'd seen, and told me not to hold back in the future but to move right in when I see it.

July 20, 1979

I've recently interviewed a mother of sons whose style of mothering is very different from mine, who has made her family the center of her life. Because she was very intelligent, because we connected on a personal level, and because I respected her, the interview called my own situation into consideration in a way that her "profile" (married, mother of five, etc.) would not ordinarily do. She holds the same world view as I, sees what I see. But she differs in that I have chosen to make myself my center, to lead a relatively self-conscious life, and that I see little hope for long-term positive social change. She puts her children, and to a lesser extent her husband, in her center, chooses to be nonintrospective, and feels that substantial positive social change is actually going on, so that we needn't feel guilt, as I so often do, for having brought children, for our own purposes and none of theirs, into this hideous world. Now the point is this: Her eldest son, much older than Daniel, seems to be closest to her, most like her, etc. Also, he was the first. So I identify him with Daniel. She speaks of that boy as if he has very little, if any, of the insecurity I see in Daniel; he seems, in her description, to be self-composed and stable, with a sense of place and understanding that I don't always see in my son. Is there a connection between Daniel's willingness to sell himself for social acceptance and my reluctance to mother him in the good old-fashioned way? I am not there for him as a constant, solid bulwark against society. Is that other boy better able to challenge and condemn the culture of male supremacy, as his mother says he does, to be an exceptional male, *because* his mother has put him before herself, *because* she has made motherhood her profession? And, if so, isn't this ironic—the freer we are of the institution of motherhood, the less committed to feminism our sons can be? Is this reasonable?

Two days later

Is this ridiculous? I'm beating myself up with recycled institutional-motherhood guilt. After all, I don't know that other kid. A lot of people think *my* kid is like that; sometimes *I* think my kid is like that—and besides, the other boy is so much older. And it's not like that woman just bakes cookies and washes the kitchen floor. She does neither, and does political work too. She's just *married,* Judith, and supported by her husband so she can do whatever she wants, with her kids and without .them. So relax. Remember, *she* feels guilty about being supported, and even, I suspect, about being *married.* So pick up your guilt bundles, girls, and move on.

August 27, 1979

I dreamed that there was a large clear cellophane sack containing three blooming purple orchid plants. One plant belonged to Thomas, one to Eddie, and one to Daniel. Daniel's plant was smaller and scruffier than the other two, and he kept saying, "Mine's getting smashed; it's getting crushed!" I take this dream to be about the fact that I don't mother him the way the other two boys are mothered. But I don't want to do it that way; does it have to be a crime against my son, a *loss* to him, that I cannot be, refuse to be, like those other mothers? Thomas's mother subordinates herself to him completely—as she does with her husband. When the boys were younger, she used to let Thomas kick and hit her; she still lets him use her body as he wishes, and gives in to all his tempers and demands; she even sacrifices her relationship with her daughter to his whims. Eddie's mother *adores* him, flirts with him; she pours all of her motherhood out onto him—to the complete exclusion of her second son. She said to me once, "You'd think I have only one child, the way I talk; sometimes I forget I have Paul too."

The dream was my guilt, and my fear that Daniel perceives himself as shortchanged, lacking and lesser, because his mother can't/won't bow before the altar of institutional motherhood, to the glory of the Jesus-boy sons.

End of August 1979

Daniel's been listening to the comic song "Leaping Lesbians" on the second Meg Christian album. As social criticism, it reminds me of Tom Lehrer; Daniel has a similar response to both artists. He's puzzled by the basic premise almost as much as he's tickled by the humor. He asked me why straight women should be afraid of lesbians anyway. What is there to be afraid of? After we talked, he said that he understood why lesbians would "feel bad and angry" that straight women are afraid of them, and then he said, "I bet if men knew that, that straight women are afraid of lesbian women, men would think it was cool." All of which reminds me to write some-

thing about how things have been changing again. The contrast between *this* summer's day camp and *last* summer's has brought it
clearly to my consciousness, but the fact is, the boy and I are
different again. Not just since the summer started, for the feeling
changed a few months ago, in early spring. But this summer program is boys and girls together, in a small group, with a leader we
chose. The whole thing rests in control of his environment. I'm
pretty certain about that now. This boy, and everybody else, will go
the way he is directed. If he's directed to call a vulva a pussy or to
interrupt girls because boys are entitled to as much space as they
can grab, then that's what he'll do. If Nelly is directed to accept having her vulva called a pussy, and to be interrupted, not claiming
time and space for herself, then that's what she'll do. While this is
somewhat depressing, at least it makes my position clear. Far better
to realize *this* than to discover that boys are irrevocably violent and
competitive by nature, sexually aggressive and woman-hating by in-
stinct. Now I know what to do. Or to continue doing, I should say.
After all, I have been constructing constructs and arranging arrangements from the beginning to provide Daniel with the kind of guidance that will strengthen him against the waves of male culture that
will break over his head, ever more roughly as he grows. I have to
be rededicated, recommitted, to keeping this boy in the heart of the
mother. I am not giving up. I am going to bring him more and more
into the parts of my life that I thought he had to be separate from. I
have been unknowingly making a sex-segregated consciousness of
my own, defeating my earlier efforts. I clipped this letter out of *New
Women's Times*—more women thinking like I'm thinking:

To have male children and to raise them with an awareness of women's
oppression is a challenge that many of us have chosen to take on. . . .
By not allowing our sons to witness and share in women's joy and pride,
we are missing many opportunities to show them first-hand how feminism works. . . . By rejecting our sons, we are literally pushing them
into a male world that will gladly take over and give them all the positive
reinforcement each child naturally needs . . . negative attitudes . . . will
only serve to strengthen the chances they will reject our beliefs and join
the patriarchy.[2]

September 1979

Daniel is worried. He's been listening to Holly Near singing "Fight
Back," and putting it together with my self-defense classes—he

came with me twice, loved it—and understands that there is a problem here. "What will happen to me and Jonathan when the women
fight back? Will you kill all the men, or put us in jail?" (Oh to be
powerful enough to do that, let alone whether we'd choose it or
not—) "What happens to us when you make what she says you're
going to make?" I explained that what she says we're going to make
is "a safe home"; and that only men who oppose that would
be shut out of the lives of the women who live there. Then I
told him about separatism, a concept that was new to him, and he
was pretty interested. He understands that not all women are
separatists—though his initial questions would seem to indicate a
fear that that extreme position may ultimately have to be taken by
all women. I cut the Michigan music festival* for you, kid, dig it!
Anyway, he knows I'm not a separatist; I'm not giving up my son
for the women either.

October 10, 1979

Will Daniel decide that he wants to live with his father all the time
—a comradeship through the bond of maleness? Will I raise him up
and have to turn him over—just give him up? And because he *wants*
to go? Will that time just come? One day, will it just come? I'll be
bitter; I'm bitter now, fearing and imagining it. I'd like to say, "I'm
not giving up, without a fight!"—but if he *wants* to go, who'll I fight
with? I'd not keep him, not prevent him from going, not beg him to
stay with pore ol' mom.

October 22, 1979

Listening to Daniel lip-sync the Stones, I realize that not only is the
main appeal in the rhythm—no surprise here; he liked the Stones
when he was three years old and couldn't make out *any* of the
words, which he often, even now, doesn't catch—but the rhythm is
violent in itself. (Is this right?) Remember, this is the child who
played his own copy of *Lavender Jane Loves Women* on a small
plaid plastic record player at the same age he first played the Stones.
The two continue to coexist in his taste. Holly Near has become
pretty special to him, and he enjoys other women's music. He used
to just listen to "Leaping Lesbians" on the Meg Christian album,
and laugh through it with the laughing audience, but now he hums

* Annual Women's Music Festival held in the Michigan countryside.

along with the other songs too. And of course, when he came home the other day to find me playing *Lavender Jane,* he requested that I play the other side for him. He tells me that they play a lot of women's music at school too, she he's getting a big shot. Maybe not big enough to completely drown out Kiss, but big.

December 1979

Daniel no longer asks the same kind of questions—or makes the same kind of terribly innocent sweet statements he made as a very young boy—when he was three, four, or five. "Mom, I'll never be like that," etc. He has now a mass of information from the media that may puzzle him, but certainly must appear to him to be the norm. The objectification, hatred, and abuse of women that he experiences as a member of the TV-watching, movie-going public is more and more a large part of his consciousness, as it is for young girls. This is what he must *understand to be* the general relationship between the sexes. Well, it's what *I* understand that relationship to be also.

Late December 1979

Daniel said to me, "When I can read *real good,* Mom, you know what's the first book I'll read? *Your* book."

February 6, 1980

Daniel needs a sense that being male is okay, even *good,* with the possibility of full humanity available. My working on *EMS* is helpful; he knows that it's "about" him, that it might help mothers grow boys into different kinds of men. But he needs models now—*new* models—and he needs more contact with the struggles of men who are changing their male identity. Maybe boys do need to be around men, especially in this society, where so much of what we are is based on assigned sex roles. But how to find the right men? Are there any? There must be—but can I advertise for them? And how can I get them to do it? Should mothers just send boys off, like in the old days, off to the men's lodge? We can't; the men aren't prepared, aren't capable—or willing to accept the responsibility, even if they could do it. Mothers have to raise boys, not just four or six or ten years, but sixteen or twenty—well into sexual and cultural masculinity. How are we going to make the proper arrangements? It is, so far, *ours* to arrange.

Daniel needs the sense that I accept and love him in his maleness, not *despite* his maleness.

February 18, 1980

Today I heard the little girl upstairs come home from nursery school with a friend, a little boy. I remembered when Daniel was in his early play group and the first year of nursery school, when they didn't know, notice, or care what sex they were. Perhaps they had no sex really; they were just children in fat white diapers. Then they found out about it, and the girls got peevish and the boys got mean. Then the girls, after being excluded and abused for a couple of years, became rigidly exclusive, wouldn't play with boys—who claimed they didn't want to play with them anyway, and they tried to keep separate while we, mothers and teachers, worked on pushing them back together. The smaller the group, the easier it is to get them to relate to each other. The more willing the adults are to make it happen, the more willingly the kids will do it. Some of them even look relieved, and lots of them are delighted, with the reunion. Some refuse to be reconstructed, of course—already set into rigid behavior/attitudes. The whole thing is deeply influenced by the *structure* in which the children are placed, and the desires/consciousness of the adults present. Girls are more free to associate with both sexes, just as they are more free to wear both costumes.

April 3, 1980

Nelly's birthday party was an excellent observation workshop, with all the adults there picking the teams, *making* them be half girls and half boys, seating them for their games alternately by sex, etc. Just the fact that she invites boys and girls together makes it unusual. Daniel is down to one or two girls in his sphere; he told me that the girls sometimes won't talk to him at school; "And I've known her half my life, Mom!" Of course, I know he joins the boy pack in the gym that excludes girls who try to play kickball, dodgeball, etc.

May 1980

Daniel asked me if he could go to an all-boys sports camp; then he said he *doesn't* want to go there. He'd hate a lot of it, for the same reasons that he quit the soccer team, nasty coach and all, disliking boys who could only relate in terms of competition, both intellectual and athletic. He loves our summer group, girls and boys together.

But Daniel may have to be in some male situations soon to fulfill his need or desire to be with boys, so that he doesn't become obsessed with it, and start to long for it in creepy ways, like for sugar, meat, and TV.

I have to find some male places, groups that won't be all macho, so he can learn from and be with good men and good boys. But look at the male organizations they've built. They're all unacceptable. Curse them. What should a "boys' group" be *for?* What might they discover, boys together? Hopefully, not "bonding" to *exclude* females, but just the pleasure of being who they are, together, without woman-hating. Just as I love to be with women, to be among Jews. Ah, maybe it's too late already. Where are we going to find men who have the goodness *and* the desire to be with children? The example I saw at Columbia College with that guy from the Men's Gathering certainly wasn't promising. The few good men we know aren't wanting to make these boys, to make children, a top priority in their lives. Men should be setting up the structures to serve this need. Well, they're not.

June 1980

At the end of the day, Daniel witnessed an episode of maternal violence that scared him, really frightened him. He told me the whole thing, but he was so upset that he was sobbing when he told it, so I don't have it all. It seems that there was this mother with a few kids, walking down the street by the school. She called to the last kid to hurry up—they were all carrying groceries—and one boy (girl? I don't know) dawdled. She shouted, "real mean," and waited for the child to catch up. She grabbed him by the arm and shook him real hard, and he ran away from her. When she caught up with him, she hit him in the face "with a big bunch of keys on a chain; I saw the blood, Mom; I saw the blood!" I held him as he told the story, and asked a few questions. I don't know why, there was a tone to his voice, or the way he looked at me, but I asked him this: "What bothered you the most, was it the blood, the yelling, the fact that she used a weapon?" He hesitated quite awhile, and then said, "I stood there, and I thought maybe my mother might do that too." This really upset me until I realized that it didn't have to mean that he was thinking that I would do what that poor woman had done, but just that he'd never seen such a thing. It had never occurred to him that a mother might do that to her child, and now it was a possibility. I remember that when I had casually spoken of my father hitting me when I was small, Daniel was amazed. Later, the first thing he said when he saw his grandfather was, "Did you really hit my mother? Why did you hit her?"

Note: What if Daniel's response to the episode of the woman who hit her kid in the face with the keys was triggered by a connection to the memory of *me*, shrieking at him, grabbing him, when he was eighteen months old and had taken *my* keys and toddled off with them? Oh—I remember it so clearly—what a nightmare mother I was that time. He took my keys, as babies do, and disappeared with them. When I demanded them back, he didn't have them, and seemed not to know what I was talking about when I yelled and pulled him about, seeking them. He probably didn't remember where they were, probably never actually put them anywhere—just padded around with them until he didn't have them anymore. Maybe not. Maybe he deliberately stuffed them down between my mattress and the wall, where I found them hours later. Perhaps he had taken them as a game, or a tease, a trick, and hidden them on purpose. But I shook him by the shoulders, gripped hard, all mean and nasty in his astonished little face. "You're not going to bed until you give me back those keys!" A threat to a baby—a baby whose "bedtime" was subject to the vagaries of four or five adults, some of whom let him stay up if he whimpers, some of whom sing songs until they are hoarse, some of whom rock him to sleep if it takes hours. Baby Daniel and the keys: the raging mother, the surprise of pain and fear, the jangling metal. Maybe our past is the source of his fear; maybe he remembers as well as I.

Later June 1980

I feel constrained in writing this book—careful not to say things that will hurt Daniel or be bad for him, make him too public so young, render him vulnerable outside of his own choice, put it to him before he figures it out for himself. This is the old problem of my needs and desires in opposition to his, but he has a great claim here, and I am cautious, censoring parts of my journal, choosing words with care for him in mind. This work has pushed me deeper into our relationship; he has come closer to my center than I thought he could. Daniel is a constant reminder that I cannot view any man only as a *man;* they are not merely male, they do not do what they do *only* because they have been entitled to whatever they can take and hold. I have been afraid of this change in me, this growing sympathy and empathy for men and boys, afraid that it will weaken me, take away my sensitivity to women's oppression. My growing acceptance of their possibilities as people makes me nervous. I have come to understand that there is not much difference, basically, between women and men. When men can be perceived as actual people—which is rare—the lack of difference is obvious, even down to genital structure and experience of orgasm. This understanding has made sex-role conditioning even *more* horrifying to me.

Still later June 1980

Am I stifling all signs of patriarchal influence in his life without enough consideration of their meaning? Like his fascination with the *Guinness Book of World Records*—that's not such a bad thing; it doesn't necessarily have to be about competition. It's fun to know that stuff. But he pretends to be interested in things he really doesn't care about, like baseball games, or insists that he's a terrific skater when he's a beginner. He wants to be the biggest, the best, the first at anything, but he doesn't want to *work* on anything to get there. (This is what all mothers are supposed to worry about; I'm just doing my job.) Am I leaving no room for him to flex, to expand, to crow? I'm shoring up the influences I perceive as good, but can I so freely attack what I perceive as bad? Am I consistent in the attack anyway? Disinterest, tiredness, changing my opinions, learning new things, forgetting—I cannot present a monolith of the right way. A little humility there, Mother.

Early July 1980

Daniel's fear and love/dependence and disdain may be the classic base for what men carry out of their relations with their mothers into adult life as the attraction/repulsion they feel for women. Does he ever feel inadequate because of being male? I wonder. He loves and admires me, and some other important women in his life, who are more like me than they are like the fake women on TV. Mostly, though, he does seem healthy and strong, possessed of self-esteem, self-knowledge, and articulate consciousness.

August 1980

Jonathan has been getting better at interceding, on either Daniel's behalf or mine, when we treat each other badly. It's more than useful to have another person around some—a person who knows us both so well—and can see what we're doing. I am sometimes bad about accepting the criticism—responding to Jonathan as a *man,* instead of who he is—unable to hear the words or let them in because I resist what feels like giving-in-to-a-man—but I take it and use it. And his criticizing me on Daniel's behalf breaks through the exclusive feeling Daniel sets up about himself and me, and creates a three-way exchange instead. I also worry about Daniel bonding with Jonathan against me on the basis of sex, but I try to go beyond that fear, to come out in another place. It's hardest to do when Daniel pulls the shit that my brothers and I used to do to my mother, making her the butt of jokes, aligning against her in games. But Jonathan's intervention helps here too, because when he intercedes on *my* behalf, he breaks through that line. Kids have so little power, though, even male kids, that we have to be careful not to team up against him. Daniel tells us when we get out of line—two adults harping on one theme—so he won't be bullied.

September 1980

Again, I am grateful that the fact of having a male child makes me admit that I might, I may, can, do—love a man. More basic than the endurance of the long-term struggle with one particular man, Jonathan, the existence of Daniel reinforces the possibil y that a man can be decent, nurturant, willing to struggle and work on himself within our relationship, fighting against and sometimes succumbing to the cultural progression toward woman-hating. Living with that process in Daniel gives me a clear sense of what it is and what it is not; what is not part of him, but is added, attached, as he grows into this culture. Now I can look at any man who will let himself be seen, and see where that attachment has taken place, see where he is struggling to detach himself, and where he is not. Daniel is the proof that decent men are possible, against almost all other evidence.

In a recent interview with two lesbian feminist mothers of sons, both of whom are committed to raising their boys, we discussed the possibilities. Their sons have asked them, "Could you ever love a man?" And they have both answered, "No, because I am a lesbian, and that means that I choose to love women—to put my spiritual, political, and sexual energy into women." This question does not arise in a vacuum of course; our sons ask if we hate men, if we'll ever marry, if we are lesbians, what *are* lesbians, anyway, and so on. So, the answer, "No, because I am a lesbian," is couched amid surrounding discussions and emotional exchanges, assurances that the sons are loved, though the fathers are not. Often the question comes up when a lesbian mother has broken off with a long-time partner: "Will you go back to Daddy now? To a man?" (One mother related her younger son's perseverance: "Well, you were married once before Dad. What about that guy? Would you marry him?")

Because they are looking for reassurance about themselves, about being male and exchanging love with their mothers, it must be very difficult for these boys to understand their mothers' answers as *feeling*, as well as principle or intellectual choice. It's difficult for the mothers themselves to work through. The answer emerges, as a position, from the intersection of emotion and politics, both conscious, both gravely considered. If these boys are lovable, and they are male, then there must be others, no? There must remain that possibility, though it may never be realized because a good man is hard to find, and because fewer and fewer women bother to look. The point is, many lesbian women choose *to love women*, rather than *not to love men*. Our sons need the explanation and understanding of that choice, so that their sense is not that males—*by definition*—cannot be loved.

Five years ago I recorded my feelings about loving the boy—knowing he'll be a man—in a separate notebook, the Acid Journal. I'd been listening to *Lavender Jane*: "It's such a pied piper; all the ideas, of course, are mine. But what about this, I want to shout—I have this *son*, you see—I love him and he is *real*. The pied-piper music tempts me to forget him—or to forget what his existence means in the future. His present reality suits all this nice MUMS and KIDS stuff—but what about tomorrow, all you lesbians with your music? I cannot think of the soul of Daniel as insignificant; how can I forget the sweetness of Daniel and Jonathan? I feel as if I have to plead for both of them; because they cannot be less than me; we cannot be separated into us/them—I can't imagine living with Daniel and Jonathan being 'the other side.' Must it come to a choice? I cannot deny them their humanity even as I have had mine taken from me. All the *more* cause not to cast off. . . . It's THE MAN, not the man, and the trap is there. . . ."

Early October 1980

Sometimes Daniel uses me as a fantasy kiss-person; he'll kiss me like he sees people kiss in the movies; and I don't like it. Interview mothers have talked about this, and some of them seem not to mind. Some think it's "cute." I don't want anybody to kiss me that way, certainly not my son. A lot I feel this way because it's phoney, and a lot because that's not the relationship I want with him. I've said to him a few times, "You're just using me; I could be a window manne- quin or a big warm blanket," depending on whether he's practicing romance or seeking warmth.

I'm not sure if he understands what I'm saying; I'm not sure he wants to. I've been struggling to explain how I feel when he does that. Sometimes he says, "I want to cuddle," meaning he wants some sensual action, hugging and stroking. But I may *not* be wanting it, not be feeling like that. When he was little, I would receive him whenever he asked, even if I didn't feel like it. I felt then that I *should* give it to him. And it was easy. I was more likely to want to do it, and my life was almost wholly designed around him then, and he was so small. But now, I don't know if there are sexual overtones to it, or that I just resent my body being used when I'm not particu- larly into it.

Actually, this isn't about sex. This is about physical comfort, and making demands. It's not an interchange, it's me giving to him for his own use, giving *myself* to him when I don't want to. He is old enough to go without gratification and not suffer from it as he would have years ago; he also can get cuddling from other people, or seek gratification of other kinds. He's old enough to be respon- sible for the request he's making; he has to be *conscious* of his request now, and of my right to refuse; that's the important part here—the responsibility. I feel that this is a transitional phase; I don't know what the next part is, though. I won't be fully accessible ever again. I was completely receptive only through pregnancy and the first six months or so; my responsiveness gradually lessened over the years. After all, I weaned him at fourteen months because I wanted to lose weight and wear real clothes again—to get out of those brown corduroy size thirty-six Levi's—so that was hardly a decision based on his needs.

October 23, 1980

I walked from the shower to my closet to my dresser, reaching for some clothes; we were dressing to go out for dinner. Daniel said to me, "Why are you walking around with no clothes on?" I replied that I was not "walking around," but getting dressed. It was a brief

interchange, but indicated something going on there about naked-
ness, about my body. He looks at me, not sure if he should, interested—as we all are—but nervous. He'll be nine next week. What
happens now? Let him see what a real woman's body looks like, instead of the unreal images the media project? But then I feel used
again. And I don't want him to respond to me sexually either. But
would he, necessarily? After all, I loved to look at my mother's
body and liked to cuddle with her, but didn't feel sexual about her.
Is that a fair comparison? Is that even true? What about all the negative sanctions on lesbianism? But had I absorbed all that by the
time I was nine? Maybe. I sure had by the time I was eighteen—but
I still looked at naked women—and men—whenever I could.

Late October 1980

It feels like it's been a long time since my acceptance of Daniel as
my child. There was that lusty first acceptance, nursing him back
into the body he'd just parted from—made easy by his absolute acceptance of me. That lasted nearly three years. Then there was an
ambivalent period, when he was three to five years old, when we
went in and out of each other; I was unable to commit myself as a
mother, especially as the mother of a son. During that time I did all
the mothering, but didn't really go all the way inside of it. Six and
seven seem, retrospectively, the toughest years so far. That was
when he went into the world, picked up a lot of masculinity, and
brought it home. And that was when I was working more and more
away from him, my life seeming to hold less and less room for the
Daniel part of it. But since seven, since the work on *EMS* began to
be *work,* not possibility, contemplation, or vague planning, our commitment has been made, has been strengthened, has grown. I suppose that's why I'm writing the book—so I can do it all better, and
more. I told him that I had accepted the commission; I'm on.

Accepting a male child as the real child, the true child of my
heart, was part of that process. I didn't want another child, and I
didn't want another abortion—these things I knew when Daniel was
three years old, and so had myself sterilized. In that process, I had
to give up the daughter dream, and I did. Some part of the desire for
a daughter had been to do it right—make a "new woman," another
part was to make a person who would be like me, and a third was to
have a child with whom I could be intimate. I see that my reasons

were, respectively, egotistical, doomed to failure, and questionable
—to say nothing of an awful set of expectations for any daughter to
face. Of course, I have come to see that my son is very like me, and
we are intimate friends. And making a "new man" is much the same
process of politically conscious mothering. Besides, the greatest part
of the daughter dream had been the desire to reraise myself. The little girl I had wanted to raise was me. I wanted to start from the beginning and give my girl the world that I, and all of us little girls,
deserved. But I found that I've *been* raising myself. I've taken myself over, taken my life in my hands. So now—I can raise Daniel;
I've put my whole self in, recognizing those places where our needs
coincide or intersect, but knowing that our lives run on separate
tracks. Ah—I just remembered that time he called out to me,
angrily—"You know, Mom, you're not me! *I'm* me!"

November 1980

Whenever I feel that Daniel is responding to me as an object, a sexual or emotional object, projecting his thoughts or feelings onto the
available woman, I move into this elaborate intellectual fantasy of
talking to him, when he's around twelve. I'll tell him about how his
natural feelings have been channeled into unhealthy directions, that
his affection for me and our intimacy, combined with his growing
sexual maturity, have come together into the now-typical male pattern, etc., etc. Why should I wait till he's twelve? Because it's so
hard to do, I suppose. I'm revving up for telling him about what's
happening, but I don't really want to, because it's so damn difficult.
Actually, bit by bit, we're already doing it—have been for years.

Very late 1980

Today, as if now that he reads, he reads Freud, Daniel said to me,
"I've got a penis, you don't." Well, this wasn't really news to either
of us, and I'm afraid my response was only a surprised laugh. He
laughed too, and there was the odd feeling that he had meant it as a
joke.

Mid-January 1981

This month I've begun to use sanitary napkins again, instead of
sponges. I've decided that I want the blood to come out like it's supposed to, not collect inside of me. So Daniel, who's been through

tampons and sponges, both with great interest, learned a new thing. I hadn't even *seen* them since I was fifteen, when there were only Kotex or Modess and the skinny white belt. I had to stand in front of a whole department of sanitary napkins reading labels and figuring out about minipads and maxipads and adhesive strips; and all the boxes have pictures of women who are playing tennis or jogging on beaches—none of them are sitting on small wooden chairs with pillows, typing. Anyway, Daniel's response to the whole thing reminded me of when I was nine myself and my older brother saw fit to introduce me to menstruation. What a contrast, between Dick and Daniel, with their sense of the female body! Here's Daniel, who used to occasionally stick a tampon into a glass of water just to watch it expand—"Now it looks like a fat white mouse, Mom"— and he's checking out the wrapping of my maxipads. I let him have one to take apart. After examining all the layers he'd removed from the gauze sheath, he stuck the gauze lengthwise, by its adhesive strips, onto the wall of his room—between the map of the United States and the poster of the African lion—and put all his loose change into it. "Look; you can keep things in it! It's handy." I thought about this for a few minutes. Is there anything wrong here? Any disrespect, or bad attitude? I found none, just healthy nonchalant acceptance that recalled the contrasting memory of that day in my parents' bedroom when my brother showed me the Kotex. I'd seen the huge box in the corner of my mother's closet many times. It was dark blue and black, and had white printed letters on it, with a capital K and an $x;$ I'd had the hazy notion that it was a giant-sized box of Kleenex, and had never bothered with it. This afternoon, Dick took me over to the closet, pulled the box forward, and said, insinuating ugliness, "Do you know what *this* is?" I tentatively offered my Kleenex theory, knowing already that I was wrong—why would he be so weird about Kleenex? He pulled out a Kotex pad and held it out to me. "This is a bandage that women have to wear. You're going to *bleed,* and you'll have to wear it." The *feeling* of that moment is what I recall, how shameful he made it seem. I don't remember how that scene ended, but I know I didn't mention it to my mother when she, just a few months later, gave me the little mail-order kit of belt, pads, and a little booklet called "Sally, Mary and Kate Wondered." But Daniel hasn't had to wonder nearly as much as Sally, Mary and Kate, knowing more about women's bodies than I did at his age.

Late January 1981

What's the big deal? Mothers have been raising male children for hundreds of thousands of years. I've only got this one little one anyway. It's no big deal; why am I making such a scene, a whole book about it? Kids are kids.

Later in January 1981

Even though I never got a regular program going with other mothers of sons, the tiny group that got together to see that disappointing movie about adolescent male sexuality was exciting. And even though my vague plans about a boys' group remain vague, I understand what I can do right now and what I can't. I can't make a boys' group, because I'm not a boy. And I can't really organize a regular mother/son group because I'm writing this book about mothers and sons, and haven't got the energy to carry it through. But I have escalated my social/cultural commitment to Daniel, and have been able to handle that, though the money part gets tough sometimes. And when I'm sitting in the audience next to him, watching him watch women sing and play, I really think that these tickets may be more important than the rent money. And, in this time, I see one answer I've been seeking. There are many women like me, feminist and antisexist, raising sons and struggling against the patriarchy's claim on them—and we have to come together, mothers and sons, socially and culturally—for here are the peers and "older brothers"—these other sons of women like me, boys who struggle to be themselves, who question the expectations of male culture.

January 15, 1981

Daniel and I went to our first mother/son acting workshop. He loved it. I loved it. When we came home, we talked for half an hour, even though it was a school night and way past his bedtime. We were peers, we were friends who had taken this class together, and out of the work at hand we exchanged impressions. We're working together; we've gone outside of our family roles to relate to each other—lucky that we like each other when we do that. I bless the night this idea came to me.

Middle February 1981

After each workshop meeting, when we're done, as the group moves out into the elevator and down onto the street, Daniel and Frank or

Daniel and Jacob spar, wrestle, and poke at each other. Sometimes the two sixteen-year-olds do it too, but they incorporate their wrestling training into their scene. They seem to be trying to make it look like an exchange of information and technique, but it feels just like what the young ones do, like an enlargement of the same thing, really. Frank is eighteen months older than Daniel, but much bigger. Jacob is three years older, but almost the same size. Daniel likes them both, likes to work with them, to improvise with them in the workshop; he likes this sparring too. Sometimes it grows serious or mean, sometimes they burlesque it, but they always do it.

The effect on me is heavy. I *hate* it. We are way past the point where I could take him out of it without his suffering a loss of face, and our suffering a loss to our relationship. I usually watch it from an unobtrusive corner or go away when what they do is disturbing to me. This sparring makes me physically uncomfortable. I see it as the masculinity training ground, the skirmishes that teach them to align themselves as competitors and adversaries. I watch to see what Daniel will do, and am relieved and miserable all at once, when I see that he can be like the others.

(I remember his second day in line on the public-school playground. I sort of lurked at the corner; he thought I was gone. As he stood there, a bigger boy, another first grader, came toward him. The boy swung his book bag close to Daniel. First he backed away. Then, when he realized the boy was doing it on purpose, he said, "Stop that." The boy swung the bag closer and closer; Daniel kept backing up and repeating, "Stop it, cut it out, take that away." When the bag came past his head—I couldn't see if it touched him or not —he yelled, "You stop that!" Of course, the boy went on. Daniel was nearly hysterical, when suddenly, throwing down his own books, he lunged at the boy, shrieking and screaming—I could hear the tears in his voice—and knocked him down. He jumped on him, pounding and pulling at him, screaming and screaming. I stood at the corner of the building, watching, crying. One of the girls in the second-grade line ran for a teacher, who pulled them apart, yelling, "You boys stop this fighting!" There was no conversation, no questioning or explaining of what had happened. They picked up their books as the buzzer sounded, and marched in, in line. I walked home, still crying, but relieved that he would wait, that he would not jump to fight, and relieved that he would not be a victim. But to *do* that, to have to *do* that, to *learn* to do that, to *have* to live in that—ahh, my baby, my boy.)

Watching Daniel and Jacob smile at each other, laugh, lock hands, and make a tug-of-war with their arms, I remember the transition; the history of boys and their bodies together. As babies, they roll around all over each other, hug and kiss and tickle each other, stroke each other's hair and skin. This is discouraged among boys after about one year—if not before. (It's allowed to continue among girls, who groom each other like monkeys until they reach adolescence, when they are told that it's queer for girls to touch each other. So the hair brushing and braiding, the arm stroking and spontaneous hugs and kisses dry up.) The boys are taught to give and receive a solemn handshake, often before they are two years old, and applauded when they can mimic that crisp abbreviation of human physical contact.

I remember that very early in the first year of nursery school, Daniel came to like a boy named Kenneth. He greeted him by touch, smiled at him a lot, and talked to him often while they played. One morning, Daniel was there before Kenneth, mixing up food coloring and water in test tubes on the main table. Kenneth came in and Daniel got up, went over to him and said, "Hi, Kenneth. Good morning." Kenneth didn't answer, ignored him completely. Daniel greeted him once or twice more, while Kenneth walked past him as if he weren't there. So Daniel went after him and punched his arm, the gesture an exact miniature of the greeting punch men use when they're "friends." "Hey, Al, how ya doin'?" Sock. If they can't hug, if they can't even talk, they hit. The hit provides physical contact, and demands recognition.

Later February 1981

I've done a lot of thinking lately about the fact that this is the end of the Parents' School, the last of our seven years. I've spent a tremendous amount of energy since Daniel was four months old, in the original play group, on keeping together day care and schooling for Daniel. For the purposes of radical education, specifically for coming as close as possible to control over the environment in which he lives—especially in hiring teachers and making curriculum—to combat male supremacy, sexism, and homophobia in his daily life—seeing to it that my voice was not the only one he heard saying what I would say. Going around to visit other schools, both when he was six and now that he's nine, recalling those two months of misery in the public-school first grade, and talking to other mothers about what they've done, not done, and propose to do have given me both a lot of grief and a strong resolve. The grief is for the loss of control, the loss of his community, and the coming of what will surely be a time of struggle, with ugly problems. The resolve is this: We cannot have what we had; it never was all that we wanted it to be anyway; it was just the only game in town, and we will do what we must do with what comes. I've made all the possible applications and inquiries; Chicago's public schools get more and more horrendous, and even those which *might* be possibilities may disappear or change before next September.

In these school visits, I've observed that the relations between boys and girls are either terrible or nonexistent, the teachers are blind to the situation or, worse, instrumental in creating and maintaining it, and the curriculum marches on as it did when I was nine years old; they're teaching the same "facts" from basically the same perspective, though with some different styles of presentation. In one "open classroom," I observed the teacher, a woman, favor the male students, call on them by name, direct all her speech to them, smile at them, make constant eye contact with them. The girls, who were all clustered around her, sitting beside her on the couches and cushions, rarely spoke, and when they did, they practically whispered. She responded to them with nods and murmurs, inclining her head briefly in their direction. It was obvious that she is not particularly antigirl, simply unconscious, oblivious to the sociopolitical patterns in her classroom.

February 25, 1981

The mothers of girls are coming to realize that the more time their daughters spend with girls—out of the company of boys—the stronger, smarter, and healthier they are. Watching Omie realize this, knowing that she might send Nelly to an all-girls' school, I want to cry. I want to scream: But what about *my* baby? What about my child, born in the same innocence, harboring no innate evil, desiring no malevolent power, struggling, in fact, not to take that place being held open for him in the hierarchy of male supremacy—what about my *boy*? Will you leave him behind? Will you leave him alone with the coaches, the hearty boy-o's of the history department, the math teachers who assume boys are interested but girls aren't? Yes, you will; maybe you should. Protect and nurture those girls, shelter and strengthen them. Teach the young girls our history and challenge them with the gift of women's wisdom, their birthright. But, sweet Goddess, how we'll miss them, my son and I. How he needs the temperance of their presence, indisputable reminder of who they *really are*—in the face of the lies other boys and men will teach him about them. Yes, girls flourish when they go to school with girls; they *need* to be with girls, but boys need to go to school with girls too. This does not admit of an easy solution. Maybe if he went to school with a handpicked group of boys, and only had the very rightest of teachers . . . But when would I work? How could I write? Write—how could I sleep, if I were in the process of setting up a feminist boys' academy? I could *only* sleep, really, because I'd be doing it in my dreams. How would we live? No one is offering me money to make such a place. Well, maybe some grants. . . .

Remember that boys in the company of girls are often labeled rough and rowdy, obstreperous simply by comparison. I don't want my kid, who is such a physically expressive person, to be constrained, to be held in. I would rather the girls pick up the body action from the boys, observe and take on some of that entitlement to space, movement in space, that boys are given from the moment they're born. Maybe the academy should have both sexes. (Is this what I want to do with my life, run a school? Run a junior high, a high school, and then a university and graduate school, just keep going until Daniel is all schooled out?)

More about the boys: How can they withstand the pressure? How can they say no to the gift of power, especially so young? They won't see the *kind* of power it is, the way it is wielded, the fact that it is power-over, rather than an expression of themselves, of their natural energy and "the way things are." How can they turn a deaf ear, a blind eye, to television, to the toys—ingeniously made to catch those ears and eyes—to the girlie magazines in the drugstores? Nothing can keep the boys from associating this junk with the girls they know—especially since it's made to create that association, to teach it; the girls make the connection too. And what about the responsibility for all of that? Must mothers of sons run interference on the whole damn culture for our sons?

March 16, 1981

I am sort of trying to discontinue tucking him in at night, like walking him to the door in the morning. Both of these are attached to an emotional separation that I don't want, but I do want to stop the sense of waiting on him. I want the goodnights and the partings to be mutually expressed, to be flexible. I feel constrained; I can't stand the position I'm put in—waiting on him, waiting for him to be ready, having always to keep aware of his needs. It's different now, he's older; this is where it's different for mothers of sons. I turn into a waiting woman, waiting on a male—no matter if he's only nine years old. This fits into the sex-role socialization pattern. Certain postures and situations arise that are slavey, and I cannot tolerate them.

Am I trapped? Can I release myself from the pattern without losing some measure, a good measure, of the sweetness and tenderness that is between us? Is there no way I can explain this to him, so that we can go on taking and giving comfort without my being *used?* I have to keep in mind that at nine, Daniel is having a hard time accepting responsibilities, giving up being a little kid, moving on to being a middle kid. He wants and needs *more* hugging and kissing lately, more time and attention, more thumb-sucking, etc. He seems to be trying to store up a bunch so he can leave this phase behind him, to get a lot in now and then go on. Like drinking a lot of cool water before going into a desert.

March 22, 1981

Yesterday Daniel told Jonathan and me that he's bound by "the pressure to be a *boy,* instead of who I really am."

March 24, 1981

Tonight Daniel and I had a fight in which he seemed so much like a man, even reminded me of his father, that I was angrier than the fight itself would justify. His fighting methods, his faces and phrases, were adult male. He just came back from his father today, and sounds a lot like him. I'm writing this still too mad to act, to do anything. Can I force myself to do right, to overcome my anger and pain to help him see the better way, to help make it right between us? Or should I let him stew awhile, see if he makes a move toward me? I realize that I'm making this decision in the same way as when

I fight with a peer, a grown-up. The fight was about the fact that he abuses me lately when I help with his homework. He doesn't like to be told he's wrong, and responds nastily, making me the butt of his emotion. He reminded me of Jonathan, refusing to come off anything, insisting on my admitting my mistakes first in the fight, while putting off dealing with my complaint against him. I want Daniel to be able to argue, but how to *teach* him while I am the one who owns the other emotional half we're discussing?

I feel bad being estranged from him like this. I want to make the connection, but I also want him to crack a little. And I just hate him, sitting there with a new book from the Jane Addams Bookstore, a new shirt from L. L. Bean, all decked out with the deliciousness I've brought into his life, and is this the gratitude I get? Etc., etc. My body is all tense now anyway, I couldn't have a good fight; there's too much else I'm concerned about—the book's progress, the late deadline, the application to Ragdale, the money.

March 26, 1981

We worked it through and found that I had forgotten about the *basis* for his temperament upon returning from his father's. He's often, about half the time I'd say, when returning on those Tuesdays, defensive to the point of offensive, surly and sarcastic, real sassy. He understands this well enough to describe it to me, which he just did, in detail. Over there—given the large family, the pressures among the boys, and this having been a particularly tough weekend in that he got very little of Michael (who had to work longer hours than usual at the restaurant)—over there, he adopts a different posture, attitude, and way of dealing. It serves him well over there, but is unsuitable for a home where he is the only child and I am the only adult. And our relationship is *our* relationship, not his and Michael's or any of the others in that family. There's always some time needed to change gears—for *me*, too—from being alone for four days, back to being with Daniel.

This time we were both needing more time and space, and neither one of us got it, so we beat each other up with words, and hurt each other's feelings. I wonder if not wearing the attitude for that house when he first arrives there also causes him pain? When I told him he fought like an adult, and that that had been part of what set me off, the sense of fighting with a man, he said, "But I'm only nine and a half." Once more, with feeling: *The boy is not a man.* The baby part was so easy! Give me that toddlerboy again, Mama, and I'll fight all the shoe salesmen in town; that was nothing compared to this. But my bright-eyed boy came off it in the grand manner. He says that the reason he gives me so much grief when we do the homework is, indeed, that he doesn't like to be wrong, and he likes to "cover the wrongness" by yelling at me, " 'cause then I don't have to think about that I got the word wrong, or let *you* know that I got the word wrong—and I think it's macho, Mom."

March 28, 1981

Last night Daniel and I went to see the Hustle (the Chicago women's professional basketball team) play at the DePaul gym. I can't remember the last time I went to an adult ball game, though I have a strong sense of high school basketball and football as social events, and have vivid pictures in my mind of the stadium and the crowds downstate in 1960. But this was another sensation. I couldn't believe myself. I knew what everybody was doing, and when Daniel asked me questions, I knew the answers. I yelled and moaned, and jumped up off the bleachers. I struck up a conversation with the woman next to me—also there with her son—we talked about the coaches' choices: who they put in, who they took out, when, and why. I couldn't believe myself. It was an exciting game— seesaw, real close. Daniel and I were both attuned to what was happening on the court. We learned the names of both teams' players, talked about those women as if we'd been coming all season. This was the last game. But next season we're going to start early.

March 31, 1981

We went to our local children's clothing store to buy lightweight pants. Five steps into the store, Daniel spotted a bright-red nylon windbreaker, and made a good case for it, so I agreed to buy one if it fit well. It was too small, and the only one on the rack that was his size was dark blue. He had really fallen for the red one, but now wanted the jacket enough to take the blue. While he was trying on pants in the fitting room, I spotted another rack of the same windbreakers—in the girls' section. These were red, yellow, and purple. Now I know this boy's taste, so I checked the available sizes, and called over the fitting-room door. "Daniel, they've got those jackets on the girls' side in *purple*—wanna see?" I've long since explained to him about manufacturers and retailers' attitudes about sex-linked color and design, so he is willing to beat them at their nasty game when he can. We are conspirators now, where before, with the rainbow umbrella, I had played defense, and blocked for him.

Early April 1981

Another mother told me that Daniel has a reputation for being a feminist at school. He recognizes sexism, calls it to the attention of the group. His teacher says he'll argue politics, making cases and defending positions on the issues. Better *that* should be his source of pride than the usual possibilities for boys his age to get attention, to make points. And he is sincere, bless his little heart. The fact that he's not perfect (like when he criticizes sugar-and-junk-food eaters, with longing in his heart for Hostess cakes) doesn't taint his genuine feeling.

April 23, 1981

Daniel used the word fag today, speaking of not being perfect. He said he didn't really know what it meant, but I could tell that he did, and was just ashamed to admit it. I came down real heavy this time, because he's too old to let that go by. We've done this one before, some years ago, and it's time to go around again. The general use of that label for male homosexuals is the same as *dyke* or *kike* or *nigger,* and I want him to see that. So I told him that it was an insult, and one that specifically affected men we knew, naming them. I had never told him that this or that or another man was gay before, knowing how it could backfire, wanting him to know them well before trying to judge them by some yahoo word. I didn't go into feminist linguistics with him, or talk about how some gay men think that word is okay, and use it themselves; he understands that concept, and he's heard about witches and bundles of sticks. I want him to understand what it means to most people, most of the time, and how it's hurtful to those men to use it as a joke, as an insult. He needs to understand that casual slang use of the word is a *weapon,* an attack. I can't even remember what the line was, so angry did I become, so quickly did we get to the core of it. Now I'm worried that I opened a closet door on somebody who wasn't ready to come out to his nine-year-old friends.

Daniel uses the word lesbian to mean any woman who seems

woman-loving and woman-identified, who dresses for herself and not necessarily in fashion, who wears no makeup or brassiere. This results in his considering many more women to be lesbians than say they are, and while that might be better than assuming everybody's straight as a stick, he needs a more sophisticated explanation, a sense of the suffering and danger, sacrifice and pain, that lesbian women share with gay men. Because he has begun to learn about the persecution and oppression of Jews, and naturally experiences his understanding emotionally, I might begin with Hitler's persecution and murder of homosexual men, comparing the pink-triangle symbol of homosexuality to the yellow Jewish star.

Funny how the major questions, about sex and death and reproduction, come around and come around again. They get asked or come up somehow once every few years, every time with greater sophistication on his part, and a fuller explanation from me. The first time we talked about gay men was when he was four, when Sam and Donald stayed with us for a week on Burling Street. Daniel opened with, "How come Sam and Donald wear earrings? Men don't wear earrings." I said, "Well, Sam and Donald are men, and they are wearing earrings. So men must wear earrings, 'cause here they are." He said, "Oh, yeah," and smiled. Simple.

May 9, 1981—written at Ragdale, a local colony for writers and artists

Last night all the writers read some of their work over at the main house. I read from the Book of Daniel, the first public airing of my journals. I was embarrassed to discover that I could not read some of it without choking up or actually crying. But with an audience of all women, and with the support I've felt from some of them, I was not disabled by the embarrassment or the tears. I just read and talked through the tears, as I do in more intimate situations. But the thing is this: Early this morning I had a dream. I dreamed that Daniel was a baby again, very chubby with his bright blond curls, toddling around in a thick diaper. He was wandering through our apartment—it was one we have never lived in, larger, older, more spacious—as I did some work. The work was not visible; I was at my desk doing whatever it was. Suddenly I wondered where he was, and went to look for him. The rooms were bright, light and airy; they had the quality of similar chambers beyond the wall in Lessing's novel *Memoirs of a Survivor*. When I found him, he was happy enough—but I saw, as I picked him up, that his upper chest and shoulders were marked with thin scratches, cuts, and tiny scars. I held him, hugging and rocking. I take this dream to be about my fear of exposing him in the book, making him vulnerable to the hurt of people knowing—and maybe using badly—these intimate things about him. I am worried about how to handle that, how to edit, how to present the journal excerpts to him. I'm sure, too, that the dream is about the basic idea of my giving myself to my work, becoming absorbed in it, and then, rather suddenly, realizing that there is this child—"where's the baby?"—that I have to care for, that I have the responsibility to watch over: it is the conflict between my work and my motherhood.

May 16, 1981

Today I went into the city from Ragdale to visit Daniel. He seems, as always when we've been apart, much older and larger. He felt more capable too, mature in a way that relieved some of my fear of next year's school scene. He seems to be able to deal with whatever the new Miss Limness will be—or do. I mean, he's still growing into himself, but that *self* is good; he's got health and strength and a fine mind. He's beautiful—dark honey hair and clear gray eyes—and he still moves easily; he bounces and twists, hops and sails along. He has it still, what Adrienne Rich calls "the beauty of little boys who have not been taught that the male body must be rigid."[3]

Another thought: I've been the "visiting parent"—like a Sunday daddy—while at Ragdale. This came clear today because I went *home*—and we were in our house together, and right away we felt normal again—the regular push-and-pull of struggle together and against each other. Previous visiting days had been awash in the romance of Ragdale: Daniel lying across the swinging bridge in hot sunlight; Daniel gowned in brocade of gold and scarlet—"the King of England" from the attic's old costume trunks.

June 6, 1981

This game that everyone thinks is so wonderful because it's intellectual, teaches strategy, and smacks of medieval culture—Dungeons and Dragons—has come to Daniel. He spent much of the evening or indoor time on the school camping trip playing this game, and is very excited about it. I love to see him so excited; passionate in the telling and explaining. But the content—of the game and the telling

—was hard to take. "What I like best is the money—and all the weapons. They have all the ancient weapons you can think of, Mom. Lances, spears, swords—all that stuff. It's *real* neat." He explained that there are monsters and dragons, many in the form of gorgons— "Medusas"—and sphinxlike creatures. I tried to keep my questions to the minimum and my tone down, not to rain on his parade, but it was tough to let all that go by—and I didn't. Here's one more game that holds a gold stash to be "success," with the stockpiling of weapons as a major motif, and uses aggression and violence, in the name of adventure, to gain its ends. Because it's done "classically," steeped in the western tradition of male fantasy and myth, it seems more acceptable than an outright war game or a money game like Monopoly; it's touted as being intellectually and culturally stimulating, etc., etc. But it's the same old story, and told—by Daniel at least—as it always has been. Chess made war a metaphor, and subdued the heavier motives into strategy for its own sake. This one seems to be wholly unexpurgated—from Perseus to Arthur Pendragon to Erich Neumann to us—the direct line of patriarchal descent.

Late July 1981

Hard times; heavy talks. Daniel is spending a lot of time with a boy whose need for masculine-style control is very great. He's nearly two years older than Daniel, and is having a great effect on Daniel's behavior. Because Daniel is a natural mimic, an impressionist, really, in the purest sense of that word—he takes impressions readily, like clay, or wax—he impersonates Frank unconsciously. He did this last year with Joseph's pronounced lisp. Worse, I fear that he may be taking on/in some attitudes and behavior. Generally, when this has happened in the past, I have *never* spoken to him of it; I watched it and let it go—which it did, in a short time. But this one unhinges me completely. Because I know that Frank has bad attitudes about girls and women, I've gone a long way out. We've had "Frank-talks," and one huge fight, precipitated by my freak-out at Daniel's seeming to be almost *possessed* by Frank; he *was* the older boy, appearing to be unable to think and feel what Daniel might think and feel. Fortunately, on that occasion Jonathan was here, and refereed us. And he was able to talk to Daniel about the kinds of consciousness necessary to keep one's male self intact in the presence of dominant boys who need to live out masculinity. We talked about losing integrity to the power of the patriarchy. I was especially upset about the way Frank treats Nelly, and I am adamant to the point of being unrealistic about Daniel's having the spiritual wherewithal to keep his relationship with his old friend, this *girl*. He's working at it, he tells me, but complains that Nelly does no such work herself, that when Charlotte (an older girl, whose power with Nelly is analogous to Frank's power with Daniel) is around, Nell shuts up, won't speak for herself; Charlotte takes over and speaks for them both, and shuts out Daniel. Though I regard the girls' behavior as reactive, I cannot excuse it, only explain it. And, since they are not my children, I cannot take their time, as I do Daniel's, talking, explaining, working on it.

August 11, 1981

I read Daniel the prologue and most of the Book of Daniel, wanting him to be prepared for what would be public. Two surprises: he was really interested only in the entries that quote or describe *him* specifically—looking at this, I don't know why I'm surprised—and he didn't want to hear my other thoughts too much; he said, "I'll read all that later, Mom. Just read me what you're telling everybody about *me*." He made only one objection, which I will edit as he asked. I had been afraid he would be disturbed by my mentioning his father, or the more emotional scenes, or by my anxiety made public. Not a bit of it. He listened with great care, commented frequently, laughed, and enjoyed matching his memory with my journal. He liked hearing himself quoted; so do I. That must be genetic. We both took satisfaction in the whole process. What a relief!

August 13, 1981

Having heard the Book of Daniel read aloud, and noting my thoughts about tucking him in and walking him to the door in the morning, Daniel initiated a serious talk. He explained that he felt pushed away, that he's not "as close to my mom as I want to be; it's easier to forget about her unless I kiss her goodnight and talk to her when she tucks me in." Though this had overtones of threat to it, it also speaks to the conflicting desires to be taken care of, babied, mothered—and to be independent, self-sufficient. So we agreed that I would continue to tuck him in at night, but that he would

come to kiss me good-bye in the morning, "unless you're real close
to the door, okay? Then you can kiss me good-bye there."

August 15, 1981

Today we were driving along in Jonathan's car, Daniel in front with
Jonathan, me in the back seat. Since I generally ride in the front, I
was surprised at the lack of shock absorbers back there. The bounc-
ing was really hurting my breasts. When I commented on it, Daniel
seemed to think I was making a bid for the front seat. Oh—maybe I
was. But anyway, I just said, "Well, I have to hold on to my breasts,
then, because this really *hurts.*" He turned around and said, with
heavy irony, "Oh, sure, Mom. Everybody's going to look in and see
you sitting there holding your breasts. Great. Let's change seats,
come on." Then I said, really meaning it, "Oh, no, it's a short ride,
no big deal, I don't mind that much; I'm not in such bad shape, and
I know you really like to sit in front. Next time I ride back here I'll
wear my running bra." But he absolutely refused to accept that, and
Jonathan pulled over so we could switch places. So—now we have
outside social criticism to deal with: the public enters the family.
My son is embarrassed if his mother holds her breasts in the back
seat of a car. Fortunately, this one is not something we're going to
be dealing with often. But it reminds me of another, recent situation
that *astonished* me: Daniel and I were going out; that is, we dressed
for the occasion. I wore some of my favorite clothes—my purple
skirt, a bright-blue shirt, those wonderful purple flower earrings—I
looked beautiful; I felt great. As we walked out and crossed the
street, Daniel said to me, "You know, Mom, everybody's looking at
you because of the way you're dressed. You look like a hooker."
What a moment! Actually I had been aware that people were looking at us; I assumed they found us attractive; we both looked great.
So many things rushed into my mind, such a conflict over what to
address first. "Whatever you may think prostitutes look like, I *know*
I look terrific tonight. Just what the hell do you mean?" He said,
right out of a Victorian drawing room, "You're wearing such bright
colors, and you haven't got a bra on," but went on: "You don't look
good in a skirt. Why are you wearing a skirt? You look better in
pants." For the next ten minutes I lectured on clothing choices, in
terms of color, flamboyance, style/fashion, taste and pride, skirts/
pants on women, the position of prostitutes in this society and especially in our neighborhood, which happens to be a heavy action

area,* and, once again, what it means when men on the street look at, call out to, or honk at women. Also, how feeling and looking good *draws* people, attracts them, even those with no evil designs. We all want to be around radiant energy. And last, never least, I wound up again with my feelings—"You made me feel bad by saying what I knew you meant as a put-down. You took some of my brightness away—and did it ever occur to you that the *two* of us were the attraction, looking so good together?"

August 17, 1981

Daniel wants to know when he'll be free to do as he pleases—stay at a friend's house as long as he likes, go out when he likes, where he wishes, eat whatever and whenever he wants, etc. He wants me to tell him an age; he thought maybe twelve. He also told me, "You have to stop thinking of me as young, Mom. I'm nearly ten." I've just learned, in this decade, to realize that I, at thirty-eight, am young and that my second and third decades were filled with delusions of maturity. But since I know he won't buy that—any more than I did —I have to appreciate his perspective. The two strongest aids I have are memories of my own sense of self—from thirteen to thirty—and my years as a high school teacher. Those students were wise and competent while they were ignorant and irresponsible; it is the nature of contemporary adolescence. And their parents—so many of them—were sad and foolish, unable to remember their own youth, unwilling to see the children as who they really *were*. I remember the few parents who got it right; they taught me lessons I'd better review now.

August 18, 1981

Daniel is seeming *older* again. This is one of the times that it strikes me, when I suddenly notice that he's different. I listen to him talk,

---

* Our neighborhood includes a strip on which, at any given moment, at least 10 percent of the passersby are prostitutes, pimps, or cops, and more than 10 percent of the cars going by are driven by johns, men looking to rent a woman. It is impossible for any woman, of any age, to walk half a block to the grocery store, which I do almost daily, without being honked at. Clothing is irrelevant. I have been honked as I carried a full laundry basket to the laundromat. Sometimes when Daniel and I stand together at the bus stop, we are honked and examined, as if we were a novelty act, mother and son for sale.

and I realize what our relationship is, and I recognize that we are becoming companions. It's early; these are only the beginnings of comradeship, especially in terms of our being together simply for the sake of being together. After all, we still *have* to be together.

Later in the same day

I read a passage in *The Waves** today that reminded me of Daniel's dilemma; it was about "the pack," the boys. They are so appealing to him; he longs to follow, to join—even when he sees their cruelty and shallowness, even when he suffers their cruelty himself. These boys are the sons of the fathers; they become Boy Scouts or Hitler Youth; they are the junior patriarchs. They will become fathers with little or no conflict at all. Unless they have the rare fortune to meet, *alone,* so that they may freely admire, a man who is tender, or a boy who is not afraid to be himself in front of them, or a woman who will guide them, or a girl who will befriend them.

September 9, 1981

Today, when Daniel came home from his first day at the new school, he said, "Mom, I don't have to worry about leaving Nelly out anymore. Today we had chances to pick partners to work with—you know, 'buddies'—and I asked her a couple of times, and she *always* said no. So *she* did it. I did it right, and she wouldn't." This was all in reference to my recent home lecture series, in which I warned him of the sexes being split in school, of the old patterns, and what I had heard about the animosity of boys for girls in this class. What I really cared about was that he should not shut himself out from *knowing* girls, and from the old friendship with Nelly. But I feel like the waters are rising; words never make it, and PEERGROUPPRESSURE is raising its ugly head ever higher. This situation is intensified by the need, in Daniel and in Nelly, to make new friends, to find a place

---

* "They are the volunteers; they are the cricketers; they are the officers of the Natural History Society. They are always forming into fours and marching in troops with badges on their caps; they salute simultaneously passing the figure of their general. How majestic is their order, how beautiful is their obedience! If I could follow, if I could be with them I would sacrifice all I know. But they also leave butterflies trembling with their wings pinched off; they throw dirty pocket-handkerchiefs clotted with blood screwed up into corners. They make little boys sob in dark passages. They have big red ears that stand out under their caps. Yet that is what we wish to be. . . . I watch them go with envy. . . ."[4]

for themselves in this group. Of course that necessitates accepting the rules of the new group—especially if you're ten years old.

September 16, 1981

Daniel told me today that his teacher says football, not basketball, will be the major sport this year in the winter months. I know it'll be touch, not tackle, but that's small comfort, if any. The girls will be *out;* they might have played basketball, but football? Forget it. I was filled with disgust and fear; this calls up memories of touch football games I've watched from the sidelines, seeing the boys and young men try to hurt each other within the limited rules of this lighter version of a brutal sport. Jonathan calms me down a bit by saying that it is possible to play touch without that happening, that he's played it many times that way, that the tenor of the game will be set by the teacher—and we don't know yet what he's like, or what he's got in mind.

Mid-September 1981

Daniel and I went to the bank today. While I transacted business, he sat in one of the cushy chairs that the officers use to interview customers. When I was done, I commented on the comfort of his chair. He pointed to the bank manager's private office, walled off from the lobby. The manager herself, a strong and dignified woman, was seated in the largest, most thickly upholstered chair in the bank. Daniel said, "Look, she's the bank manager's secretary; that's why she gets to sit in his chair." He understood that the chair's location, size, and style symbolize power—but he has learned that no woman may be that powerful, so he short-circuited the logical inference, the information his own eyes gave him, i.e., that the woman *is* the bank manager.

September 23, 1981

Today Daniel called me from school, just about the time he should have been walking in the door, and told me that he and three other boys were robbed—"mugged"—on their way to the bus stop. Two teenaged boys threatened to beat them up if they didn't give them money. He told me another mother was on her way there in a cab to pick them up, and that he would be home as soon as he could. I was both frightened and relieved. His tone had been rather ironic, that crisp, sarcastic tone he's been coming into lately, and I'm sure that here, as elsewhere, it's a defense. When he got home he said very little at all, less still about the robbery. His pose pulled me up short; I couldn't comfort him if he revealed no need; I couldn't help him talk about it if he gave me no opening. Is that what creeping masculinity is about? I have to keep myself from blaming his response on Frank's influence—Frank's defensive stance is a wall—he's just closed. I'm sure all of them were frightened, and I don't want their real emotions to get lost in the need to be cool—and I don't want to harp on, or emphasize, *fear* to the point at which it will disable him. Later that night, when he was unable to do his homework, unable to think, he finally blurted out, "I was mugged today!" And we talked. He was able to say that yes, he was afraid when it happened, and that he was afraid it would happen again. I did not handle this as well as I should have—whatever that means—oh, what it means is that I knew as I was talking to him that I was coming up short—that my own fear and anger were short-circuiting my ability to be his comforter and source of strength. But by bedtime we had come to a better place, and he was able to sleep soundly, for which I was very grateful and glad.

I'll look again through Violet's book about children's emotional needs/problems;[5] it will help me to help Daniel with the aftermath of this fearful experience. This raises, besides all the worries about machismo and boys' emotional blocks, the old issue of living in the city. We are mad to stay here. Pimps on the corner, robberies at the bus stop—should I take my kid and run?

October 15, 1981—back at Ragdale

Last night I dreamed Daniel was in jail. We were in England—the ever-present Anglophilic fantasy turned sour. He had been picked up and locked in for his behavior—being obstreperous and loud, singing and dancing, running and jumping—being too free, basically. I waited in a hot stuffy cigar-smelly room, high walls paneled with old dark wood, hearing official police business go on around me—doors opening and shutting, staplers and typewriters, clanking keys and handcuffs. The police were all men, dressed in black wool overcoats. Finally they brought him out to me, very subdued. He was thrilled to see me, but visibly checked his joyful response. One of the overcoated men gave me a sheaf of legal papers, filled with print. I glanced over them and read the end, which said that he was to be released to me, after having been held two days "to teach him a lesson." That line has three meanings: First of all, it is the classic patriarchal threat—the father says, "I'm going to teach that boy a lesson." Second, Daniel and I use that line all the time as a joke; e.g., if he reads in the newspaper of someone having a disastrous experience Daniel will say, "Well, that taught *him* a lesson!" Third, the idea of being taught a lesson is directly applicable to the source of this dream—his time of getting used to the discipline and routine of his new school.

(In the past several days I've been trying to decide if I should go home from Ragdale, to be with him while he suffers through what I had thought would be a pretty smooth transition between our freewheeling little school and the "real world." It's not nearly as bad as it *could* be—and there are, as Jonathan points out when I get really crazy, some values to his learning to organize his work, to plan, and to correct himself. The question is—as usual—is *this* the way to learn those things? The answer is as obvious as the question—*no*—but we've no other choice. I want his world to be a place where he learns these things because the need for them grows out of real work, out of tasks with meaning and value, with connections to his life, where the pressures are not the result of his teacher's temper or insecurity, but organic to the tasks of his own life.)

At the end of the dream, we went home, and inside, once the hugging and kissing subsided, he began to dance and leap about— showing, no doubt, my conviction that the world cannot crush it out of him—what Jonathan called yesterday the creative sense, his ability to think up stuff, to imagine and make worlds of his imaginings. But I hate to think of these children held down, held in— *Oh! Enough!* I lived through it; he'll live through it—and that's what the dream means.

October 23, 1981

Daniel says he wants to stop taking Aikido. He says he's "just not interested anymore." Well, of course this statement isn't good enough; he has to explain *why*, why he no longer loves it, no longer loves the idea and the costume, and doing the forward rolls—all of which he was crazy about just four weeks ago. So I pursued the subject, though it was clear that he felt there was no more to be said, and also seemed to feel that his views wouldn't count anyway, that he would be *made* to go on studying Aikido. (Of course, coming back from Ragdale for only one day, hearing this from him, I'm in a bad position to judge the situation. If he won't tell me anything, I'll be in *no* position to judge the situation.) Finally, I asked him if it was the style of instruction, the ways of the teachers, or if it was the content, the actual *art,* that he wasn't interested in anymore. Then, as I suspected, we got somewhere.

The first day Daniel enrolled in this program, I sat and watched the whole class, which takes an hour and a half. I was seriously disappointed in the style of teaching, appalled by the attitudes displayed by the instructors, and sorry to see that the newcomers were given no information about the art, what it was for, where it came from, what the philosophy behind it was, and so forth. The main man, about my age I'd guess, a black belt who wears the hakama, the formal black skirt, personally instructed Daniel through much of the lesson. He never paid any attention to Daniel's body, to the boy's own sense of balance or movement. He manipulated Daniel's limbs as if he were a mannequin, putting him into the appropriate positions, telling him what he should feel. The kid was off balance the whole time, rarely had a chance to just *move.* I wanted to call out to them—"Just show him what to do, watch him do it, and *then* give him criticism on technique." But I bit my tongue. I watched a young man, a yellow belt, instruct/assist the small boys in exercise. His attitude and demeanor were military and punitive; the exercise regimen struck me as more suitable for the Marines than for Aikido. But I gritted my teeth, watching Daniel drag himself across a huge mat by his elbows. Maybe I wouldn't have known the difference, and thought Aikido was just another variant on the macho martial arts craze among boys his age—but I've seen exhibitions, and I've read a bit, and of course heard Jonathan talk about it for years—as has Daniel. So I knew that this was all wrong. Here were these little boys making the obligatory bows of respect to Morihei Ueshiba, and they didn't even know he was the man who created the art of Aikido. But—I held my peace, and said nothing, because Daniel said that he loved it. The next lesson, he also said he loved it. The third lesson—I was out at Ragdale already—he threw up during class. The fourth lesson produced headaches and nausea. And now he doesn't want to go anymore. Now, I never told him what I thought about the teaching methods, though I talked my head off to Jonathan, so disappointed was I that this dojo didn't have it right.

When Daniel says he doesn't want to go anymore, I have to know if those guys with their Bruce Lee style of teaching have already killed his interest, or what. He finally answered me. (The length of time it takes to get him to say what he's really feeling seems to be growing.) He said, "I don't like those guys! They twist my body all around, pull my hands and feet up and down, and when I say that they hurt me, they say, 'It's *supposed* to hurt!'" And so forth, quoting this, that, or another fellow, who all sound like the coaches at my old high school. This cannot be what Morihei Ueshiba had in mind. When I think of Aikido, I picture that beautiful old man; I imagine *him* teaching Daniel, as in that sequence in Maxine Hong Kingston's *The Woman Warrior*. Now we have to see if there's another dojo where children can study, if it's reasonably priced, if it's on a direct bus line, and if they teach in the style that the art requires. This had seemed so easy; I should have been suspicious—and it's already paid for, damn it.

October 27, 1981

I always expect Daniel's birthday to look like the day he was born. This one's all wrong. The sky is gray and overcast, and there's a chill indoors. The morning of the day he was born, the sky was brilliant blue and the day was hot, the air warmed by a yellow sun, shining on the colors of the leaves. So as I write, I keep looking out the window, wanting the clouds to clear off and reveal this day to be the same as that in 1971. It *snowed* on his fifth birthday; the flakes were enormous and slow, far apart and silent, falling through no wind at all. We walked among them on the way to Sarah's house, where his playgroup met each morning before kindergarten. Five years seemed a lot then; this is a decade. Where's that sunshine?

The first few weeks after he was born, I still wasn't sure I was really his mother; how could I be somebody's mother? Even on his second birthday, I could still get a laugh by looking in the mirror and saying, "I am the mother of a two-year-old child." It seemed impossible in the moment of the statement—though it was real enough in the days of my life.

Today he'll get out of school a bit early to meet me; we're going to see a Marx Brothers matinee—*A Day at the Races* and *A Night at the Opera*. At 4:10 P.M., ten years *to the minute* since he came out of my body, we'll be sitting in the dark with Harpo, Chico, and Groucho. I wish they'd been with us in the delivery room.

So he'll celebrate presents and sweets—and being *ten!* I'll celebrate the memory of his small head between my thighs, and my domed stomach collapsing as his shoulders slide out.

2

Raising Sons

Now I see Eve covering
her breasts with her hands
and I know it is not to hide them
but only to keep them
from all she must know
is to follow
from Abel on one,
Cain on the other.

—LINDA PASTAN[1]

What do I think of raising a son? With any luck he'll do a
little yard work.

—JENNIFER STONE[2]

Women create men. We carry them inside of our bodies, feeding
them with our food, sharing our precious oxygen with them. We
labor to bring them to birth, then lift them up into our arms, and
hold them warm against our breasts. We soothe, kiss, cuddle, and
sing to all the baby men. We dress them, give them toys and books,
make them peanut-butter-and-jelly sandwiches. They grow from babies to boys and then to "young men." Soon, before we realize it's
done, they are adult men, culturally empowered to dominate us.
How does this happen? Are we a pack of demented masochists, urging them toward misogyny? Do we deny their maleness, hiding
behind "baby" and "child" until we find the dried semen in their underpants and bed sheets—and *have* to recognize that they're men?
Are we unwilling or unconscious maternal repositories of the party
line, believing that anatomy is destiny, that boys will be boys—every
mother's son of them?

What *does* a woman think of when she thinks of raising a son? What can it mean to a woman in this society, to push a boy out of her body—and then watch him grow into a man? I asked this question of mothers, looking for immediate emotional responses, philosophical positions, whatever the words evoked. Several women spoke first of what it meant for them to be mothers, to experience motherhood. They needed to speak so, before they could go on to the sex of their children. Their motherhood is, after all, the starting point.

The social worker at the child-guidance clinic told me, "You know, you're very conscientious and do all the things you're supposed to do, but you never talk about enjoying your children." And it's true. It was so hard. You know, when they were little, I was just exhausted all the time. I would have sold my soul for one night's sleep all the way through.

There are a lot of problems. Finances. I have a real minimal amount of support, and the court can't get me more. I don't buy any clothes but shoes, boots, and winter coats. Money has over and over again been the issue. And also all the years I worked and dropped him off at the day-care center. I worked all day and then had to pick him up; I never had time away from him. When I went out for the evening, I came home, grabbed him up, and took the sitter home. I'm so sick and tired of calling and asking, asking for help.

Those two mothers were among those who were able to speak of the feelings mothers usually hide. We hide them because we know we aren't supposed to *have* them; we're supposed to be mothers of perfection, and to embody the institution of motherhood with no consideration of money, stress, or time.

Someone said to me when my oldest son was four, "God, I can't believe he's four already!" And I said, "Well, you might not be able to believe it, but try 365 days times four." I feel like I've been putting in a lot of time with them, and there's still a lot of time to come. I see lots of joy out of it, but I'm also tired. It's exhausting. I could be doing a whole lot more with my life—like I'm ready to fly and they're not ready to have me gone. I still need to be home at night; I still need sitters. Their needs are immediate and they grow more complex. They need more time with me. They get in bed at night and they want to talk and I'm so tired, or I want to spend time with my husband. I feel like I'm being pulled in a lot of directions. If I could do absolutely what I wanted to do, it would be to be by myself more.

As I get older and look back, I think I should have worked harder; I just sort of went with the status quo. Why didn't I start immediately, saying, "Go make a sandwich; I'm getting out."? I just wondered, but I didn't do it; I stayed home. When I gave up my name, I knew something was wrong; I felt it immediately. But it was so vague; I didn't verbalize it: I knew something was cooking, but it wasn't in my head yet. It was a gut reaction. That was the program and I just went along with it. I was married so young, nineteen, barely had begun to develop and then—plowed under. Now I always feel like I want to go away for a month; I want to go to graduate school. I was hoping they'd take me at the University of Montana so I could go away for nine months.

Raising itself is a funny word, isn't it: all I can think of is just watering them. Maybe that's part of it; you just have to water them.

What some women said may seem shocking in that they were able to describe the reality of their motherhood without the traditionally applied romantic filter. The same kinds of conflicts and contradictions appear when mothers speak of raising *male* children.

These women are diverse; their past lives and present situations are as various as their faces. Aged twenty-five to seventy-two, lesbian, straight, and bisexual, Black, white, Asian, and Latin, welfare recipients and upper-middle-class housewives, students and teachers, artists and office workers, mothers of one boy and mothers of girls and boys, they talked about what it meant to them that their children would grow to be men. Most of them are not feminists. Some are women who say, "I'm no women's libber, but . . . I believe in equal pay for equal work," or "I believe that women can do any job —if they're trained as men are," or "Abortion should be a woman's decision—and safe." Some of these women were unaware of the contemporary usage and meanings of the terms *feminism, sexism,* and *women's movement.* And yet, their words are deeply influenced by their experience of the antagonism between the sexes. Whatever their conscious politics and vocabulary, these mothers are *emotionally* aware that their children are male.

Oh god—the feeling that you must always be receptive, whether you feel it or not. You are always on, you are responsible, this is it. That is the strongest force in my life, being responsible for the boys. When I'm pissed at men in general, which happens, I find myself thinking, you goddamn motherfuckers, I'm tired of it. And I cut them off. Now it's Ernie, firstborn child, poor child, he's at that age. I kind of dismiss him in my mind. Male. I also use the flirty kind of manipulation women use with men on the boys. You might try that with a girl; I don't know. But I need more space. As they get larger and larger they take up more and more space. Their possessions are uniquely male; a girl's junk would probably bother me just as much, but I don't know. The bats and gloves around all the time seem to consume so much space. And noise. Boys are noisier than girls. All these male voices are so *loud*. And they're more physical. When they're watching TV or talking to each other, they wiggle all the time; they kick their feet up and down or they toss a ball or they shadowbox or they're punching at themselves or somebody else or the wall all the time. And they eat a lot. Girls don't eat like that. God, it's like a shovel. It's almost repulsive. It really is. It's five sandwiches before dinner, and then if they stay skinny you can't say anything about it. There I am, I can't even have a piece of lettuce without bloating, and they just eat a cake and a half. Anyway, they do eat.

This next mother of two sons, a housewife, has accepted the teaching of the male role. Her acceptance is completely unself-conscious, though quite deliberate in action.

Raising a son is the upbringing of a male figure. Showing him the difference between a female and a male. Just showing him the difference between a boy and a girl is the basic raising of a son. Like in the toy stores, the girls' toys are separated from the boys'; they're in different sections. That's one of the ways he can tell that girls are different. In school the little girls have to be in one line and the boys in the other. In any public place there's different toilets. So he's surrounded by things that remind him that there is a difference. And then his daddy is always telling him how mommies are sweet, and mommies are a bit more tender and sensitive and soft, so he's exposed to that. I show him, too, like waking up in the morning and putting makeup on. He looks at me and says, "Oh, Mommy, can I try that on?" I tell him it's only for mommies and not for boys. And I've often put the deodorant under his arms even though he doesn't need it, so he sees that. He also sees that the mommies have to shave their legs and men don't have to. The mommies don't have to shave their faces; the dads do. And I'm the one who raises them, more than my husband. They see that; I meet their needs in terms of making food, making sure their clothes are clean. These are the ways my boys will learn.

Many mothers begin to struggle with their sons' maleness when the boys begin to change into men. These mothers talk about size, and strength. This is a corner Daniel and I haven't yet turned. In fact, *most* of mothers' negative responses come as sons appear more and more to be *men*.

My son is dominant. There was a period of time in there when there was no adult male in the house and he would attempt to dominate me. That would make me very angry. He would want to tell me how to cook, and what to do, that whole trip. At a certain stage he just became domineering, just became that right before my eyes. At the same time he grew taller and weighed more, so there was force behind it; it was incredible.

I don't find my boys difficult, but when I think that they will turn into seventeen-year-olds, that makes me nervous. They can just look at me and say, "Fuck you." They are more apt to be defiant, and do things that are dangerous to themselves—the cars and the motorcycles. Not that a girl wouldn't do it, but a boy is more likely. Sometimes I sit here in this living room and look around at them and think, Oh my god. The rest of my life with these three men. That's the farthest I get with it, the best I can do: Oh, my god.

Sexism has manifested itself between us more than I had imagined it would, in comments and discussions with his friends. I find that alienating, but I really don't think I can change it in any great big way. He responded, for instance, to the yowling of a cat, with the remark, "Oh, he's saying that he wants a woman. I'll tell him about women: They're always there when you don't want them and they're never there when you do." Or something to that effect, anyway. He knew that by saying that he would get a rise out of me, but he also meant it. He was about to get more outrageous—his friends were there—but my husband cut in, and that stopped it. Another thing is that when Mona went to camp, I was uncomfortable to be the only woman in the house. I needed for Mona to be there. I understood that it was important for her to be where she was —and she needed not to be home. But oh, I missed my daughter.

I find their being teenagers increasingly difficult. *Teenage* boys, not boys, you see. This is emotionally difficult, to be constantly faced with confrontation about everything. My husband and I were joking about this; nothing is okay. You think you're an okay person, and all of a sudden you have these big angry people running around the house, just looking at you and saying, "What are you anyway, who are you, what are you doing? Why? Why does it have to be this way? Why aren't you doing it differently?" Everything you are and everything you believe in is in question constantly. It's exhausting. We are going into high gear for the most difficult stage of their lives, made difficult by outside pressures. There is a dynamic at work that makes it very hard for a mother and a teenage son to communicate without clashing. I don't know what it is. Maybe it is, to get Freudian about it, a deliberate rejection on the part of the sons. Then, too, when they get big, as big as you or bigger, that causes problems. They know that they are stronger than their mothers, and if they decide something, we cannot push them, can't stop them. It's a physical fact.

This next mother has understood that *something*, what she calls "the outside factor," comes between mothers and sons. That *something* is a major theme of this book.

One of the things I thought you were going to ask is if I have a personal investment in making a difference with these boys. These boys represent all men. I had a little bit of that. Not that I was seeking revenge, but I wanted to make sure my boys grew up and didn't feel like this: My father's words to me when I got married were, "Obey John." Well, I wasn't going to argue with him, yeah, Daddy. He really thought he'd be doing mankind a big favor by telling another woman to obey her husband, fine. So when my boys came along, I thought, here's a chance. But . . . It's difficult being open with the boys. With my daughters, I have a terrific rapport. They go into the world, they're subjected to the usual treatment for women, they come back home. Since they're the victims, they come home and tell me how they're victimized. But I get more resentment from the boys. Maybe it's because I'm labeled Mother. Maybe I should have made them call me Maryanne. Or lied to them and said I wasn't their real mother. Who knows, who knows? They don't want to respond to me naturally. There's some outside force that interferes—that's right, an outside force. What I have with my daughters is natural, but the boys, I use the same approach, and the outside factor comes between us. *Mother*. There's something in their heads about *mother*—about me. I say to them, I'm just a person, I make mistakes, can't we be friends, can't we break that down? But no. They can't see me. Now my husband has the same thing with his mother. They could have gotten along better but he has this same conflict about boys and mothers. Maybe it's sexual, I don't know. Something they're trying to avoid. Can the love for mother be *different*? Maybe they're afraid that if they love their mother better it may be nearly incest? I don't get it. There is some sort of tension there, something holding them back from what would be a natural response to their mother. But I'll tell you something, it's them; it's not us. I mean I'm trying and it's not working, and I cannot deal with whatever this is.

When a woman is pregnant, especially if the pregnancy is planned and the child wanted, one of the major considerations is the sex of the child. Despite our denials of its importance, the sex of the growing fetus is of far more than passing interest, and to more people than just the mother. Fathers, grandparents, and friends—often total strangers—speculate on the genitalia of the child growing beneath spreading shirts and elasticized pants. There are locally famous midwives and nurses who have reputations for accuracy in sex guessing; they are consulted periodically through the nine months. There are formal questions for the sex-guessing game: Does she carry far forward? Is the child lying across her hips? Does she sleep on her back? Is the child active, noisy; does it seem starved, does the combination of craved foods seem "feminine" (like strawberries and cream) or "masculine" (maybe a sausage pizza and a beer)?

A great many pregnant women, especially during their first or only full-term pregnancy, pretend that we do not care what sex the child is—but might admit later, as in a confidential interview, that we cared a great deal. How could we *not* care? Sexual definition is a high-ranking distinction in this culture, and a woman who produces males in male supremacy is rewarded and praised.

The experts still tell us that women *prefer* to have male children, that women express the wish for boy babies. They cite the statistics of female infanticide in China and India, they interview college students, they talk to couples in prenatal training classes. In my own work, interviewing mothers of daughters, I found that the majority of women who wanted children preferred to have female children, or children of both sexes, though most understand that making males does garner more praise and status. Certainly those women understood that I would not disapprove of their desire for daughters and they may have been telling me what they thought I wanted to hear. But, interviewing mothers of sons, I found many women who said that they wanted to have male children. It may be that mothers believe that if we admit we didn't get what we wanted, we will be disloyal to our children, who are what they are, no matter what their mothers wanted.

Had some fortunate researcher been granted the right to interview Catherine of Aragon, Anne Boleyn, and Jane Seymour, the first three luckless wives of Henry VIII, and asked those ladies which sex they "preferred," what can we imagine them to have answered? Catherine, who was scholarly, wise, and politically astute, suffered several miscarriages and a stillbirth, eventually producing one daughter. She was divorced,* put aside in relative penury, and finally—it was rumored—poisoned, for bearing only Mary. Anne, who was aggressive and clever, also suffered a miscarriage—a son, in fact—but bore only Elizabeth, who was probably the most brilliant monarch England has ever known. So Henry annulled the marriage and cut off Anne's head, to seek his male heir in the body of "good Queen Jane." Jane managed to produce the precious boy, Edward, but he died at the age of fifteen. His mother was spared the grief of this loss, however, for she herself had died only twelve days after the birth of her son, more fortunate than her predecessors.

When asked to explain why they want male children, mothers' answers are illuminating; they are far more interesting than what simple statistics might imply.

I wanted a boy. There were two reasons. One is that I have a sister; my father never had any sons, and I always wanted to name a child after him. Secondly, in the third month of my pregnancy, my father-in-law passed away, and if our child was a male, he would be the only one of that family living within the continental United States. And I felt that it would be very important to carry the name through. I was elated when he was born. I really was. That was what I wanted.

I clearly preferred to have a boy; I had been socialized out of my skull. I was one of three girls. My father was very kind, just a pleasant person who was always terribly disappointed—after all, he had been socialized too. We did a lot of talking in the family about how bad it was that there had been no male child, that we were the end of the family name.

I wanted a boy because my husband wanted a boy and his family wanted me to have a son. My husband didn't *say* it, but his mother did. She always made it clear that her son was more important than her daughter,

---

* Henry so desperately desired a son that he created the Church of England when the pope refused to grant his petition for divorce from Catherine. It is more than sobering to realize that the origin of the Anglican Church is to be found in that king's search, through the bodies of women, for the replication and extension of his power in a son.

and her grandson more important than her granddaughter, and that she wanted, her phrase was, "a son from a son"; that's what she would say.

I had a slight preference for a male child; it was real clear that that's what I should do. It was the first child; that was what our parents expected. A son. It was a joke; Richard would say, "Well, when my son is born . . . ," and I'd say, "Well, what if it's not a son," and it was funny. Really a joke, hahaha. When Francis was born, my father sent an immediate telegram: "Congratulations on the sex" were the words of the telegram. Stopped me right in my tracks.

Poignant and sad, expressing a desperate vulnerability to the power of the husband's favor, are these words from the old testament: "And Leah conceived, and bore a son, and she called his name Reuben: for she said, 'Because the LORD hath looked upon my affliction; for now my husband will love me.' " (Genesis 29:32)

Another common theme, among those mothers who preferred sons, was the desire *not* to bear a daughter—the attendant reasoning just as disturbing as that above.

The next two mothers explain that their sense of what women are, and what woman can be, was very limited when they had their (preferred) male children.

I did want boys and I think I felt I would be more comfortable with them. I was afraid that if I had a daughter she might turn out like my sister and be all frou-frou and weird and I wouldn't know what to do with her because I, I can't cope with that kind of femininity. So I was nervous at that time about having girl children, and was happy when they both turned out to be boys. Now, of course, I wish I had a daughter, because now I would know how to raise her. At that time I was very insecure myself and worried about how I fit into the world.

I really didn't want a daughter. I wasn't at all sure that I could handle a daughter. I'm very prejudiced in favor of men. I was also terrified that I'd be jealous of my daughter and I didn't know how I'd handle that. I also thought something about how it would not be near as much fun to have a daughter as a son, because I really enjoyed the playing that boys did—traveling in spaceships to wherever and talking about what it was like when they got to the edge of the universe. At that time in my life I had not had any opportunities to play like that with other women.

This mother's fear of lesbianism extended to a fear of intimacy with her own child:

I had this funny thing about breast-feeding Jeremiah. I breast-fed him until he was about ten months old. I realized that I had wondered about what it would be like to breast-feed a daughter; I thought it might be harder to do, not as comfortable, you know, because of having that kind of sensual relationship with another female.

This mother's "ambivalence" was strongly political:

As a matter of fact, at that point I probably did want to have a male, because I was very unhappy and there was no women's movement. I know how to bring up a male, but what the hell do you do with girls? If you bring them up to fulfill their potential, they're gonna be destroyed: "Better to expose them on the mountainside than to die the death of a thousand cuts." So maybe I was ambivalent. And when I had a boy, my husband was upset for three days, because he wanted a tiny little girl, so he could bring tiny little dresses with tiny little ruffled panties, pervert that he was.

This last mother has come to a conclusion that is perhaps the saddest of all:

Well, I wanted a boy with Gabriel very much, and with Gideon, I wanted a boy again. I remember thinking at one point in the second pregnancy that I was for sure going to have a girl, and I just couldn't believe it. I got very excited. Then I had the amniocentesis and found out it was a boy again. I was a little disappointed, but at the same time relieved. You know, I had always wanted the first child to be a boy, as long as I can remember. But it was for different reasons. It was definitely the status thing then, you know: I am like Cleopatra, I have wide hips, I will bear you many sons, that kind of shtick, but, much later, when I was actually going to be a mother, my reasons changed. By then I had undergone psychoanalysis, and I did not want to have a child my sex because I was sure I'd have the same things happen with her that had happened with me: I'd repeat the patterns. I thought that having a different-sex child would change that. [She chuckles.] Well, now we know that in fact I have visited the same patterns upon my son as I would have with a daughter. But with this current baby, I was very overwhelmed with feelings of being unsafe in this world as a woman: Vulnerable. Safety things were big in my mind, and I felt that it was just easier to be a male in this society. I would be so worried with a girl child, and that was real scary for me. I think it's a real act of self-confidence to want to have a girl child at this time.

Yet women do want to bear daughters, some quite consciously, despite socialization, statistics, and the need to satisfy the male hierarchy's requirements, despite the prizes awarded and the punishments avoided by bearing sons. In counterpoint to the previous quotations are the words of these two women, the first a forty-year-old mother who has borne three sons, the second a seventy-three-year-old mother who bore three sons and a daughter:

With the first one I was positive it would be a girl; after all, there were no brothers in my family. With the second, it just seemed preposterous to have another boy, and having a girl second would be orderly. With the third, I longed for him to be a girl; really, really wanted him to be a girl. It took a couple of weeks before I accepted the fact that he was a boy. It was lucky that he was a real clunky boy, a real boy-boy-boy from the beginning, because I couldn't trick myself or fool myself in any way whatsoever.

I wished, I hoped that I would have a girl. But I never thought I would; I'd had four brothers; I was the only girl. I just thought I'd never be so lucky as to have a little girl. She was a dream to me.

If all were well—if wishes were horses—then women who chose to be mothers could greet the birth of a child of either sex with joy and curiosity: What a delight—a baby! And who are you, my baby? But all is not well, and wishes are only wishes; and we mothers, who must consider and face the complicated values of "female" and "male" attached to our babies, face no such pure pleasure. We must pay careful attention to the defined sex of our children and its impact on our own lives as well as theirs.

In times and places where women have been unable to live full lives, held relatively powerless by male supremacy, having sons has been an avenue to power and self-expression. Though no women said they *wanted* a son for this purpose, many made it clear that they believed their dreams could come true in the lives of these boys; the mothers could be powerful; their presence in the world would be known, through their sons. Linda Wildmare explains: "Before Matthew was born, when I was pregnant, I wanted a boy child. Now I know that that was because I saw women, I saw myself, as powerless. A male child could do all of the things I'd only dreamed of doing and never felt I could."[3] Again the potent words of the old testament echo, for these dreams and the needs they represent for women are exploited there, to urge chattel women to accept the domination of the fathers and the father god by offering them power once removed, through their sons: "Sarah shall be her name. I will bless her, and she shall be a mother of nations; kings of peoples shall be of her." (Genesis 17:16)

In more recent history, there have been countless queens and princesses, royal women whose bloodlines were negated by the male hierarchy, which often advanced feebleminded men, cruel and vicious men, even men whose lineage was questionable, in the place of women. But women frequently ruled or directed policy through their sons, effecting governmental and social change on both national and international levels. They were many, and they were the mothers of sons we have been taught to revere, sons who became the fathers of this culture.

Olympias, the mother of Alexander the Great, "worked to ensure his succession to the throne" despite the violence and uncertainty of her husband's reign in the fourth century B.C. Plotina, whose husband Trajan had been Emperor until his death, was not allowed to rule Rome herself, and so "secured the throne for her favorite son, Hadrian . . . [and] continued to be active in government through Hadrian until her death in 120." Flavia Julia Helena, who was divorced by her husband when he became Emperor of Rome in 292 (she was a commoner), "saw to it that her son was proclaimed Emperor." Helena then became "Empress Mother," and wielded power and influence with her son, Constantine.

Theodora II of ninth-century Byzantium, Melisande of twelfth-century Jerusalem, and the tenth-century German queen Maude held sway until they suffered the loss of their power at the hands of their envious sons, as did Adelaide of Burgundy, who had the misfortune to marry Maude's son, who apparently taught their own boy to treat her in the same fashion. These women, to the manor born, were perhaps more polite then Fredegund, who died in 597 in France after a life in which she rose from the peasant class as the bride of Chilperic, who had murdered his wife to wed her. After bearing a male heir, she is "said to have planned and executed [her

husband's] assassination"—not having taken his example lightly—
and "became sovereign and the guardian of her infant son, holding
this position for thirteen years."

Bertha, Queen of the Franks, "was responsible for her son
Charlemagne's education, and many of his later religious policies
can be directly attributed to her influence." Many popes were sons
and grandsons of Theodora the Senatrix and her daughter Marozia,
whose influence "was so great during the tenth century that popes
were chosen and disposed of at [their] bidding."

Outside the palace, but still notable enough to have been
recorded, the mothers of John Wesley and Francis Bacon were
similarly influential in or responsible for the work that brought
credit to their sons. Susanna Wesley (1660–1742) taught all of her
nineteen children at home, and, eventually, hundreds of others. She
wrote religious textbooks and conducted services for the children,
though she was opposed by "the local curate, as women were forbidden to preach." Her son is credited with "founding" Methodism—
and it's not hard to see where he found it. Anne Bacon
(1528–1610), mother of essayist and political theorist Francis
Bacon, was a "scholar, translator, and tutor and governess to Edward VI of England." Her translations, in particular, were important
work, earning her an international reputation.

These examples are deliberately taken from those societies
which have been traditionally considered the primary sources and
influences of this one, but I cannot go on without writing of
Kaahumanu of Hawaii (1772–1832). After her husband died, she
"dressed in warrior's clothing and announced to her son, who was
heir to the throne, that his father wished that they rule together.
After learning to read and write, she helped establish schools and
educational rights for women and then passed laws to rid the islands
of the abuses of the traders, who had brought drunkenness, venereal
disease, vandalism, social disruption, and sexual exploitation of the
women."[4] This queen was one of the mothers who used the maternal
power behind the throne to put herself and other women forward—
to the throne itself.

Kaahumanu went far beyond merely hoping that a son could be
a woman's passport out of powerlessness. For most mothers of sons,
the benefits of having male offspring are considerably less than those
the great queen achieved. Her own triumph depended, at least to

some extent, upon a responsive, affectionate, and respectful son who accepted her as an equal in power.

In this interview group, sons responded candidly when asked what their mothers' hopes had been when pregnant; several said they hadn't the faintest idea. But those who responded with a guess or a sure feeling were divided pretty evenly between the sexes. Several of the men who said they believed their mothers wanted a male child simply said, "I'm assuming she had a preference for a boy, since she already had a girl, my sister." The majority of the others in that group attributed their mothers' desire for a boy to sexist socialization. For example:

I think women at that time thought if they had a son it would be much more pleasing to the husband than a daughter. The daughters were very much second best. When she had me, she was very pleased. Firstborn son, right, which was traditionally hoped for.

The rest of the family, she's told me, sort of said this better be a boy. I think that's partly made up, though. Her pressure on me to have children to carry on the line—whatever that might be—because I'm the last surviving male, shows that she believes in it herself.

She wanted to have a firstborn son. And she said that she wanted to have a second son and a daughter. That's what she said. She said she wanted just what she got. I don't know if I believe it, no. She used to tell me she didn't want to have children; maybe she says this other stuff now because she doesn't want to hurt me. I mean I couldn't believe it; it was kind of hard for me to believe that was exactly what she wanted. It doesn't happen.

Few of the sons mentioned, or seemed to consider, that having a male child would not only "be better," in terms of what would please the husband and in-laws, but could improve the mother's situation in terms of higher status, greater influence, or stronger representation to the power structure. Is this because male privilege, as one of the interview mothers suggested, is virtually invisible to men? Or is it that they don't believe that power once removed *is* power?

No man said of his mother, nor did any mother really say of herself, that she wanted a boy because she wanted to make a man, because she felt an affinity for boys and understood them, or because she wanted to help boys grow into good men. Apparently it is no longer possible for even the most male-identified women, even loving mothers of sons, to make such statements as this one: "I know many people think boys are a nuisance, but that is because they don't understand them. I do, and I never saw the boy yet whom I could not get on capitally with after I had once found the soft spot in his heart."[5]

One reason for this, as for the words and attitudes conveyed by mothers speaking of males, is that most women today, whatever their political persuasion, understand that there is a terribleness between females and males. Even the sweetest little face beneath a cowboy hat can quite suddenly take a shape that shocks a mother into the recognition that boyhood is brief: ". . . how can a woman feel? What can her stance be toward the creature who . . . created this mess, this murderous predicament [the world situation], and who even now stands blocking her off from the right to make a human contribution to its solution? It seems possible that now . . . women in substantial numbers hate, fear, and loathe men as profoundly as men have . . . hated, feared, and loathed women."[6] Even those women who insist they like little boys better than little girls will pull up short at descriptions of men.

When asked to generalize and to describe young boys, many mothers had positive views of the lads, sympathetic and affectionate. Some, in fact, had *only* good things to say. They said that boys were active, happy, outgoing, adventuresome, daring, romantic, easygoing, energetic, smart, bright, challenging, inquisitive, loving, constructive, cute, happy-go-lucky, sporty, free, sweet, frank, fresh and lively, and "have a mind of their own."

Psychologist Jean Hubbard gave me, in conversation about this book, an explanation for that offensive expression, "He's all boy!" She said that what it means is this: "People believe that boys embody assertion, aggression, confidence, and even that charming copping to *not* being confident—for a moment. They are world-changers; they're willing to engage in physical violence to win or make a point. There is a charm in two boys having a fistfight on the street: they fight, and then they become best friends, and walk off together."

Though this definition might seem to have been influenced more by Mark Twain's boys than *our* boys—the kids who are really out there beating and being beaten up in the street, with absolutely no charm at all—she is right. That is, people *do* mean what she says they mean; even some mothers of sons, who have perhaps the best opportunity to know what boys are about, subscribe to this Tom Sawyer definition of boys and boyhood.

Most interview mothers did not give boys unqualified rave reviews, of course. Many compared the lives of boys, and the social direction they receive, with the lives of girls, who get female conditioning.

Boys have an attachment to their mommies; they seem not to be as mature as little girls the same age. Girls are not as mischievous; boys are out to have fun. They seem to get into more physical stuff, sports and building things, and they are less verbal. (Every time I say that I think of all these people I know who don't fit the generalizations!)

The male needs a whole lot of praise. It seem like my boys need a whole lot of "Honey, you're wonderful." But then everyone needs that, so I can't be sure. I have a friend who has two boys and two girls—I've just got this troop of three boys—and she said the boys are the troublemakers in the family; they give her the most trouble. That could be just the way it is with those kids, though.

My boys were noisy and they were dirty. They were more physical and more outgoing, stronger, often more outwardly responsive; I could see their reactions more easily than my girl's. The boys would just charge in, they were boisterous and loud, more assertive. They indulged in braggadocio more than girls do.

Boys are much less together than girls. Girls seem to have a social sense, a sense of behavior. They know how to deal with social situations that boys don't know how to behave in. Also, boys need a lot of exercise at the age when they're just beginning to turn into men. But then, so does my Stephanie, who's just turning into a woman.

I always thought of little boys, if I thought of them at all, as playboys—not serious children. In my generation, we always thought the girls were serious and the boys were more or less playboys. They like their bikes and they like to play ball.

In the early teenage years, when they start to put on a show for girls, they're dumb. They kind of stay behind; they're just not as sharp; they're not willing to expand their minds; they slow down. They pick up on the girls again in the late teens. Actually, all males, as if they were a separate species, are more insecure than girls and women. They're not as strong as girls. They stay immature for a much longer period of time. They can't seem to handle things as readily and as well as girls do.

Boys are frightened of everything that's new. Sometimes afraid to venture out of their own neighborhood. I see that in the older fellows, seventeen, eighteen, nineteen. I think they're more frightened of life than they let on —more than girls. These boys, especially Black boys, are petrified from the time they are little until—some men I've met—as old as forty. They're frightened. Men and boys, they just seem to be frightened of everything. Women and girls just do it.

By the time they're five years old, they've received all kinds of messages about what it's not okay to be if you're a boy. And they receive all those messages no matter what we do; it's an enormous battle for them to hang on to being human; the messages are dehumanizing. Girls aren't hit with it so strongly until puberty. Think about it, little girls can wear pants or dresses to school; they can wear what they want. Little boys cannot wear dresses to school. They can't even wear pretty shirts to school. In most situations, they can't even have their hair slightly long. Little girls can do any of that.

They are aggressive, pugilistic, freer physically than girls; they have better and bigger muscle development because they're allowed to play. I believe that they are forced into all of this. I honestly don't believe there are any differences except those that we superimpose on them.

Other mothers described the choice boys are given; they may take on the heroic stereotype for themselves, or they may choose another, admittedly less desirable but still acceptable, male role. These choices are delineated by movies and TV, and learned quickly and easily by boys. A classic example is the movie *The Man Who Shot Liberty Valance*. John Wayne is the main man; a rancher, he embodies the first choice: physically powerful, emotionally undemonstrative, contemptuous of weakness and propriety. James Stewart is the second choice; a lawyer, he is an eastern intellectual (though he learns to accept and even attempt brute force); he does women's work, and he wins the woman's love by teaching her to read and write and appreciate "culture." Though there are other types, they are variations on this theme, which depends on the power dynamic between the two men: football player/college professor, explorer/

farmer, sailor/shopclerk, etc. Though second best is okay, boys
know that second is not first.

Mothers' analyses of this situation are less dramatic, and more
thoughtful; the source of the role's duality is examined below:

They can be very sensitive; they'll be sensitive to you, and to your needs
and wants. And they're not afraid to deal with those needs and wants—
yours or theirs. It's after twelve or thirteen that they get into a thing
where it's not *cool* to do those things that can turn you on emotionally,
that are about real stuff between people.

Boys are active, noisy, boisterous. I think they are overcompensating. I
don't think that they're insensitive, but I think that they are terribly
frightened of their feelings. They're also terribly frightened of the power
they have, that society hands over to them, and all of a sudden they realize they can wield. Boys are afraid.

I see two separate types. The kids that Bobby relates to are the ones I
like. They're just basically nice kids. They help their folks, they get along
with people; they get excited, but nothing bad. The others are the wild
hell-raisers. They swear all the time. These are young boys who don't really like anybody except kids like themselves, and Bobby just shies away
from them. He had this one little friend; they started school together. But
now it's at the point where Bobby won't even talk to him, because he's
gotten into this role of being a tough kid, and Bobby's not.

I see a real change since we've moved from a city to a small town. His
city friends were more serious, and so was he, quieter, somewhat fearful,
more circumspect about where they were going. Now, that he's in a more
open situation, less physically threatening, it's all different. They're loud
and boisterous, they take their bikes anywhere; they do the things I'd
heard that boys do, but I'd never seen before.

Boys are also described by mothers of sons as aggressive,
strong, reserved, athletic, fair, tough and open; but these get mixed
in with sloppy, loud, smart-mouth, destructive, wild, insensitive,
pushy, dirty, disrespectful, rowdy, selfish and demanding. This combination, considerably less appealing than the first list, begins to suggest the connection mothers feel between boys—even our own sons
—and men. Though some women do speak of socialization, and believe that boys learn to be boys, many make the assumption that
differences between the sexes are all natural; the distinctions are not

seen as a result of sex role stereotyping. . . . Baby boys are seen as men in miniature, with feelings and sensibilities at odds with their mothers' *by definition*. Eve herself, when "she conceived and bore Cain . . . said: 'I have gotten a man with the help of the Lord.'" (Genesis 4:1, 2)

But though these children are male, they are not men. At birth, they are not yet *boys*, for this word is socially defined, like *mother* or *son*, and, as Margaret Mead showed us decades ago, boys are made, not born.[7] It is a mistake to endow male babies and children with the attributes of grown men. Surely they are helpless infants; their license to wield oppressive power has not yet been granted. As mothers, we cannot afford to define the sons as we might define the fathers. One mother who made this error said, "When he was born and the doctor held him up in the palms of his hands, all I could see was *prick*. It looked enormous to me. When he was a tiny baby, on the changing table, I remember feeling he was a little *king*. Because of his penis, his maleness, he had a power over me, he intimidated me."[8]

Pregnant mothers of sons, we are females holding males within us, their bodies hidden inside of our own. They emerge, newborn, with swollen penises, with penis and scrotum big—out of proportion —unlike their tiny fingers and delicate toes. This swelling, normal in newborns, makes a blatant display; a male child is born. From that first moment, we must be conscious of the impact of social conditioning. Respecting and understanding the power of our own preconceptions, we have also to be aware of and actively combat the conditioning of others who act on our babies. For as soon as his genitals are visible, before the cord is cut, that baby is labeled and treated as if he were all that male culture expects him to become. "Well, Mother, you've got a football player!"

The mothers in this group said, over and over again, that they didn't want their boys to be like "most men," that their grown sons were different from "most men," that they were dissatisfied and unhappy with the behavior and attitudes of "most men." When asked to describe "most men," these mothers, though sometimes hesitant and ambivalent, were quite critical:

They're less verbal than they should be; they're not in touch with their feelings. They do have cooler heads than women; they cut through the personality to the issue at hand. I don't think they're as sensitive as women are to people's feelings, to nuances in relationships. Now in that particular area, I think I've made some headway with my husband; it pleases me that he is less typical in that area.

They're self-contained, job-oriented, work-oriented. They have difficulty with ego problems; they're assertive, adventuresome.

Men are boys who have put on a grown-up mask. And I hardly know a real adult man. In fact, the ones I like best are the ones who simply drop the mask and let themselves be more like boys. I don't think boys are given the chance to grow up in this society, grow up healthy, liking themselves. There are a few men who like themselves, but they seem unhappy somehow, not at peace.

They are totally unaware of male privilege; they have no notion of what it is. Boys, like my son, do know; he knows it very well; he could verbalize it if you asked him. But a man can't any longer; they do not remember when it came to them, and they don't tell the truth about what it was for them to be children. The main thing I notice is the total lack of sensitivity. Maybe one or two men really have their consciousness raised; they watch themselves all the time. That's what it amounts to; they carefully keep themselves in check.

These next two women are generalizing from their personal experience—and while we all do this, sometimes the generalization is only a mask for the need to relate one's feelings.

Men are egocentric. Somehow they believe that women owe them something. They all think a woman has to serve them on hands and knees. Most men are very inconsiderate people. Although they are more considerate with their male friends than with women—even their wives—and children.

They say they're more flexible than we are, but they're not; they're stubborn, inconsiderate, and they can be very selfish. I see more selfishness in men than I do in women. They seem to be able to just take, not feel any shame about how much they're taking. Like hey, you're gonna give it to me; goddamn it, I'll take it all.

The following two mothers are clearly women who've put in some serious time comparing the behavior of women and men.

I sympathize with the way that man's role is so rigid and so proscribed. I feel sorry for the male principle. Now, I might take the time to try to rap with men, but at some point I see that the eyes have glazed over and I just think, you know, screw it. Men don't go around saying to one another, well, my wife and I were developing our relationship along these lines, but it doesn't seem to be working so we're going to try. . . . No, you don't see two guys walking down the street having that discussion. 'Cause they don't. Women do; men don't. I feel very sympathetic to men in our society; their role is so rigid, and breaking out of it is always perceived as being weak. They have to fulfill so many requirements as men before they can get to the point of saying, "I'm not going to do this anymore," without being perceived as weak by the rest of the guys.

1 tell you, my whole view of men has changed in the last few years. They're not honest with themselves; they can't face their own feelings. Most of them are not too bright—or if they are, they hide it or something. I've seen men fall apart, and they can't put the pieces back together, but women who've had a much harder blow, dredge up every bit of strength, who knows from where, and get it together and make it. The men sort of sit in the corner and suck their thumbs. They're lonesome; they're frightened; they can't seem to face up to things.

Men are closed off; they expect women to take care of them. I guess I generally don't trust men, with real specific exceptions. Meeting a man for the first time, I do not assume that this is going to be someone I may get to know and like and trust.

Men are scared, defensive; *scared* keeps coming up; it's blocking out everything else. Rigid; they're rigid. Once, in counseling, *I* got really scared —the only time—it was when my counselor said, "Frank is going to be a man: you have a boy child there, you know." I said, "Why'd you spoil it? Don't tell me."

Here is one of the few interview mothers whose personal observations have been deliberately filtered through a radical feminist analysis.

They can't help being sexist if they're raised in this society, unless they are willing to spend a lot of energy overcoming it. Some of them spend a minimum of energy and they overcome the rhetoric, so they sound wonderful. But most men—I go to get my car out of the city garage and I want to make this turn, and I ask the attendant and he says, "Oh, you can only do it if you give me a kiss." And I go jogging and this guy starts screaming, "Hey baby, hey baby," and you know, that stuff is ordinary. So I think of them all as rapists—I mean they don't all jump out of alleys and hit you on the head. But they have this enormous sense of entitlement, and women don't have any. And they sort of feel that women are on this earth to gratify their needs—whether it's to sit and listen to their life story for two and a half hours, even if they just met you, or to fuck them or cook for them or whatever. That sense of entitlement is what seems to be coming through all the information on violence against women. I think that even the exceptions have it, but they control it; that's what makes them exceptional. But as a class, they're dangerous to women, children, and other living things.

Knowing men well enough to make such profound observations, mothers cannot then make the assumption that little boys may be left to patriarchal socialization, that it is positive for them, that only girls present the necessity for painful struggle in raising children. It has been suggested that we should seek "the emergence of a social and cultural order in which as much of the range of human potential is open to women as is open to men."[9] In fact, very little of that range is open to men, and they experience, as boys, a process of severe and crippling constraint. The false and misleading notion of equality is responsible for this thinking. We should not begin to raise girls to be like "most men"; and we shouldn't raise boys to be like them, either. We don't need *two* sexes raised to be emotionally unresponsive, spiritually undeveloped and obsessed with power; we do not, in fact, need one.

Mothers of sons are not responsible for who our boys are, nor for the men that they become. But we have, obviously, great opportunities to influence the process of their growth, to contradict the messages purveyed by the culture's lowest common denominators. We have a responsibility to obstruct the general process of sex-role stereotyping—just as mothers of daughters have begun to do.

Twentieth-century American mothers have been accused for decades of doing ill to our boys. Inspired from outside their profession by Philip Wylie's infamous *Generation of Vipers*,[10] psychiatrists and psychologists went beyond their Freudian base and began a wholesale condemnation of mothers in the fifties. Ironically, but not accidentally, this was the same decade in which women were being encouraged to regard homemaking as a career, and never to work for money outside their homes (middle-class mothers), or to feel terrible about the consequences to their children when they did (working-class mothers).[11]

In 1950, the "schizophrenogenic mother" was invented, defined as rejecting her child at the same time that she parasitically attaches herself to him. Mothers of autistic children, already painfully burdened, were accused of being "obsessive, over-anxious, cold and inhibited,"[12] thus causing their children's autism. Soon enough, mothers were being blamed for psychosomatically inducing asthma, ulcerative colitis, coeliac disease, ulcers, and more. By the mid-fifties, researchers had blamed mothers for causing schizophrenia by being "seductive," and had "found" that schizophrenics hated their mothers.

Perhaps it has been to defend ourselves against such attack that some of us have come to say—and believe—that we haven't the power to make a positive impact on the characters of our sons. Perhaps the "experts" have succeeded in filling us with fear—especially of the dreadful crime of raising a "sissy."[13] We have come to believe that mothers are often a negative influence—especially in terms of sex-role identity and sexual practice, which used to come under the deceptively simple category of "manliness." We've come to fear that even a single maternal "mistake" might ruin our sons' lives. Many of us are now reluctant to try to be a positive influence, to activate our personal convictions about the inappropriate, negative, or damaging results of male socialization. After interviewing feminist mothers about raising sons, Van Gelder and Carmichael asked, "If women felt it was within their power to turn their sons into transvestites and homosexuals, why did so few feel they could turn boys into non-sexist men?"[14]

We have been frightened; we are afraid to wield our power, for it has been discredited, labeled evil—and many of us have ceased to believe in it. Afraid we'll go wrong, we go nowhere. We are terrified of depriving our boys of "acceptance" and their "proper place" in society—and then being blamed for doing so. But what does that mean? Should we encourage them to be just violent enough to be accepted? Just a bit cold, just a shade inarticulate, contemptuous of women just short of actual rape?

What is the "proper place" for my son? For this boy whose sensibilities nudge him to lean over and whisper to me (as he watches *Star Wars* for the fourth, fifth, or whateverth time), "Luke is crying because he's scared and sad; he thinks Obi Wan Kenobi is dead. He

doesn't realize that he'll be with him always, does he, Mom?"
Should this boy grow up to ride the bull at Gilley's? To drop napalm
on El Salvador? To taunt women about their breasts as they jog the
park paths on Sunday afternoons?

Why should we raise our boys to fit into a pattern that is detest-
able, frightening, and brutal—that cuts them off from their essential
tenderness and warmth, their compassion and intuition? Do we want
them to fit easily into a world of poison and pain, violence and rage?
Many mothers of sons—including some who are highly conscious of
sexist oppression—have fallen prey to the fear-mongering experts
who use the "homosexual threat" on us "every time we challenge the
patriarchal system that keeps men in a supremacist position."[15]

The basic assumptions behind the use of this threat are that no
one should be homosexual, that no mother could tolerate her son's
being/becoming homosexual, and that mothers, in fear of homosexuality, will be terrorized into allowing full-scale socialization of
our sons. Rather than steer our boys away from violent behavior, repression of emotion, and exploitive treatment of girls and women, we
have been told and taught to concentrate on keeping them away from
playing with girls or creating intimate friendships with other boys,
and to encourage them to participate in competitive athletic programs. This will assure them of "acceptance" and their "proper
place."

Mothers may well fear homosexuality in our sons because we
understand that homosexual men suffer in this culture; we may also
fear the blame and guilt that will be our portion of that suffering.
But while we fear that our sons will be condemned and ostracized,
we may also be afraid that they might take on the style of woman-
hating, the sneering and contempt for women demonstrated by a
highly visible minority of gay men, along with their apparent adoption of the most oppressive external aspects of "femininity," i.e.,
high, shrill voices, confining clothes and shoes, vanity, etc.

We may then fear that our sons will be unwilling or unable to
appreciate women. In this vein, feminist mothers fear our sons'
growing up *straight,* because *that* usually precludes their loving
women *or* men in trust and tenderness, unstifled by homophobia.

I don't want to be held responsible for my son's "sexual
preference"—an unfortunate term for his sensibilities, his personal
alliances, his choice of people to be intimate and open with. I
wonder—if I introduce him to a way of being that allows him

behavior and feelings that are not considered masculine, will he be incapable of acceptance among boys and men? And will he be "lonely"—or *apparently* so? And would that be a bad thing, worse than being like "most men"? Is it better for him to run with the pack, no matter what its character and purpose, than to run alone, or with gay men, or with women? Or might such "queer" sensibilities, and his sense of society's rejection of them, render him incapable of running at all?

There were only two mothers who responded totally negatively when asked, "How would you feel if your son had male lovers?" They said:

I would be terribly upset. I have no reservation about it. I would be really, terribly, upset. Don't ask me why; I can't tell you why. I don't know; I just would be terribly upset. My sons are teenagers; this is an age where they must beware and not allow themselves to be influenced; it could mess up their whole lives.

I'd be very disappointed. I suppose I would tolerate it. I would not be proud of it. Disappointed is the word. I would feel that he was unhappy with his role in the world if he had male lovers. I'd know that somewhere along the way I'd failed him and was responsible for bad influence. It would certainly have to do with his upbringing. But I can't believe that he could have the men he's had in his life and have male lovers; they were such good men! [The ironic contradiction in this last line, and her self-blame, are so sad.]

The majority of the mothers, to my surprise—and perhaps to theirs—responded with concern, rather than horror or disgust. They expressed fear, anxiety, doubt, ignorance, ambivalence, and, often, a willingness to face "the problem" and deal with it.

I would wonder if he was searching for something he missed as a child—the closeness of a father. I would wonder if it was coming from a real choice or alternative, or if he did it because of not having father care, and he was looking for that. If I had the sense that he really wanted it, I could probably deal with it. There's a lot of difference between people who have thought they were gay since they were very young and people who are claiming it now, which is very popular.

I was concerned about Jeff when he was little, that maybe he had homosexual tendencies, latent feelings that he didn't know how to handle. He was quiet and reclusive, even though he was also very active. And he did not have a lot of friends. He had one little boyfriend, and they were inseparable. When that boy moved away, Jeff had one more little boyfriend most of the time, I remember thinking, gee, I wonder if he has homosexual feelings about this little boy. I wonder what they do when they're locked up together. I know it's always perfectly natural and all that, but somehow it was of concern. Maybe it was just his build. Or his nature—he was warm, very touchy, not what you envision a little boy to be. And yet, on the other side of the coin, he was all boy—climbing fences, falling out of trees; one time he brought a turtle home that was as big as that couch. He found an old safe in an empty lot and he hauled that home. He was always bringing these relics home—like little boys do. But somehow there was something feminine about him too.

I probably would find it a little difficult to accept. But if he would do that, I would probably make a study of it and find out about it. I've often wondered, is it physical or is it emotional? I don't know anything about it. But no matter what, I would try to find an avenue of help and see if I could guide him through there. I'm sure at his stage of the game he's not gonna accept any guidance from me anymore. As a child it was one thing, now it's another. And he's too wise for me to camouflage it as guidance; he would recognize it. So there wouldn't be much I could do other than learn about it, so I could talk with him.

Now, see, I looked at Simon—I wouldn't say this to my husband 'cause he'd have a stroke—when Simon was younger I said to myself: Now this one's going to be that sort of a person, the sixties type, off catching butterflies, following birds, you know. I just knew it. And I want him to be what he will be. As I watched him, I thought, I don't know if there is a list of characteristics for homosexuals, and I don't know if he's going to be a homosexual, but Simon shares some of those characteristics. I said to myself, they may even say he's a sissy when he goes to school. He may be the kid who bakes cakes and decorates them while other boys play football. I realized then, not only that Simon but any one of the kids, maybe one of the girls, may choose to spend the rest of their life with a person of the same sex. So I should learn more about this. Even if I don't approve, at least I'll know what I'm doing. I have some white friends whose kids have brought home Black boyfriends or girlfriends, and I thought, you've got to be prepared; it's a new world. They may bring a cat home and say I'm going to spend the rest of my life with a cat. Be prepared. Just so it's something they really want, not that they're forced into or just doing because they're rebelling and choosing this instead. And I'd ask right out, "Is this someone you're in love with, or is there some problem you need counseling with?" 'Cause I don't know if it's a disturbance or what the hell it is.

I've thought a lot about that. It's been real hard for me to deal with. I've had a lot of negative feelings and a lot of fear. I've talked with some of my friends who are gay, and they helped me sort this out. Fear of the unknown, fear of having to deal with it. Wanting grandchildren. And wondering where I'll be if he ends up marrying another man or living with a man his whole life. I don't know, but I kind of wonder if my older son didn't have some homosexual experiences when he was younger. That's when I began dealing with it because I knew I was going to be real harmful to him if I didn't get it right. So, I think I'm okay with it now. I could live with that. It would be difficult but I would want to talk it through and deal with it openly. I'm not sure but what all people are bisexual anyway.

I've thought about it, and his father and I have talked about it. Not lately, about two years ago. At the time I felt I wasn't sure, but now I feel it would be okay with me. It wouldn't cause me grief. Right now I feel that what would cause me grief is if he got married and moved to the suburbs. That would cause me grief.

You know, I guess I'm supposed to say something abstract here, but the first thing I can think of is, if he did, okay, okay; I don't see that as being a reflection on me. That's a very fucking personal choice. Once he has decided that's what he wants to do, shit, he's still my son. My cousin has disowned her son because of that. He's changed his name to Sheila, and goes in heavy drag now—the whole bit. But my cousin can't take it; she's unable to talk to him in public; she doesn't know how to handle it. But that's her *child,* you know.

Not so much a male lover, I mean, I think in terms of "gay" and there's a difference in my mind. I mean, experiment all you want, honey, but when it comes down to it, don't decide, don't do nothin' foolish. But to be gay—it seems to be the straw that'll break the camel's back for a Black man. I want as many options for my sons as possible. But I'd be totally and utterly supportive of them. I would not love them one iota less. I suspect I might love them a titch more—'cause you have to when somebody's taken on a bigger load.

First of all, what I'd want to know is "Why have you made this decision?" I'm sure it would be very difficult, but he's my son and I would try to understand it. It might take me awhile to adjust to it, but if it was that important to him, and if he felt that that was the way he wanted to live his life, rather than lose my son I would learn to accept his preference. I'd have to, to keep my son.

Well, I thought about that. As I talk to women nowadays, we raise questions about whether or not our sons are homosexual, or have homosexual tendencies. Something out there has everybody running scared. When my mother was raising my brother, this is a question that never occurred to her. I saw a couple of Donahue shows about the subject, and my first thought was, "Oh, god, what would his father do?" Not how would I feel, but what would happen with his father, if that were the case. When I got to me, I just thought, gee, I hope I never have to deal with that. I remember when the kid next door brought home a male lover, and his mother—she was an alcoholic—beat him up. I mean, I heard the screaming from next door. But even she came to grips with it, because those young men came back. Apparently it's something you have to deal with. I don't know that I would have as much trauma now as I would have had at one time. So many things have happened with my young people; it's like, what would be next? [Laugh.] Well, I'm certainly not concerned with grandchildren. No, I have a lot of homophobia that hasn't been worked through. You're just giving me an occasion to get in touch with it, and look at myself.

A minority are radicals on this issue, remarkable for their positive response to the possibilities of their sons' sexuality.

I don't think it would bother me; I really don't. If that's what would make them happy, if that's what they wanted; fine with me.

If my sons had male lovers, I'd think: Lucky them!

Fine. [Laugh.] I guess I'd feel fine. I don't know, it hasn't happened yet. It may happen. He has a wonderful friend now who is almost a queen really. I'll tell you what is scary. Since my sister and I are lesbians, my father is obsessively terrified that my son will be gay. It won't be easy for these kids to grow up. Very hard, that's how it'll be.

If my son had male lovers? Oh, I would celebrate; I would celebrate any bisexuality in the children; I think it's more normal. I'd be so sorry if he stuck himself *anywhere* with his sexuality; he should allow himself the fullness of his sexuality.

As both mothers and sons well know, a man doesn't have to show up for Thanksgiving dinner with his male lover in drag to demonstrate his low rating on the masculinity scale. One simple test, a sure sign of danger even in young boys, is crying. Of all emotional displays—and displaying all emotions except anger is pretty much forbidden to men—weeping, sniffling, sobbing, "having a good cry," is the most dangerous for males. For a man to cry, especially in the presence of other men, is to show that he is not only vulnerable but weak and pathetic. Though other animals, such as wolves, cats, and monkeys, use a display of vulnerability to deflect aggression and violence, to ingratiate themselves to others who could otherwise injure or kill them, male humans must contend with the opposite reaction. Men grow to understand that demonstrations of vulnerability should be avoided, for they will *heighten,* not lessen, contempt, anger, or physical violence in other men.

Crying alone is not so dangerous, of course, though many men feel shame and self-contempt on these occasions, because they have taken on the values that condemn male crying. Crying in front of a woman or a male lover may elicit comforting, and is indulged in by those men who can bring themselves to do it with a safe person. Some would say that if a man cries in front of a woman, he is open and candid, trusting. But that is a more likely conclusion if he cries in front of a man who is not his lover. Crying in front of a woman may be just another way to get her to take care of him—or even, with some women, to *admire* him.

It is true that there are special situations, and even particular roles, which hold a license for crying. A man may cry at the death of his mother, father, sibling, or child, less at the death of his wife or lover. The amount and style of the crying will be noted, however, and "excess" will be commented on, or punished by the withdrawal of support from others. "Pull yourself together, mac"; "Be a man, Jimmy, your father would want you to be strong," and so on.

A man who has demonstrated extraordinary masculinity may be allowed greater leeway than other men. Professional ballplayers, men whose jobs have come to symbolize masculinity—such as lumberjacks, or drivers of diesel trucks, astronauts, actors who consistently play tough guys, and high-ranking politicians or businessmen —these men risk less in crying where other men can see them because they are symbols of, or actually wield, power and influence over other men. The more power a man has, the more leeway he gets with the rules. Green Bay Packer Jerry Kramer wrote of coach Vince Lombardi: "He gets misty-eyed and he actually cries at times, and no one thinks less of him for crying. He's such a man."[16] The irony here is that such men, Vince Lombardi notwithstanding, have usually given up or destroyed much of their ability to feel or reveal their emotions, in order to *become* powerful.[17]

Mothers understand the dangers of male crying; we too learned that "boys don't cry." Maxine Hong Kingston explains *how* we learned this, by the scientific method:

I invented a plan to test my theory that males feel no pain; males don't feel. At school, I stood under the trees where the girls played house and watched a strip of cement near the gate. There were two places where boys and girls mixed; one was the kindergarten playground, where we didn't go any more, and the other was this bit of sidewalk. I had a list of boys to kick: the boy who burned spiders, the boy who had grabbed me by my coat lapels like in a gangster movie, the boy who told dirty pregnancy jokes. I would get them one at a time with my heavy shoes, on which I had nailed toe taps and horseshoe taps. I saw my boy, a friendly one for a start. I ran fast, crunching gravel. He was kneeling; I grabbed him by the arm and kicked him sprawling into the circle of marbles. I ran through the girls' playground and playroom to our lavatory, where I looked out the window. Sure enough, he was not crying. "See?" I told the girls. "Boys have no feelings. It's some kind of immunity." It was the same with Chinese boys, black boys, white boys, and Mexican and Filipino boys. Girls and women of all races cried and had feelings. We had to toughen up. We had to be as tough as boys, tougher because we only pretended not to feel pain.[18]

But, as with homosexuality, many mothers' feelings and attitudes transcend or contradict the social rules and requirements. Asked "How do you feel when you see a man cry?" again only one or two gave negative responses.

Well, on a theoretical level, I feel fine about it. Crying is perfectly fine, a good way of expressing feelings and letting things out. I can accept it if that's what I feel a man is doing, letting out his feelings. But if I see it as a sign of his weakness, then I can't accept it. Now I could with a woman; with women I can accept it on any level. There would never be a man in my life who broke down. I would never allow it to get to such a point. Never.

A large group of mothers spoke of their pity, their sadness, their desire to give care and comfort when faced with a crying man. The responses of these women show the deeply held conviction that men shouldn't cry, and that if they do, there must be tragedy in the well those tears flow from.

My response is terrible pity. If a man cries it's somehow worse, because I realize what it means for them to do this, to cry. It makes me feel terribly sad.

I just feel pity, is that what you mean? I feel sorry for them. My heart breaks when it happens to my husband. I couldn't stand to watch my sons cry, though I have seen one of them. The others, never; they weren't letting it show; they didn't want me to see them. It would be so sad. They are very self-contained, so it would have to be so serious, and I couldn't stand that sadness. When the one son did, years ago, when he was in college, he was crying because we didn't understand what it was like to feel what he felt. I couldn't shake it for weeks.

The most unnerving to me is to see my father cry. My husband doesn't cry often, and when he does, it's unnerving to me, too; it's so out of character for him. Probably men in general should cry more. But, given that they don't, it sends up a red flag to me. They are truly upset, and the times they cry I can't do anything for them, so it gets more upsetting. Joe's mother died—so what the Christ am I gonna do? You know, I can't undo that; I did comfort and console him, but what good is that?

A third set of responses demonstrates a growing understanding that "letting it out" is healthy—even for men—but that woman's role in man's emotional development is not only to sympathize. Some women feel used or manipulated; they are suspicious of crying men—and their motives in crying to women. Others experience fear and relief at the same time. These women would welcome a greater emotional range in men, but acknowledge that we're not yet prepared; we've precious little experience with men who don't "hang tough."

The alienation of women from men underlies this woman's response:

I feel real moved and touched because it is so hard for them to cry. It's not allowed; all their training has been to not let those feelings out. When

I see a man cry, let's say in a therapy group, or somewhere else where it's okay to cry, I'll feel real supportive and touched. Now with the same man just completely out of control, sobbing on the street, I feel real scared, because that means things must really be bad. With a woman, I'd be scared for her too, but I'd go up to her, which I wouldn't to a man.

These next two women feel that they can sense the difference between genuine feeling and just tears.

I used to get all torn up inside, and think, oh god, he's really hurting. Now, I know it hurts, you got to cry, and the man is truly a man, a *person*. If he cries in front of me, he either really trusts me, or he's the world's greatest con artist. And you can always tell, you get that feeling when you got a real one going. Those are few and far between, men that'll just bring out a cry that way.

I have two feelings; I am delighted that he can let himself go to do it, and there's the enjoyment of being allowed to see the inside of another person. The other part is real resentment. He's only crying in front of me because I'm a woman. I don't like that feeling of being used as a mother, a soft touch.

This woman admits that her ambivalence is based in a fear of having to be responsible *for* a man.

Well, I love it and it's very scary. It's so unusual for a man to have that depth of feeling, and that's good, but then there's this part of me that still wants my man to be strong and take care of me. The scare comes with that—like if he's crying, my god, then what am *I* gonna do? Am I going to have to be the strong one? Yet I am supportive, and encouraging for that to happen.

This next woman's admission touches me. There is so much about which *all of us* don't know any better.

I feel two things almost simultaneously. Hurrah, you broke through that one—and very maternal; I hope you're going to be able to deal with what this is going to cost you socially. I have occasional flashes myself of being real weepy, and occasional flashes of thinking, am I going to be sexist about letting this man cry; am I as accepting of this as I am about letting a woman cry? Oh, the truth is that my deepest unconscious feelings about men crying are reflected in the fact that my son finds it extremely difficult to cry. I taught him not to cry; I did that when he was a child, because he was a boy. I didn't know any better.

It hurts a lot to see a man cry. My husband has cried many times, and so have my sons, and it hurts me to see them. I don't always know what to do. I feel just like crying along with them. It shows the humbleness of a person, that they can actually cry. The idea that men shouldn't cry is crazy. It's from the idea of that macho business—just what my dad was, cold. That's not healthy. It's good to show another person how you feel. If a man doesn't cry he could lose his mind, and go wacky. If you feel like crying, you should cry.

Other mothers unstintingly expressed pleasure, relief, and excitement at the prospect of sharing the world with men who can show pain, sadness, pity, and their appreciation of the profound, through tears.

It's wonderful. It's real, thank god—let it out, do it again and again. I mean, I'll even sit through it. (People don't, they feel uneasy when other people cry.) I think it's great. I know they're going to feel better after. Now I don't see men cry very often. My husband told me that he cried in a movie we went to, but I didn't see him. Now my older son, he'd try to stop himself when he was upset. I'd say, "Cry, for god's sake, cry. What are you holding back for?" Then that'd make *me* cry.

It's just beautiful. It's the ability to express a depth of feeling and do it openly. My father cried in front of us. He would cry often at sad movies, or he would cry when someone he cared about was hurting. And once, when I won a prize at the state science fair, he came to pick up me and my friend. When he saw the blue ribbon he started to cry; I was so embarrassed. Years later, I talked with my friend about it, and she said she had been very touched by that, that my father could cry. I went with a male friend to see *The Deerhunter*, and when we came out, he wept. He was crying about the politics of the war, about his own struggle with being a man in this culture. It's human; it shows the integrity of the man if he can cry and not worry, just be a person.

In the last two groups of quotations, several mothers made the connection between crying and essential humanity. They've said that when a man cries, he seems more like a person; his tears reveal that he is a human being. Perhaps they mean more like a *person* and less like a *man*. Many of them have suggested that there is a link between men's learned inability to cry and that quality called masculinity; that is, masculinity and humanity may be in opposition to each other, or mutually exclusive.

I asked mothers to define masculinity, and to explain if it meant the same as *male,* or *man*. We talked about whether all men were "masculine" by definition, simply because they were people with penises, or if women could be masculine. Several women contrasted their ideas of masculine with the (generally regarded as opposite) idea of "feminine," as well.

The fact is, people have simply made up masculinity. It is a social construct, a creation of words and concepts rather than an organic reality, like having testicles or producing semen. Unlike organs or hormones, the idea of "manhood," the concept of "manliness" is a result of human culture.

This first large group of mothers simply named the concept, accepting it as a fact of life, assuming it to be natural in males, instinctive. They state the social value of masculinity and associate it almost exclusively with grown men, but not with their sons.

Well, we've always equated the male with some sort of strength. There is just as much strength in many women, but the word makes me think of a man who is strong and reliable. Masculinity also has a sexual overtone; it's about sex appeal. Not in a woman, though, a woman who's masculine isn't appealing; she's probably large and doesn't have a female walk.

I've tried to learn about it. It has to do with focus. Focusing energy and generating it into directiveness. Traditionally, it's had to do with being adventurous, a risk taker. Being strong and protective of others also. There are some things that are inherently masculine and some that are inherently feminine. Psychologically so, and yes, women can develop those things in themselves. I don't think there's anything that a woman can't do.

I have found that there are a great many men who don't strike me as being very male. I don't mean in attitudes, I mean in mannerisms. Maybe it's a different body language, but there are an awful lot of them that I would call almost borderline bisexual or even homosexual; yet they have all the appearance of conservative heterosexual lives. The men I met when I was growing up struck me as being more sure of who they were, comfortable with what they were. It's different with women, of course; *feminine* is used with a different kind of connotation—the frills and ruffles and all that.

Those three women defined masculinity by comparing it to femininity, or by comparing men to women. Others relate masculinity to sexual acts, or sex organs.

At this particular phase of my life, masculinity means a really wonderful body and a good fuck. Besides that I have no use for the concept.

For me, it's merely sexual. It's part of the sex act, part of the attraction. In heterosexual sex, there is a masculine role, and the act of penetration.

Masculinity is having a penis, and no breasts.

I tell you, I don't know if I would ever use the word, but today, you're either masculine or you're a homo.

All of this next group of comments seem more reflective, influenced by active change in their own lives as well as in the culture at large. We have to remember that though some of these women are feminists, *most are not*. They are ruminating as they speak, doubting the old definitions, demonstrating the effect of the women's movement, relating their feelings about men in their lives. A few of these speak only of men.

Kind of a macho man, a tough guy, like Bogie. Inside, they're good people, but still, they don't cry, and they're very big. They can handle things and control things. They can take care. They are sort of rough-hewn daddy figures. That's the kind of man I used to look for, to admire, but I've begun to change.

In the past we had the myth that the man had to be the provider, the strong one, the unbending one, the unyielding one, the one that wouldn't break down and cry, wasn't emotional. His life's work was to make money, to take care of the wife and children. He used "pleasure outlets" to get back into shape so he could face work again on Monday. His involvement with the children was limited, giving them money, being a discipline figure, but not close to them at all. Now men are moving away from that definition of masculinity.

Oh, Jesus. Oh, well, you know, it's a biological gender thing; to a certain extent men are born with it. No, that's not right, because all men are not masculine. So overriding the gender thing is socialization.

But most recognize the implicit relationship: to have the concept of masculinity, there must be the concept of femininity; so the mothers discuss, once again, both of the sexes, and both of the required forms of behavior.

As a sociologist, I understand that the crucial thing about being socialized a male, being masculine, is not to be like a girl. That's what they learn. Not so much to be like a man—except they're taught never to show emotion—but *never* to be like a girl. So masculinity is not being feminine. Maleness is a biological state. Masculinity is the cultural expectation of people in that biological state.

This next woman is strongly conflicted, resenting the implications of female weakness, but subscribing to them herself:

I just hate this whole thing. A real man would be strong, powerful, in touch with himself, be able to be affectionate, caring, have good relationships on equal terms with other people. And all those things I would say for a woman too. So what is truly masculine and what is truly feminine always just does me in. *Masculine* does make me think of someone who is the protector, the powerful one of the two. To be sexy in a particular way can be masculine. The word shows power compared to *feminine,* which means weak or frail, needing protection; I really reject that description.

This mother has tried to figure out the difference between what's learned, or gained through social experience, and what's inherent, or comes with the body. She is challenging one of the most basic assumptions about the essence of sexual difference.

I don't believe in masculinity or femininity. I just think that physically a man is different in his organs and that's where it stops. Maybe a man is stronger. I play a lot of sports, and I play with men. Women's endurance is longer, better. But men are stronger, because most of us have played later in life. If I get my daughters going early they could match a man's strength. Now I've played tennis three times a week for eleven or twelve years with all kinds of men, with different stature and strength, and I can endure it longer. But I just can't get some of those fantastic shots, those serves. All of us women played late in life, after children were born. These men have been playing all their lives, encouraged to play, schooled in the hand-to-eye contact, and practiced in the coordination. I never had that, so I could never do what they do. Even though now, after all these years of athletics, the joke in our house is that I can hit the garbage every time, no matter what part of the kitchen I'm in. See, if I had played basketball as a child, like they do . . .

This next woman has been bedeviled by the definitions for years; she's doubted her own integrity on the basis of sexual stereotyping, but she retains her strength of conviction.

I've been told that I'm masculine so many times that I've gone to the mirror and touched myself, and I still don't know what it means. Aggressiveness in a woman can make her masculine. They say that women are dominant who speak their minds or tell their husbands what to do; they're masculine. But if you're so secure in yourself that you're not afraid to speak your mind, that's fine. We *should* be that way, and men should be that way too.

Finally, this last mother speaks to the issues of expectations, appearance, charisma, and energy, explaining that gender is defined only by structure—having a penis, for men—and that all the rest may be something else: a game perhaps, or a mask.

Oh, god. I don't like that word. It feels like a mask. It feels just game-ridden—like femininity. That one is easier for me because I've been asked to be it. They are both words that are related to expectations. There are expectations put in men to be cool, to keep it together, to know how to organize things, to know how to run things, to have everything under control. Control is a big component. It also includes their looks, their appearance, their charisma when they walk into a room. Robert Redford. Or Paul Newman. Or Travolta. I do believe that there's a male energy as opposed to a female energy. If you're of the male gender you carry more male energy, but we all have both in us. Gender is decided by having a penis, and all the biological structure that goes with it.

Asked, then, if they believed that their own sons are masculine, a few mothers said yes, and seemed entirely pleased or satisfied to find them so.

I love it that they're masculine; they are. It has something to do with their delight in their deepening voices, with their occasionally wanting to come up to me and put an arm around my shoulders and point out to me that I am so much smaller than they at this point. And with the fact that they feel they will grow into men.

Neither one is effeminate as that term is used hereabouts. Both are well developed, healthy, thin, muscled within reason and athletic to some degree. I have to admit I would be disappointed if they were flabby or physically unfit. This is radically unfair because I am very much overweight and yet I expect them to be in shape. (This is perhaps more a matter of youth than of gender.) I would also be very disappointed if people didn't look over my older son to see if he is my gigolo. The younger one is too casual to be mistaken for anything but a local kid.

Some mothers were disconcerted, disturbed at the developing masculinity in their boys.

Sometimes I look at him and think of him as a little man, and it doesn't bring me pleasure. I must, at those times, be thinking of him as masculine.

Yeah, in some ways he is—the physical, all-boy stuff. I don't mind him being a jock, so to speak, as long as he's not—as long as he doesn't put down boys who aren't, or put down little girls. As long as he doesn't have that fucked-upness about it. I do mind that, and if he's "cool." He *is* kinda cool, emotionally a little cool, and insensitive. I don't like that, and I try to work on it. I don't know if that will ever be worked out. It might just be the way he's gonna be, and have to work on it throughout his life.

Some of our friends and relatives have said that they see it happening in him, the development of a macho kind of appearance. There is a masculine stance, which includes standing in front of the mirror showing his muscles, which transform the personality, but it's not there all the time in my son. It'll make the next few years intriguing for him, but it's relatively mindless, and soon after that it will become very much a burden.

And, naturally, there's a group with the proverbial mixed emotions; aware of their sons' masculine appearance or behavior, but not entirely unhappy to see it.

Robert is a boy now, as opposed to a baby, or a toddler. He is a little boy. And there are things he doesn't want to be bothered with about his mother anymore. He doesn't want to cook in the kitchen with me anymore. That's for mothers to do, he thinks, and I regret that. I can't dress him up anymore and take him down to the Walnut Room at Marshall Field's for lunch. He used to like to do that when he was little, but he doesn't want to go there now. I could still do that if I had an eight-year-old girl; oh, maybe I'm wrong. But I see that gap getting greater as he gets older. My homework has started now, on what *he* likes —football, baseball, and things like that. I'm glad I like them, because he wants to do those kinds of things.

If the masculine elements in him are used to control me, or to use power on smaller beings and all of those awful things, then I'm terribly enraged and fearful; there's a lot of anxiety with it. But if it comes out in his going out and taking on the world, then I identify with it and I love to see it. If it were a girl child, I'd be thrilled. I don't think I'd be thrilled to see a girl child be mean and aggressive in the negative sense either.

At thirteen years old, Frank has not been victimized as an individual as a result of racism. He has been victimized as part of the race in terms of what living in America is, but not crippled, and that will determine what happens in terms of his acting out the sexism. White Americans never allow Black men to be masculine. That's the reason sexism is so strong in the Black community—the whole business of calling fifty-year-old men *boy*. The masculinity thing has another context in terms of the racism. So with Vince, I understand that his macho stuff is reflective of a sense of powerlessness, but Frank can play the game because he's been lucky enough to have a sense of total self *and* of his Blackness. Vince is a victim of his time and his period; Frank is a survivor. What that means is that the younger boy is free to redefine some stuff. At the same time, he's not going to be victimized by the society because he will be found masculine *enough*. That becomes the key in terms of survival. Now I can tell, when Frankie comes home from school, or from playing ball, it's going to take about an hour before he's livable with. 'Cause he's got all the uh-uh-uh shit that's been laid out. But it ain't him. And the key for *me* becomes to hang in, and make sure it doesn't *become* him. Frank doesn't want that to happen any more than I do.

These were all mothers who considered their sons to be generally masculine. There was a good number of mothers who did not, or who said their sons were both feminine and masculine in combination, or another thing entirely.

I see my son not differentiating between girls and boys as friends. Not looking at a woman strictly as a sex object, but as a friend first, a human being. My son can still cry, at the age of seventeen, and not feel that he's lost his "manhood." Yet I do consider him to be masculine, and I feel good about it.

Now my son was always secretive around my husband, did not share with him any of the masculine camaraderie around "I screwed six women last week," or what have you. There was none of that. So for a long time my husband was worried and asked me, "Do you think he's a homosexual?" He asked often enough that it became a concern for me, though it hadn't been before. I can remember a couple times my husband telling him that he needed to go pick up a whore, or something like that, explaining that he needed it, that that was why he was acting a certain way at home, and so on. Yet, I don't think that was it. My son was into sex, but he wasn't into whores.

Some of my male friends were concerned that my son was going to be gay. So I got concerned and asked a lot of people who know us. But they couldn't see that this was who he is, these characteristics that they called feminine characteristics, that they were saying were negative. They didn't use the word *feminine*, they used other words; it's just awful to remember that. He's just full of life, my son. That stuff has to come from the outside; the badness is in the minds of the people who say those things, not in Jeremiah.

These last two mothers have been driven to concern, or fear, by the men in their lives, men whose own masculinity was perhaps threatened by the supposedly feminine behavior of these mothers' sons. They are in contrast to these next two, who seem to be able to accept, even to welcome, what might be seen as feminine or androgynous behavior in their sons.

My sons are kind of androgynous. They don't come off macho. They act kind of macho sometimes, especially around sports or being rowdy with each other. But they come off mostly as rather nurturant, gentle young men.

Both boys are relatively street-wise. Neither of them are victims. On a broad scale, they're softer than most. They're intelligent and intellectually aggressive, both quite sensitive. They both tend to look like regular boys walking down the street; their classmates would not single them out as sissies, no. They might single out the older one, Martin, and say he's different because he's so intellectual, but no one would ever single out Arthur. He looks so much the part of a pig that no matter what comes out of his mouth or what goes on in his head, he is never ostracized for his sensitivity. But I am certain of its existence. Because I listen. Maybe that's how it'll always be for him, 'cause that's certainly the way his father does it. Jerry does not take his upsets, his feelings of justice in the world and compassion for people, around with him a lot. He carries it all inside himself and then spills it out where he knows he'll get a sympathetic audience.

Ultimately, and aside from definitions and social theories and cultural expectations, the question is, will your sons grow to be like "most men"? Are the grown ones already in that category? In keeping with their previously expressed views of men, the most common response of these mothers was a fervent wish that these boys would escape or transcend sex-role stereotyping and male socialization.

I don't want him to get bothered, so I want him to fit into society. I hope he'll be one of the good men, though. I hope he'll be an understanding person, and not one of the macho type. I just hope he's one of the good ones.

I am waiting for him to come out. It feels, on the outside, like there is nothing there. But I know what is on the inside, so I am waiting for signs of what he really wants to be to come out. Like he went to a dance class, and he really liked ballet, but there was no place for him in the neighborhood to dance after that one time. It was real hard to follow up on. I would like to show him things so that he could have a bigger choice, and not just do what the guys on the street do.

I'm beginning to think that the reason he takes all these women's-culture courses in school is that he's trying to save himself from all that. I do notice that, as a young male, he makes these pronouncements. I hear him talking, and I think, "Who's this?" And there's no point trying to discuss it with him because a pronouncement has just been made, however wrong, or however misconceived. The only thing you can do is try to bring to his attention that it is a *pronouncement*, so maybe he'll rethink it. Somehow this has to do with male hormones and their body strength, and how they're trying to contain it, but it goes to their heads. I tell you, it does go to their heads, and to their sexual organs. Somehow they think they are absolutely the smartest person in the world, invincible, because they've read a few books. Women, on the other hand, do not perceive themselves in this way. My daughter has an aggressive and cocky attitude, but you can put doubts in her head easily.

I don't expect them to become that way. I hope they don't. Oh, I hope they don't, and I hope that I have something to do with it. But they just might end up like that, if things continue as they are, with the poor mold that boys are supposed to fit into, that says this is what it means to be a man. If that continues, and my younger boys go to an all-male high school like my oldest son did, that may just repeat another vicious cycle. I'm only one person; I know that. I say things to them, and they say, "Oh, Ma." But, see, what I say is not reinforced by anything outside, by another adult, by a teacher, so it's not going to mean anything. Just that *I'm* a kook.

This next mother speaks my own greatest fear—and implies that there is no hope.

What*ever* I might want, or hope, my sons have already taken into themselves what our culture holds up to be masculine.

But some mothers said that their sons *have* changed the pattern, that they are already different from their forefathers and different from many of their peers. These hopeful mothers suggest that the newly male actions and attitudes embodied in their sons are a healthy sign for the future—not only for the boys and men who are their sons, but for humankind.

Well, I have to admit that both of my sons have a lot of those qualities and the younger one is probably going to be like most men. But my first, Edward, is beginning to be different. He's learning how to talk about his feelings, at the age of ten. He sees that it's okay. He'll bring it up at bedtime, so I know that he may try to use it, but he's really learning how to do it, how to say what he *feels,* even about himself. I see that as a major improvement, for a boy.

No, No. [Laughter.] I don't expect that of them. I mean they really aren't that way. They do get invested in football and baseball and that stuff, but they also are real, really warm, feeling, expressive people.

I expect that in many ways they will be like their father, a man who was not socialized right as a male. Who does not have the expectation that the women he relates to will assume a passive role, or that he must assume an aggressive role. In some ways I expect them to be failures at being men, just like Jerry. They will opt out of the world on some level. That's something both Jerry and I have done, in choosing not to play the assigned roles. The boys will relate to people real responsibly, and they'll care about themselves a great deal. Not in a selfish way, but in a thoughtful way. (All of this is hope, you know.) After all, in this world, men carry all the power, and what comes with that power is a view of the world that is limited and oppressive. But even among people who were not raised by feminists, there are lots of men, like my boys' father, who, for whatever reason, escaped that. What I hope is that more and more men will become misfits in the same way that more and more women are, and that it will be jumbled up somehow. I just hope that my sons will be misfits in the way that their father is.

Brian and Jeff and their generation are far ahead of most of the men between forty and fifty that I know. They come out of a different era. They're not as brainwashed, and they're not so scared of their feelings. They've learned to treat women differently than the older men did. I certainly see justification for the hope that my sons won't be like the men I described to you, most men.

Hope can be a mighty inspiration, but it is inadequate without concentration, struggle, and high consciousness of the task at hand. We need to understand what mothers and sons are, in ourselves and for each other, and what we are expected to be. We must learn to differentiate between the institution of motherhood and the experience of mothering.[19] The daily lives of mothers—what we do, how we feel, what we think—are very different from the generalized social definition of motherhood created by the "experts." The *institution* we learn to call motherhood is not only different from our reality but goes a long way toward negating and denying our actual *experience.* One of the primary reasons for this is that, while the raising of children in this culture is solely in the hands of women,[20] the form and requirements of the task are laid down and policed by men—male obstetricians and pediatricians, psychologists, psychiatrists, priests and rabbis.

Men, no matter how sympathetic, no matter how willing to do child care, no matter how many studies they've read or done on the subject, have never been mothers. Despite the now fashionable use of the word "parenting," the raising of children has remained *mothering*. The motherhood institution men have created is built upon their memories of dependence, and on the needs, desires, and fantasies that boys and men have developed about women. Perhaps as a result of that dependency's leading to the awe and fear, jealousy and anger we find in the mother/son relationship, perhaps born of the wish-fulfillment of men whose power and prestige allows them to realize their dreams, the constructed institution features mothers whose energy and passion devolve upon their (male) children, whose love is boundless, whose approval is constant, whose admiration is total, and whose anger is aroused by and directed toward only those who threaten her child, never the child himself.

Through the motherhood institution, women are required to maintain physical and emotional intimacy with children at least from infancy through adolescence—which grows longer every decade—and sometimes throughout the life of the mother. Required to maintain that intimacy, women—and our children—accept the official definition of the relationships that may exist between and among us, no matter what our actual desires, needs, or hopes. Women who are mothers are always trying to live up to the expectations of men—who are, of course, sons. "It is the mark of women's oppression that while [we] are held to be . . . the only ones legitimately responsible for baby and child care, [we] are also held to be insufficiently worthy to instruct each other in just how babies and children are reared. Males who have never raised children, who . . . profit personally from the undermining of women's strength, instruct mothers on how to care for and manage their young. . . ."[21]

We know we mothers really do get angry at our children, feel tired and need time alone, disapprove of our children's appearance and ideas, or dislike their actions and attitudes. But we've learned that to feel these things is unacceptable, is not motherly. So we mostly keep quiet, feel guilty, and try harder to be "good"—to be what the institution says that mothers are.

This required goodness is applicable not only to the definition of mother, by the way, but to the definition of daughter as well. The two major roles women play in this culture are not merely biologically or structurally defined, but carry the admonition to be a "good girl"—a good daughter and a good mother. Though mothers may similarly hope that their sons will be prosperous, well-mannered husbands and fathers, deferential and loving to their mothers, this is not necessarily expected. A son is expected simply to be "on his own," and "his own man." In contrast to a mother's expectations of her daughter, if a son does not live up to the standards of behavior for men of his generation, class, and race, his mother is not stunned or disgusted; she does not disown or deny him. The mother in the song who daily visited "her erring but precious son" in prison, who "told the warden how much she loved him," for "it did not matter what he had done,"[22] was perhaps a sentimental representation but remains an archetype nonetheless.

Because of his maleness and the latitude it implies in this culture, a son may be acceptable where a daughter has gone beyond the pale. This does not mean that sons bear no censure or disapproval from their mothers. They do. But their behavior may deviate from standard, appropriate behavior far more than that of daughters and still be acceptable. Often, in fact, mothers expect trouble from sons; many women told me that men—sons, fathers, husbands, lovers— mean "trouble" for women. Some of the sons interviewed for this book, and some of the men whose writings and research I've been reading, complain that their mothers expressed disapproval, or set standards at the highest bar. But sons' complaints, often generated by the "counseling" of therapists, are less in quantity and intensity than those voiced by daughters. Moreover, they are frequently surpassed in bitterness and passion by the sons' recounted memories of *fathers'* standards and expectations.

It will serve us well to realize and remind ourselves, whenever we try to understand who we are, and what "human nature" might be, that the definitions of the roles we play are not definitions of us. These definitions generally have more to do with the ideas of the people who create them, and the expectations of our friends and relatives, than they have to do with who we actually are, as individual mothers or sons, women or men.

We are used to thinking about the roles in movies and plays as make-believe; we realize that actors are doing what is required for the part, the situation in the drama. But though we use the same word—*role*—to describe the acting out of our relationships in social situations, we often forget that there is a difference between the person and the role s/he is playing. Further, we tend to forget that social and family roles keep changing as decades and centuries pass, as new experts redefine them, and as the economic and political needs of society rearrange themselves.

We speak of the ties of kinship—for instance, closeness between fathers and sons, or between wives and husbands—as if these had always been what they are today, as if there'd always been some sympathetic bond, some sense of belonging, among all these folks. Not so. Especially in regard to the relations between females and males, the role of fathers, and the sense of what the family actually *is*—social arrangements and structures have *not* always been as we know them here, today.

"In our society, founded upon the individual family, kinship stems from biological or genetic relationship. But in ancient society, founded upon the collective clan system, kinship expressed a social relationship embracing a whole community."[23] Though ancient people knew who their biological mothers were, and perhaps their fathers as well, this knowledge did not mean for them what it does for us. The emotional grounding, security, and acceptance that we have learned to expect from the patriarchal nuclear family were formerly attributed to the collective family, the clan. Relationships within the clan were, naturally, defined differently from the family relations we know. All women were potential or actual or spiritual mothers to the *whole clan,* and were considered sisters to each other. Fathers were outsiders, or unknown; they were not even kin.[24]

Mothers and sons related to each other within the context of the maternal clan. In many earlier cultures, when boys were old enough —anywhere from five or six years old to puberty—they were sent by their mothers to the men's lodge or to the men's side of the village. They did not live intimately with girls and women as boys and men of this culture do. Though the boys counted kin through their mothers, traced their allegiance and ancestry through them, and lived in their mothers' villages, they did not really live with their mothers as our sons do. This practice did not necessarily estrange boys and men from women, or from their mothers' people. Adult men took part in the raising of the clan's children, especially their sisters' children, and served as guardians of those children and protective allies to their sisters. So a male alliance to mothers' kin did not lead to the dominance of boys by women that is so often feared or disdained by contemporary men. The mothers and brothers were cooperative groups within the maternal clan.

Our own lives and kinship patterns are, obviously, very different from these ancient forms. Many women and their children are dependent, economically and emotionally, upon one man, a father or a mate, for much of their lives. The relationship is rarely truly cooperative, given the social reality of male supremacy. Even those of us who live in families, households, or communities which include no adult men still are bound within a culture that is made and governed by men. And women have fathers and grandfathers; many have brothers, cousins and uncles, as well as bosses, employees, co-workers, landlords, tenants, and neighbors who are male. When ancient peoples physically separated males from females, they honored that separation as appropriate and natural, and did not necessarily institutionalize a denigration of either sex. In contemporary nuclear families, however, wherein the sexes live intimately, our closeness both denies and fosters what we jokingly call "the battle of the sexes," an antipathy which is now ordinary, and considered normal. We separate under male-defined conditions that mark "women only" as lesser.

This concept of *lesser* has been applied to motherhood. It is the underside of the institution, and generates a great contradiction.

Mother is condemned for thwarting her children, repressing them, raising them for selfish purposes, and refusing to let them go —even dominating their emotional lives after she is dead. This condemnation of the woman who is also defined as the primary source of warmth, tenderness, forgiveness, acceptance, approval, and love-without-end can only be understood in terms of the conflict between woman-hating/mother-blaming premises, and pietistic reverence for the false motherhood of the institution. Despite the fact that many men see mother as "controlling, erotic, castrating, heart-suffering, guilt-ridden, and guilt-provoking,"[25] they still maintain that mother "only exists for one purpose; to bear and nourish the son."[26]

Men in general often refer to themselves as "every mother's son." The irony of this label in a misogynist society is intense—as intense as the impact of the most common epithets used by men to defame each other: bastard, son of a bitch, and motherfucker. Though all of these are considered insults to the man so named, they also slander his mother. She has borne a child outside of marriage; she is (no better than) a dog; she has engaged in carnal intercourse with her own son. Though most men would not regard them as such, these are, in fact, mother-blaming epithets. They all mean, "You're no good because your mother's no good." The "blame" for whatever action or characteristic led to the insult is not cast upon the man, but upon his mother.

From birth, our children are completely dependent; they naturally develop strong attachments to the people who respond to them with care and nurturance. Given that dependence, and the fact that mothers are the people who generally do the caring and nurturing in this culture, we should not be surprised to find that despite the contradictions of institutional motherhood, or even embodying them, there is a deeply abiding connection between mothers and the sons we raise.

Yet the constraint of institutional motherhood becomes a model for the oppression of women to the demands and benefit of men. Baby girls require the same work, the same exhausting devotion as their brothers, but in doing so they are not fitting and reinforcing a pattern for the society at large. Though children of both sexes put their mothers in the position of servants, and all mothers find themselves in humiliating postures and situations, mothers of sons are, whether we feel it in the moment or not, inadvertently reinforcing the sexist premise that women exist to serve men.

Though we love our sons and understand the basic truth that, as children, they *do* depend on us, and thus we agree to "serve" them, we may experience a sense of double vision on such occasions as these: in that uncertain time between my having to dress my son and his dressing himself, I found myself, more than once, standing and waiting, like a human coatrack, with his pants, shirt, or jacket in my hands, while he bounced on the bed, played with a toy, or even left the room. Or, worse yet, I'd be kneeling at his no longer adorably tiny feet, tying or buckling on sneakers or sandals, while he twisted over backward to turn on the radio. When I say that I "found myself" in these situations, I am not speaking metaphorically. As a mother, I naturally developed the capacity to be in many places at once, and would often come to and find myself doing something or being someone that, had I been wholly present for the decision, I'd never have chosen to do or be.

The sense of being *used,* if not outright duped, was strong. I was not just a doting mother, I was a subordinate woman. If Daniel *could* keep me walking him to the front door to kiss him good-bye every morning—which act necessitates my being attuned to his movements rather than going about my business—he *would,* long past the time he needed me to open that door for him. His outright resentment at my suggestion that he get himself together (bus fare, keys, lunch, wallet, homework, etc.) and come to kiss *me* good-bye, echoed the deposed lord: "But you're *supposed* to kiss me good-bye at the door!"

Men learn from infancy to expect and solicit selflessness and cherishing care at the hands of women. Most men spend their adult lives, after separating from their mothers, relentlessly seeking another nurturant woman who will belong exclusively to them—as their mothers did, or seemed to, or were "supposed" to. Daughters learn from our mothers to *be mothers,* to give in that disastrously self-destructive way that has been honored by men as true motherhood; sons learn *to expect such treatment from women.* Mothering—behind sex, behind the "helpmate," behind the "good personality" all those boys in the fifties said they looked for in a date—mothering is what they're after. A twenty-year-old told me:

You know, I've thought about this once or twice, laying there in some chick's arms, thinking—this is just like being a baby again.

By the age of eight, my son had already learned that when he wants to be comforted and cuddled, he should solicit those actions in the perverse, inside-out style of adult men. That is, rather than tell me of his upset or pain, he will display a *bad mood,* surly, sulky, snotty, silently demanding the laying on of maternal hands.

The concept of love, as defined by the terms of heterosexual romance, has, strangely, been applied to the process of mothering, to the relations between women and their young children. What can this mean? Can there be love where there is complete dependence? What does it mean for a child, a tiny boy, to "love" the woman he depends on for his life and security? Beyond the small warm bodies and sweet cuddling with infants and toddlers, what is "love" between mothers and young children? Is it simply a feeling of physical security, from the womb out, that men are seeking, expecting, and demanding from women as they grow older, having learned—being mothered—that that's what women are *for?*

Fully understanding that not every woman is a mother, nor even motherly, and that not every man seeks warmth or satisfaction from women, we can yet acknowledge that even women who do not radiate maternity are nonetheless solicited for mothering by men, and that many sons who find their lovers among other men also seek maternal nurturance from women.

Mothers need to recognize the ways in which we, as the people who raise boys, have either failed to recognize or have ourselves internalized woman-hating and mother-blaming. More important, because of the great danger to us and our sons, is that we understand the powerful primary and peer-group sources, those unrelenting purveyors of masculinity and patriarchal consciousness that daily fill the minds and senses of us all, educating us to accept—to *desire*—the definitions and roles that are "masculine" and "feminine."

3

Making Men

Ralph Waldo Emerson says, "Men are what their mothers made them." But I say, to hold mothers responsible for the characteristics of their sons while you deny them any control over the surroundings of their lives, is worse than mockery, it is cruelty! Responsibilities grow out of rights and powers. Therefore, before mothers can be held responsible for the vices and crimes, the wholesale demoralization of men, they must possess all possible rights and powers to control the conditions and circumstances of their own and their children's lives.

—SUSAN B. ANTHONY[1]

There was a farmer in Mei Chia village, who knew that he would be drafted. Recruiters told the hungry farmer about the food, clothes, and shoes the army would give him free. He could send all the pay home to his mother. Whichever army reached the village first would force him to fight on its side or shoot him for an enemy, so he might as well volunteer. His mother told him that she did not want that money. But the farmer said he would have to get some sleep if he was to go to war in the morning. That night as he lay sleeping, his mother stabbed his eyes out with her two hairpicks.

—MAXINE HONG KINGSTON[2]

As mothers keenly feel, and sons sense early on, boys may not simply grow up, getting bigger and bigger, and then, one day, realize that they have become men. Rather, as they grow, there is a gradual and pervasive pull within the culture, which removes boys from their mothers' influence, taking them into arenas of male interest and action. The same effect, produced through more abrupt means, has been observed in simpler, "primitive" cultures, in which a boy is "wrenched from the domestic sphere in which he spent his earliest years, by means of a series of rituals or initiations that teach him to distrust or despise the world of his mother, to seek his manhood outside the home. . . . For a boy to become an adult, he must prove himself—his masculinity—among his peers. And although all boys may succeed in reaching manhood, cultures treat this development as something that each individual has *achieved*."[3] (My italics.)

Women made people, our ancestors observed, and they considered the process a miracle. Those ancient people saw that the earth and the sea were mothers, that life came from the water and the soil. They saw that woman, with her bodily tides and cycles, her seasons, shared the secret of creation with the earth and the sea. Just as the original creation myths feature the Great Mother and explain Her relationship to Her son, so the world's mythology has given us the story of the male theft of women's magic and power. The focus of that power, and the purpose of that magic in the hands of the men who stole it, is the making of *men*. The "rituals or initiations" that characterize a boy's passage to manhood, though they sometimes came to include terrifying violence and tense competition, are based in male envy and emulation of woman's birth and menstrual magic.

Originally, as represented in our mythic history, women made men, giving birth to males and teaching them the arts that made us all human, so they could be men rather than animals. Male initiation rites, eventually closed to women, may well have been created as celebrations, designed to spiritually transform male animals into human males. These initiations ultimately became the process of turning *boys* into men, but began as a means of turning *beasts* into men, taming the male of the species.[4] "Beauty and the Beast" is only the best known of many versions of this universal story, the male being saved, humanized, reborn, restored to human form, through a woman ("He needs the love of a good woman"). The mother of the beast, a powerful fairy or a queen, is usually retained in the story, often appearing in dreams, directing the action.

When men stole the magic from women, they claimed the ability to create life, to "make men" for their own. "They get the male children away from the women and brand them as incomplete until the men themselves have turned the boys into men. Women, they have to admit, make human beings, but in their belief only men can make men."[5] In most initiation ceremonies, many of which last days, weeks, or months, the most striking feature is that not only are the men pretending to be women, playing midwife or pregnant, laboring mother, working out of or sequestering the boys inside of shelters designed either in the shape of female genitals or huge female animals[6]—but the ceremony itself often consists of marking the boys so that they will appear to be like women.

We know that men have historically defined circumcision in terms of religious sacrifice. To the question why?—why that particular act, why the foreskin of the penis should be removed—there has been no clear answer. But if we think of the penis as the male's equivalent of the vulva/vagina, from which come both the sacred blood of life *and* human beings, and if we learn that circumcision is actually a lesser form of mutilation, related to and modified from the operation of subincision, then we can begin to recognize "the element of male compensation for woman's primary role in nature."[7] In subincision, practiced in several parts of the world but probably most studied in Australia, men slit their penises to resemble vulvae, and the cuts are called "penis-wombs," or "vaginas." The longer the cut, the greater the bloodletting, and the greater symbolic similarity to a woman, the greater pride a man may take in himself. Elizabeth Fisher cited one tribe in which the men periodically cut their penises with a shell, even calling the process menstruation or male menstruation.

Circumcision becomes easy to understand as a step away from the pain, possible infection, or even death that must have accompanied those bloodier initiation rites. Thus, if subincision was a male attempt to emulate women, circumcision appears to have been a female attempt to save young boys. Anthropologists have discovered that not only was the circumcision ceremony often guided by (usually old) women, but the most efficient tools were sometimes said to have been designed or found by the women, doing less harm to the boys, lowering the operation's mortality rate.[8] Though tattooing, body painting, scarification, and haircutting or head-shaving have made the sacrifice easier yet, many modern males are still circumcised, the operation being performed in hospitals as a matter of course soon after the birth of a male child, and justified in terms of "hygiene." The mark of circumcision became socially crucial because most women refused to mate with or marry uncircumcised men, and spiritually important because the initiation ceremony was a metaphor of death and rebirth, sons being reborn through the agency of their fathers. Born again, like their contemporary christian counterparts, such men could revere a male god and claim to have been created by him.

As boys came to be taught by men in the old time, taken over by them for initiation into manhood, so are they trained by men—by male culture—today. The training, the conditioning or socialization process, is different from raising. Mothers and sons both agree that mothers are the people who raise sons. A few mothers gave credit to their husbands for helping or sharing, and a few sons, who seemed to define raising as child care, including occasional play and teaching, also gave credit to their fathers for a share in the process. These situations were contrary to the norm in the American family.

I would say both my parents raised me. My mother made sure I ate, was well groomed, had clothes that fit me, took care of me that way. My father took care of me in different ways, like teaching me to work hard, to be dedicated and honest, to keep studying and to take care of myself physically, to watch out for myself in the world. He would put the trains up, and teach me about carpentry. But he always worked at night so he would sleep in the day, and he was always busy. They both worked, but my mother was around a little bit more.

I would say I raised myself, but I would have to qualify that. My parents both raised me, my mother doing most of the work, my father securing the money. And my father did shopping, vacuuming, preparing meals, serving food, telling stories. My mother did those things too. She did them a lot more visibly than my father, who worked construction and only did them, say, on Saturday or Sunday. My mother was very fastidious; she did it every day. But he always helped her.

Both my parents did, really. My father had been a teacher and he taught me tons of stuff about the world of science. They both were around almost constantly. He did a ton of work, about sixteen hours a day, but the basement was where his major shop work was, actually. He would make an appearance, but he was also gone a lot of the time, away.

All of these preceding remarks describe situations in which mothers still carry the main load, but the sons seem to want to obscure that fact, to make the work appear to have been equally shared. Perhaps this is the result of their having learned, as adults, that shared child care is desirable. But the great majority of the interview sons, predictably enough in this culture, explained that their mothers had raised them. Interviewing women for *Our Mothers' Daughters,* I found a tiny minority who said they were raised by their fathers, so it was especially striking that *not one man* in this sampling said that he had been raised, nurtured, or brought up by his father. Men, ranging in age from twenty-two to fifty, said:

Up until I was thirteen at least, it was a one-person effort, and she was the person.

My father did the teaching; he'd come over and expend a little wisdom. Raising is making breakfast and making sure that you're taken care of when you're sick. My mom did the raising, almost without question.

My mother actually was the one who raised me. He really didn't have any part in it. When I was very young he worked a whole lot. I saw him very seldom. The first times I remember spending any time with him were when he'd do a lot of traveling and we'd travel together. But it was a lot of driving and being left in the car waiting, nothing like real interaction. I think it was obvious that he expected her to be the parent. The rap would come down once in a while from this guy, but that wasn't parenting, that was "the rap."

Oh yeah, my mother raised all of us, all the kids. But my father's presence was always felt in the household. The decisions that were made by my mother, everyone knew they were contingent upon what my father would say. There was very little approval from him. He left the whole household and the raising of the children up to my mother, even though he had the final approval—whether it be about what's going to be on the table for dinner, whether I could go out for a sport at school—it had to come from him. She knew what her guidelines were. We got into his car once a year, and that was to drive down to Louisville with him on business, for this big fair. He was, other than that, outside of the family.

Oh, yes, she's the one who raised us. He was never around. He was around for punishments, he was around at the dinner table; that's it. Occasionally he'd take us for a car ride on Sunday. But even the rides were to see some land he was interested in buying, something like that. It was never to go *out*. And when we went, it was always four o'clock in the morning.

Pretty much I was raised by my mother. My father would do a little bit; he helped me with my homework sometimes. He also did some of the bedtime things. He would often put me to sleep, sing me lullabies. But, in general, my mother was the one who was there. He wasn't there, so my mother did most of the raising.

Oh, Lord. He didn't really raise us. But then she was around all the time and he wasn't. If he wasn't working, he was on the golf course or he was playing billiards. He was in a retail business, so he worked late on Mondays and Thursdays; we might not see him 'cause we'd be in bed by the time he got home. I would say that my mother did 95 percent of the child rearing. She was the one you went to if you fell down and skinned your knee. Whatever it was, she was there.

Unquestionably she took care of me. Oh, unquestionably. She was very responsible. Momma would work all day, come home, wash clothes, clean, this type of thing. My great-aunts helped; when my mother was at work they took care of me. I loved both of them. My daddy did his share, which was financial. He paid the bills and whatnot, and he'd bring home all these baseball bats, softballs, footballs and all. They'd all have P.S. 73 on 'em. He'd say, "Now, y'all scratch off this P.S. 73." It was good stuff; he worked at that school.

Even in families where the mother worked outside of the home, she was still known, by her son, to have been responsible for raising the children. While women have understood this for a long time, men have ignored it or taken it for granted, so it is gratifying to hear men recognize the situation.

I'd have to say my mother. From the time I was able to remember, my mother took care of me, always made sure my lessons were prepared for school, and packed a lunch, fixed dinner, fixed breakfast every morning and all that sort of stuff, took us places. His work schedule didn't much coincide with our schedule. Her work schedule, working in his business, sort of fit into ours, my sister and I.

These next two speak of fathers entering their lives on an "intellectual" level; i.e., *after* they'd been raised, he could talk to them.

She raised me. He was around. He was a sort of a partner in it because he was there, but his role was secondary to hers until I got to a certain age, around fifteen. The older I got, the more direct his involvement was, the more he affected the content, the more the content was mental or intellectual. More and more it came off the daily stuff and on to what's going on in general.

Well, he certainly took a special interest in the intellectual side of life. We were never companions until I got out of college. Dad was very busy when I was a child. He was the director of one of the government bureaus in our county, and I guess that was a very demanding job. He was never home very much, although he did take an interest in our schoolwork, and praised or blamed us when we brought home our report cards. And, of course, if there was punishment to be done, he would do it. She simply reported at suppertime to Dad. Corporal punishment wasn't common; we were dismissed to our rooms and supposed to stay there. Mother raised us, that's right.

Raising all these boys, do mothers have any part in the process that makes most male babies into "most men," into aspirants to masculinity? In the previous chapter, mothers' voices were heard criticizing men and denying the supposed values of full-out masculine behavior. It is not mothers who generate and support the Green Bay Packers, *Playboy,* and the Pentagon. As a group, we don't really want our boys to grow up masculine.

Just as mothers bemoaned and regretted the behavior and attitudes of "most men," so might we respond to the following list, culled from the work of predominantly male researchers and writers, who have been studying masculinity, male character, and sex-role stereotyping. Despite the fact that most men never completely fulfill the requirements, and their attempts remain more common than their successes,[9] this list stands as rules to live by for most men. Boys learn, as young as one or two years of age, to strive for these goals—or the appearance of them:

To be self-sufficient and independent;

To be strong and aggressive, physically and socially, in work and in personal relationships; to be brave—never frightened, worried or anxious, never revealing these emotions when they do (as they must) occur;

To be emotionally insensitive, unaware of what others are feeling, and refusing to respond to others' feelings if they are perceived; to show no feelings but anger;

To be able to demonstrate anger by arguing, fighting, shouting, or injuring other people, showing no physical or psychic injuries of their own;

To be wary of each other, competitive to the point of ruthlessness, regarding everyone, but especially other men, as adversaries; bonding only with power equals or men more powerful than themselves, never men who are weaker, or women, or children;

To be "winners," to achieve, to be "at the top";

To dominate other people, exploiting or abusing women especially as a demonstration of power and strength, or as a release of tension;

To be athletically competent and knowledgeable;

To have "freedom" and use it, doing as they like with space and time, moving unobstructed over the earth;

To be heterosexual;

To regard themselves as superior to women, by definition.[9]

Some of these goals would be considered positive in another context, but pressed unremittingly, in combination, and with none of their complements, they are crippling.

We mothers have other goals, other dreams and desires for our sons. Some of these are acceptable to traditional masculinity, and would not necessarily fly in the face of the list. Often they reflect the secondary male role, James Stewart, as opposed to John Wayne.

I want them to have lessons in lots of things, when they are young and can develop proficiency. Probably music, not the violin, but music. And sports, swimming, and maybe dance.

He'll be a humanitarian. He will have kids. He'll be well liked; he'll be very well liked. Very well sought after by people because he tries to work things out and make things just right for everybody.

The closeness of family feeling is what's important; that's what I'm trying to impress on them. My kids have heard me preach dozens of times: I don't care where they are or what they're doing or what happens to them; if one of them needs the other one, they'd better go. Brian and Jeff are separated now by many miles, and though they beat up on each other many times when they were little, with bloodshed and broken bones, the closeness that's occurred in the last few years is amazing. They really want to be with each other whenever they can, and they get a lot of pleasure out of being together when they are.

I want him to be a good person, be kind to others, to value people—preferably more than things. I've made some headway there. When he is kind he is reinforced and when he isn't kind, I explain to him what might have been a better thing to do or say.

I want them to have the feeling that it's not a good idea to give up on things quickly. There is this tremendous feeling of instantness around: if it doesn't work right away, just go somewhere else. But I feel that a lot of things are worth working for. They don't work instantly. I also want to give them the sense that commitment is very fine and that warmth, love, and understanding within the family are valuable. How do I show this to them, teach it? I go through what I suppose every mother goes through always, the working mother, the horrifying anxiety and guilt because I'm not doing it, whatever it is I'm supposed to be doing. [Laughter.] My own mother did it by talking, because that's her thing: she loves to talk. But I also do it by example. I am fortunate in that my husband and I have a genuine warmth—which I'm coming to think is quite rare—which we rather take for granted. Obviously we also have very violent misunderstandings, quarrels and all the rest of it, but that undercurrent is always there and the children know it. Occasionally I try to arrange not to quarrel in front of them, but we can't possibly avoid it, so they know when we quarrel and then when we make up.

More often, what we want for our sons is in direct opposition to the requirements of the list. In fact, if we mothers could see to it that only *our* expectations were met, rather than those of male culture, the list would disappear.

These first mothers stress their own part in the developing of their sons' character.

If I could go around again, I would have been freer. I wouldn't have been quite so rigid with them. I would have enjoyed them more. I wouldn't have been so careful about the impression we all made. I would like to have been more my own self; it was always so circumscribed. And I'd have gotten out of the suburbs sooner, exposed them to real life sooner. Then my sons would have had more of what I want for them.

One thing I'd want for him, if I could give him anything, would be to change some of what I did. I sure would not have led him to believe that he could depend on the promises of his dear father. I would have been more confident in what I believed in; I distrusted myself.

I want them to be human beings, to feel other people's sensitivities, to be honest with themselves and others, and I want them always to have a sense of family. As far as their being men is concerned, I hope they'll always have the strength to do what they think is right. I expect them to do mainly as their gut tells them, and follow what feels right for themselves. I sound corny, I know.

Sensitivity is the most important thing, a sense of caring beyond oneself, and a sense that you can make a difference. The real happiness and satisfaction come from outside of yourself, dealing with other people, making a positive contribution.

A lot of what I want to give him, I already have given—or he was born with it. He cares about people. He knows that it's as important to have a happy body as it is to have a happy head. In fact, he doesn't distinguish between them. I want him to understand that it's a trap to try to make a lot of money. Even if you do, it's still a trap to make more; there's never enough. And I want him to know that putting a high priority on money is immoral, as well as a great waste of time and almost definitely bound to disappoint him.

Flexibility. And the ability to just go out there and trust people.

I'd like to teach him to live life as directly as possible, to be very close to how he feels about things, and live from that. That's what I want for myself, of course, at the same time that I want it for him.

All of these next mothers care about their sons' relations with women, presenting themselves as models for their sons.

I want him to be a good person, good in the sense that if he ever gets married or has a female companion, I want him to do right. A lot of men are very inconsiderate; they leave the whole responsibility of raising the children up to the woman, and I don't want him to grow up like that.

My son comes in the kitchen with me and stands on a chair and washes the dishes. My husband says, "What do you want, to raise a sissy?" But I want my sons to know about everything, how to sew, wash a pair of pants, make a meal.

I want him to have a sense that, between people, things can be worked out, resolved. I would like him to have healthy relationships with women and men. One of my concerns is that he'll fall into the trap of being protective, rather than letting women be who they are. It really bothers me when he repeats stereotypes, things that contradict his own daily life. Like saying men are always bigger and stronger than women. [Laughter.] When he's got a real big strong mother. Or women like to cook—and I have never liked to cook, and he knows it.

I want him to understand that being a white middle-class male is a source of privilege. I want him to understand what that means, in who he is and in relationship to the rest of the world. That's too abstract to say to him at this point, but I feel that in changing the way I live my life, having him see and be a part of what my life is, I can give him a sense of what I mean. He knows what women are about.

This last mother says many of the same things as the women preceding her, but she is making a deliberate feminist statement; she has acted upon her philosophical position.

I want them to feel good about being male, about being who they are. So they need to realize, to recognize, that a lot of what men *do* is not necessarily what men *have* to do. I want them to be able to cook, to be able to sew, to take care of their own stuff, do their laundry, clean their own rooms, order their own lives. I feel that the men I know are so incredibly dependent on women to take care of their daily lives. I want them to be strong emotionally and not lean on women for their sense of being or their ability to feel. I pay a lot of attention to what I could give them, as a woman, as a model. It's very important that they should see a person who is capable. I've read Adrienne Rich, and she talks about how mothers give up their sons to the patriarchy. Well, I've vowed not to do it. It's been real important to give kindness and gentleness and touching, because you know there are so many screwed-up attitudes in this culture. I mean, my god, the Oedipal complex! I'm their parent, I need to touch them. I need to be touched by them. I need to have physical contact with them. And it's not okay with me to turn them over to the armament industry or the marketplace.

Men say that their mothers raised them; mothers say we don't want our sons to grow up in accordance with the list. How does the discrepancy develop? How is it that we raise boys, but don't make men—or, at least, make them the way we want them to be? Are we contractors rather than architects, following specifications not of our own design? To a greater extent than we are always aware of—yes. After all, women are relatively powerless in this culture, and though we raise the children we bear, almost none of us are free to bear and raise them *if or when we choose,* much less *as we choose.* We know that role expectations for children of both sexes, and the attitudes adults are required to maintain toward and teach to them, have been designed and regulated by men. Asked if their mothers held specific expectations and goals for them because they were male, some sons replied that their mothers had, more or less enthusiastically, passed on to them the culturally accepted notions of male behavior and required masculine traits.

Yes, there were clear stereotyped responsibilities to being a male in my parents' home. For instance, I shouldn't cry. I shouldn't get weak in a crisis. Being the eldest male in an Italian family also meant I should be driving around in a Coupe de Ville by the time I was sixteen and a half, you know.

She would say to me, "Be a man, Bob." That meant that you have to do the best at what you're doing, be strong physically, emotionally, and spiritually.

There was some of that "Because you're a boy, you don't cry" business. You've got to be strong. Boys have to be courteous and open doors for ladies. A boy stands when a girl comes into the room. There was an emphasis on being, not exactly butch, but being strong—a good, firm handshake. Manliness. I was prepared as a boy to be the breadwinner.

She talked to me about boys don't cry, boys have to grow up strong, and sooner or later you're going to have to be the head of the household. I remember several talks about how I'd have to go into the Army. Raising a family, being the breadwinner, those sorts of things. And that girls weren't as smart as boys. How did that go? That girls were initially smarter, but somewhere along the way we'd catch up and then we'd surpass them because they have emotions that interfere. Girls will be mothers or nuns. She's still that way. That's one of the things we argue about. She hands my son a blue bunny and my daughter a pink bunny. Specifically with the crying I can remember her holding me and trying to comfort me and alternating comforting words with "Boys don't cry." Seriously, she was rocking me and just saying things off the top of her head and that's the mix that came out. It made me crazy. I could never understand it. But these words kept coming down, girls do this and boys do that, and I would wonder why, but I'd never vocalize that question.

She expected certain things of everybody, boys and girls. But of the girls she expected other things as well. Everybody had the basic things to do, but the girls had extra things. They were also expected to talk differently; well, she expected them to be like her in the sense of being submissive around males. Also I remember her saying when I was a child that she never objected to my father's smoking and drinking, but that it was disgraceful for women to smoke. She criticized one of my aunties for smoking, thought she was disgraceful. Wouldn't permit a divorced woman in the house—quite a different set of expectations.

A few other men said that their mothers did not deliberately socialize them, but that the ideas were in the air, and that their mothers personally followed the rules though they did not deliberately apply them to their sons.

Nothing was overtly stated. But she bought dolls for her daughters and trains for her sons.

See, I was an only child, so they didn't have to be sure that I only played with fire trucks and not dolls. I wasn't involved in that; I only had the fire trucks. They didn't buy me any dolls. And they never made a big deal out of it if we went to someone else's house and I played with the dolls. But I had to learn to do things because I was going to have to go to work because that's what men do. And I was supposed to have this family and support it.

No, not outwardly. But she reinforced those traditional kinds of male things, she gave a lot of support to that. We weren't supposed to drink or smoke, we were supposed to be straight sexually, no messing around with drugs. Now she never said that there was anything in particular expected because I was male. But when I grew my hair long, let it go, in college, here's what she did. She took my senior high school picture, which has a crew cut, and she put it up on the mantel when I came home with the long, crazy, incredibly unkempt hair. It would always be there, and I hated it. There would be references to it from time to time.

But the largest group of men said that their mothers had not subscribed to sex-role stereotyping; they couldn't recall even subtle, unspoken exhortation to be "men" when they were boys.

I didn't get it from my mother; I got it everywhere else. The schools were like that. The lines were separate, gym was separate, recess was separate. Obviously, from kindergarten on, you know something's going on here. As kids we didn't pay much attention to sex until they divided us up. And I only became aware what a problem it all makes when I was in high school. It was just out on the streets though. From the examples of the fathers, from the life around me, I could see what men were supposed to do, and not do. It didn't come from my mother.

Oh Lord, I really don't think that she did that. Obviously I got it—I got it from the culture. But I don't think I got it from her.

First of all, I was such a goody-goody that I met all of her expectations; there was never a problem with me. I was never out late, she always knew where I was; it was terrible. You're laughing, but it's true. The nuns loved me.

Her main expectation was that I get a college degree, and I did it. She didn't care what I did as long as I did that. As long as I didn't turn up—like some of my friends—with a prison record, I'd lived up to her expectations.

Honestly, not that I know of. Due to the fact that there were no girls in the family, since she was only dealing with boys, there was no "This is what the *girls* do; this is what the *boys* do." It was all just "This is what people do; this is what *we* do." Now I know she desperately wanted to raise a girl, so there must have been some difference in her head, but it was not evident in the raising.

Well, she never *said* what she expected of any of us; it was known, however; it was *indicated*. But the indications weren't about what men do, they were about what *we* do. And when it was verbal, it was inclusive: We cooked, we cleaned. We scrubbed the floors, we washed the dishes. We sewed—we did all those things, my brothers and I, that women do.

She was probably upset or disappointed that I am gay, but she never said anything, nothing negative that I ever noticed. She must have known, I know she did, that I caught a lot of flack in high school for being different, but she never suggested to me that I be an athlete or that I should live a certain way, do things a certain way; she's just not like that.

My father had those expectations, not my mother. He gave me this: Be strong, be a man, don't take anything from anybody.

I don't think my mother cared about that really. My father was the one who wanted me to excel. He wanted me to go to Yale, and when it became clear that they wouldn't have me, my mother stepped between us. My mother kind of fended off my father's expectations of me, which I thought were unrealistically high. She did express her anxieties about, her terror about, guns and destructive things. At the time I thought she was really paranoid, but I see what some of my friends have done to themselves over the years and she was right. She was not disappointed in me at any time. She thought that I was gonna do all right. Her role was a reassuring one, rather than directive, very supportive, yes.

And one young man of seventeen, in the vanguard of this sample, explained that maternal pressure in his life was brought to bear *against* the tradition of masculinity.

My mother expects me to be liberated, to be an exception, to be honest. Mainly just to be an exception. She has an idea of what American manhood is, and she certainly doesn't want me to be like that. I agree, but I don't like the pressure. Like if I do something that isn't consistent with that goal, there's pressure on me to change it. An example is that last year I dated Gracia Steele, and every Friday night I drove my little car out there, paid for all the gas, paid for dinner, paid for movies, paid for everything else. And my mother didn't think that was appropriate, especially since I'd never arranged it verbally with Gracia. We finally did that near the end of the relationship; but my rationale had been that I had a job and Gracia didn't, and she got like two dollars a week from her parents. But my mother thought there should have been a discussion between Gracia and me about it. I just didn't like the pressure she put on me. I agreed with her principles wholeheartedly. Part of the reason I didn't like the pressure was that I already felt bad about it myself.

Just as we mothers have socialized our daughters into roles we have found oppressive and demeaning, so we have allowed ourselves to assist in male socialization that oppresses and demeans women, and lessens the humanity of men. Some of that assistance is deliberately contrived to protect our children from penalty, to ensure that they will be safe and successful adults. Just as mothers of daughters may reach a high pitch of anxiety if their daughters do not bear children, so mothers of sons might desire that their boys be athletes or soldiers, and thus acceptable to the male power structure. But even those sons whose mothers do teach or encourage them to follow the rules will learn how to be men primarily from direct observation of, and paternal instruction from, adult males; from other boys, especially older ones; from the communications media—television, movies, newspapers, magazines, and books; and from commercial merchandising, both through the products offered and through advertising copy and design.

Mothers are lesser agents in the socialization of sons than of daughters. Because sex distinction is basic to the identity of the individual in this culture, the same-sex parent, in this case the father—despite his greater absence and lesser personal involvement—is ultimately a stronger influence and "culture bearer" for boys. The father *as a symbol* replaces the father as a person. The fact that fathers are just not around much compounds the problem and confuses the situation, because boys are left without a model when they piece together, as well as they can from their various sources, the puzzle of what a man should be.

A 1959 study of boys' socialization suggested that, since fathers have had little role in the raising of children, small boys depend on older boys for their role models; "both the information and the practice . . . are distorted. Since [their] peers have no better sources of information . . . [than the younger boys themselves], we find overemphasis on physical strength and athletic skills, with almost a complete omission of tender feelings or acceptance of responsibility toward those who are weaker."[10] The study suggests that the images presented to boys, by boys, are pictures "drawn by children" and "not enough." The researcher seems to be saying that boys, left to their own devices, will create such models for each other out of themselves, with no external influences, presumably because such models come naturally to boys. In 1982, with increasingly pervasive electronic media as image producers and purveyors, compounded by the heightened power and constant presence of advertising, we know that the images young boys flash for each other are rarely pictures "drawn by children." They are, rather, copies of the images men have made: Starsky and Hutch, the Fonz, and the whole crew of insane Saturday-morning cartoons. Young boys did not create the "overemphasis on physical strength and athletic skills" with which they become preoccupied; they are only following the pattern that's presented to and expected of them.

When male children are presented with a different pattern, they grow up different. Margaret Mead's early study of three tribes in New Guinea gave evidence of this truth.[11] The Arapesh men were nurturant and cooperative; they demonstrated hurt feelings with much the same style of expression we have long associated with women. The Tchambuli men were vain and lazy, doing almost none of the actual work of the tribe; that was done by women. The Mundugomor men were much like contemporary western men, but so were Mundugomor women. Many other peoples whose sex-role definitions have been different from the ones we live in are known to us. But even if they were not—even if Mead's study were the only one—or even if only a dozen men on earth were known to be *other than* what men in this culture are supposed to be—we would know that masculinity is learned, not born into men.

Despite maternal opposition to the list, despite the fact that what we want for our sons cannot be gotten by following that traditional prescription, despite the fact that we raise boys and live with them, mothers are making scant headway against traditional male socialization. The primary reason for this is that basic sex-role conditioning is not in mothers' hands, but in the hands of the men who've made this culture. It is the job of men to socialize boys, and their conditioning permeates the cultures men have created. Male supremacy and the concept of masculinity are basic in terms of controlling the point of view, the social perspective, i.e., what is visible and available in the culture at large. As feminist scholars have shown, the definitions and explanations of what is meant, for instance, by *art* or *history, sport* or *entertainment,* and what is found in these areas of study, work, or appreciation, are male concepts and constructions. There is art, and there is *women's* art. There is the history of the world, and there is *women's* history—separate, as if the latter action had taken place upon another planet. The male representation of things as they are pretends to be the body of general *human* knowledge; the female representation, *if given,* has the status of a petition from a special-interest group.

A riddle, popular with third- and fourth-graders, illustrates this point: A child is struck by a train, rushed to a hospital, diagnosed as needing brain surgery. The surgeon on duty takes one look at the

child and says, "I can't operate. This is my son." The surgeon is not
the child's father. How can this be? Of course, the surgeon is the
boy's mother—but the point is this: only in a culture where the perspective, the point of view, precludes the possibility of a female brain
surgeon, could such a riddle *be* a riddle. There's no puzzle without
the sexist bias.

The bias which defines and constructs this culture in terms of
men's needs and desires permeates our lives to such an extent that
even the birth experience has been distorted. For the infant, being
born is more than a rude shock—and by no means simply because
he must leave the womb. For the mother, the experience of giving
birth is also traumatic, designed so that it alienates her from the
child who has been her most intimate companion for nine months.

Beyond the birth experience itself, there is a constant stream of
suggestion, directed at both mother and son, that leads them to further alienation. Though a certain amount of cuddling is deemed appropriate in the early months, the mother is instructed, mostly by
child-raising authorities, as well as friends and relatives, not to
"spoil" her baby, not to weaken or sissify him with maternal
caresses. The boy is encouraged early to shun physical affection,
told that "kissing is for girls." The form of this discouragement becomes more rigid and threatening as the boy grows; by the time he is
six, seven, or eight years of age, his reputation for masculinity is on
the line, and his mother risks accusations of being seductive, or of
willfully risking her son's "sexual adjustment," especially his (presumed but apparently tenuous) heterosexuality.

Past infancy and early childhood, sons are more fully instructed
in their rights and powers as males in patriarchy. They readily
develop contempt for women simply by observing the way women,
and images of women, are regarded and treated in the society. Men
have learned that mothers, like mother earth, are repositories of rich
and precious natural resources, which exist only to be mined by
their sons, to be emptied, to be used up.[12] Sons are never to be
turned away empty; it is the mother's destiny to be left hollow when
her sons have plumbed her depths and gone beyond her.

Though that tradition is by no means dead, a new form, created
by television and refined by the movies, is growing. Where mothers
were previously used up and then discarded, soon there will be no
mothers at all. In this transitional period, existing mothers are being
erased, removed from the family. There are no real mothers on TV

(it may be argued that there are no real people on TV, but that is another issue), and Hollywood—spurred perhaps by that great widower Ben Cartwright—is now producing films that eliminate mothers altogether: *Kramer vs. Kramer* and *Ordinary People* are the prizewinning examples in this new genre. They portray mothers as coldly willful and selfish, Freudian nightmares, emotional debris in the wake of the powerful father-and-son alliance. What with scientists making people while movies teach fathers and sons how to get rid of existing mothers and/or live without them, this may become more than an interesting sociological observation. So far, though, the situation breeds only confusion, for scientists and filmmakers aren't going to raise those kids. Dustin Hoffman and Donald Sutherland may *act* like mothers, but they remain *actors*.

In the old days, when mothers were mothers and men were men, such an erasure would have been unthinkable; every soldier had a dear old mother, every gridiron hero made a touchdown for Mom, and every mother's son who went to the movies aspired to be a man like John Wayne. Wayne was a man who became an idea, who met the requirements of the list so thoroughly as to define them, whose death was mourned not because he was a well-loved actor but because he embodied a way of being that was exemplary for male culture. Some feared that his death was a symbol of the passing of American masculinity. Sadly, they were wrong, for patriarchy dies harder than the man who, for nearly forty years, performed as its metaphor. News of his death spanned nearly a week of newspaper coverage, on the front pages and in the editorials. One man's eulogy began, "God, what a man he was," and went on, inevitably, to call him "an American legend."[13] Another, describing him as "a symbol around whom works of art could be shaped," tells us rightly that John Wayne "was not an actor. He was a force."[14]

John Wayne was an icon to the culture that created the list. In the lives of most men, the qualities he personified will be much less fully realized, and far less romantically displayed. They will be exhibited and employed blatantly in two areas of male activity: sports and war. Even when men do not actively participate in athletics or battle, they relate to them as ideas, as social institutions, as required concerns *for men*. Small boys, playing at manhood, pretend to be soldiers and ballplayers, coveting the full-dress uniforms of both.

Perhaps most of the appeal of these two can be found in the license they allow. In sports and war, men may touch each other passionately, even lovingly, experiencing extremes of deep emotion. In war and the most common team sports, the ball games, men find their greatest license to propel themselves through space and toward each other with vigorous power and direction. In both, men may come close to true male friendship—the emotional intimacy otherwise so elusive as to seem illusory. They are also free to compete, viciously and murderously, in league with comrades against an opposing group of men. Though other activities may call forth the passion, the drive, the energy, or the force of sports and war, few require all of these, and few may encompass them all. Not every man goes to war. But every man learns, from his tenderest years, that "games" are required and to be desired. He also—à la Vince Lombardi—learns that pleasure, fun, and enjoyment are *not* the point.

To that point, little boys, middle boys, big boys, and young men are confronted by the social expectation that they will play, and that they will play to win.

The role of sports has been significant in my life, though I play less now than I used to. When I was a kid I played sports all day, or just about. Really, for years, until I was in college. Then, when I was in college, I was a sports writer. And since then I've done a lot of sports writing, TV sports journalism, and I go to sports events all the time. I did go through a period when it wasn't cool, and I didn't have any sports in my life for that time, but I broke out of that. That was the late sixties—you know, "How can you go to the ball game when there's people dying?" [Laughter.] Now I go to the ball game all the time. Baseball. I'm a part owner of a team, put together some money and some people to do that. Yeah, sport is real important; it has been real important to me.

Okay, the first sport I got into as a kid was swimming. That's the first thing I learned. And I was very good at that. And then I progressed to baseball, but that overlapped swimming; you couldn't do both. I was an excellent baseball player (and I'm modest, too). And after that came tennis and golf. I couldn't stay with golf because of working in the summers, but I still play tennis today. That I really enjoy. Now spectator-wise, I like to watch football, and on TV I like to watch hockey. But I go to football games; I have a season ticket. I've been in that stadium every Saturday for the past ten years. I've missed only one game. But when my team loses, I'm not crushed. No. Well, maybe I'm a bit sorry they lost. But I don't get emotionally involved in it. I root for them; I'm an avid fan, but I'm not a *rabid* fan.

Some men present a serious rationale for the value of athletics, of continuing to exercise, practice, and play.

Sports were very important when I was a teenager, and then at about twenty or so I dropped them. I went through a sort of intellectualized period and then picked up again. It's pretty important to me now. If I didn't play tennis, I would not die, but it's important. I don't think of running as athletics; it allows me to eat more ice cream. Activity is important to me, and I enjoy the friendship that comes, with the other men.

Yeah, I was on a Little League team. My father more or less encouraged me. When I was little I collected baseball cards and all that. It was always something we had to do to balance out the scholastic kind of work. It was a mind-and-body kind of thing. You play baseball or ride a bicycle because you need the exercise. There wasn't anything masculine about it, like hunting or that sort of thing. Nothing macho, just that you will feel better if you do exercise.

The next four men are particularly clear about the value of sports for men, mostly for masculinity.

Oh, yeah. I played football and I played baseball. I was a very good golfer all the way up until a few years ago when I slipped a disk, and that wound up the golf. And I love to dance—always. I won prizes dancing, incidentally, way back. Sure, sports are important. The association, who you do it with, the competition. All men like a certain amount of competition. Even in the business world, your sports experience helps you; you want to get in there and go, to be top dog.

Sports have played a very big role in my life. I never wanted to be on the bench. That was my greatest fear. I started as a goalie for the soccer team at this private school where they didn't have football, but I kind of rebelled against that, 'cause I thought it was a sissy sport. I wanted to play football 'cause I was used to rough sports. In high school I had participated in track, wrestling, and football. I was the smallest defensive tackle on the team, but I was the starter. I really felt good about it, got an honorable mention when I was only a sophomore. Coaches never had any regrets about starting me over some big guy. If he was bigger, I was quicker. If he was smaller, I had the muscle. After I went to the state college, I started to think twice about my size, though, because if I was going to get broken bones, that was the time. I got out while I was still in good health. And I found that the more interested I got in my education, the less and less I did any work on my body. I'm going to pot here in the city, so I have to pick up my old health habits, and do sports again. Contact sports—especially football, and wrestling is really good too—are my emotional outlet. Those were all the years that I never let myself cry, that I was holding in all the crying. I always thought that it was a release, to hit somebody as hard as you could, and make them hurt worse than they could make you hurt. It was such a challenge.

This man, in his late thirties, repeatedly alludes to the way sports can satisfy the need/desire for sensual contact among men.

Sports have played a very, very big part in my life. Still do. I always think of D. H. Lawrence's terms: it's a phallic and cerebral thing. And it's a nice way to get away from the hubbub of teaching and thinking, and it's also keeping myself in shape. I always feel a lot better, so it's a good sense of myself. And in high school, all the way through. It was a real sense of relationship with guys. It was terrific. I was in football; I have always been involved with some kind of team activities. In a lot of ways it was probably a surrogate thing, the sports activities.

I was always clumsy, and then I started doing athletic stuff. I was never really good; I was just below good, because I was clumsy. And now that I've gotten through the clumsy stage, I don't have time for it. But whenever I do do something, like go down to the park and play soccer on Sunday, I'm really good. I'm what I would call good, and more coordinated. I would have been a lot more clumsy and uncoordinated if my father hadn't put me into sports. My father mainly got me into sports stuff; he knew, although he never told me, that my clumsiness was a problem, and the sports really helped out my coordination.

But of all the men who spoke of the role of sports in their lives, fully 40 percent recalled pressure, pain, fear, and humiliation as their portion on the playing fields. Some of these—by no means all —were able to make a go of it in one sport, or came again to athletic exercise as adults, reluctant or surprised to find success and pleasure after early disappointments.

When I was a kid I was real poor at sports. I did that deliberately, I can see now, because I clearly could have excelled. All through high school I managed to get out of gym class by using a doctor's statement that I was asthmatic. In fact, I induced a little difficult breathing from time to time to demonstrate to the physician that I was incapable of sport. Later on, in my adult years, I have wished that I had done more. At this point, I have an appreciation of the physical skills of sports. I don't like the macho image that goes along with it, but I love swimming; I love exercising. I have much more a sense of responding to and caring for the magnificent machine of the body—and one way to do that is through athletic exercise. I have done almost a 180-degree turn on it.

Very little sports—or very little importance to sports in my life. I have a hard time walking into a room without falling over. No coordination. In certain situations, I feel uncomfortable because men are expected to play sports. With my wife's family, for instance: she's one of eight kids, and she's very athletic. They once, all the brothers and sisters and cousins, challenged another set of cousins to a softball game. We were all out there, about ten million of us; we had bottles of champagne, and we had all these children, and the children were running all over the field. I told my wife, "I'm not going to play." I hadn't had a bat in my hands since I can't remember. And I get embarrassed when I can't do what everyone's expecting me to do. I make myself even more uncomfortable than I necessarily have to be. Several people asked me, and I said, "Oh, no, I'm not going to play." They finally talked me into it when the game was halfway over, and I was *terrific*. It was amazing. I couldn't miss a ball. Where did I come from? I was a different person that day. But that was *that day*.

Sports have been very important in my life because I was so bad at it, or thought I was. The rejection was terrific. At school, a boy's identity and status is determined almost exclusively by his athletic ability, and the physical-education classes were all very competitive, and that's the way it works. For example, where I went to junior high and high school, you'd never be popular, really, if you weren't athletic. The less athletic, the less popular; that's the way it went. I was pretty bad at it. Now I realize that I wasn't as bad as I thought, but I didn't feel like I fit in with the other boys. My father never encouraged me, and the first contact I had with sports was in the schools. I played mostly with my sisters and brothers, not in the neighborhood kinds of experiences that teach you how to play those games. So of course I defensively rejected it all. I was very sarcastic and negative about everything. I had a bad attitude in college. I got bad grades in my phys-ed classes—not because I was so bad really, but because I was so snotty about it. I made nasty remarks, I resented having to take the classes, I resented getting grades, and the teachers knew it. It's only been in the last four or five years that I've become interested in doing these things for myself. I've been exercising at home—for my health and for cosmetic reasons, to be frank—and since starting that I've had a much better outlook. But I still wouldn't go to a health club, or exercise in public.

For others, the experiences of their youth simply remain sources of unhappy memories and bad feelings that have accompanied them into adulthood.

Negative—always ghastly. Sports don't teach you anything except the sport. It doesn't teach you teammanship, patriotism, stuff like that . . . it may teach you some male chauvinism. I dislike team sports intensely. There are some individual sports, gymnastics, swimming, occasionally ice skating, that I enjoy watching for the aesthetics, but sports, for the most part, turn me off. My brother was in sports and he was pretty good— even though he was younger than me. He wasn't too bad about that, though, maybe snickered a few times. But the bad experiences I had, myself, were what turned me off to sports.

No sports. As Oscar Wilde said, "I have sometimes played chess outdoors." It was because I was afraid of intimacy. I did, as a child, play sandlot baseball and that sort of thing. Also I was very fond of skiing, fishing. But an intimate sport for which I had to undress in front of the other boys in the high school gym locker rooms, that sort of thing I avoided. Not because I was afraid of sports, but because I was afraid of physical intimacy with boys. I was afraid that I might betray my inner feelings and so forth. I was conscious of that from about age ten or eleven. Therefore I avoided situations in which I might be moved. And the result was that I was insulted for not showing an interest in basketball.

Well, I have never been what you would call athletically inclined, in terms of any game that has anything to do with a ball. I was on the swim team in high school. I went out for football one semester, and that was trauma. I don't know what I was trying to prove, but I proved it wasn't for me. But I do like the White Sox, and people say, "Well, you like the Sox so much, you go to so many games, why don't you play?" I am just not a participant. I am an observer. I like the beer and the hot dogs.

I was just miserable at sports. I couldn't do them. I liked to read, and most of all I liked to watch TV. The Flintstones, and Woody Woodpecker. Other people made me feel bad. I could have got along if they'd all just said, "Okay, Joey, you're not good at this; go inside and watch TV." But people make you feel bad about that stuff. I used to walk home with my head down between my knees, just looking at the ground all the time. The worst was that I had this friend who used to jeer at me because she was such an excellent kickball player. We moved from the city, where we played baseball, to the suburbs, where they played kickball. I had never seen it. It was a damn foolish game, I thought. I couldn't kick it; I'd run it up, but I'd miss the ball. I'd be crushed and then my friend'd chase me home and tell me what a lousy kickball player I was. She'd say, "Look, this is how you kick it." She'd kick it, and it would go off to Japan. "Why can't you kick like this?" I wasn't made to kick like that; I was made to read books and watch TV.

I was really talked out of it by the system. I hated brutishness, and when I was in boarding school, the experience was awful. Then public school had poor programs, always forced me to do things, to participate in things I wasn't good at. That pissed me off, and then John F. Kennedy finished it by making me jog an hour a day. I won't lift a finger again, *ever,* for the purpose of exercising. I consider myself fairly active, but it's hideously boring to me.

Mothers of sons are sharply aware of the importance of athletic prowess as a symbol of masculinity and competence—even normalcy—in boys. Many interview mothers, despite their apparent acceptance of this requirement, did see some of the inherent problems in the masculine sports system. Though sports for boys seems to be business as usual, some mothers implied or openly expressed the fact that the situation, as is, is less than desirable.

Yeah, they really are athletic. It's real important to them, but I worry about its being too important, especially the whole team thing, and winning—though I love it when they love it. But I would love for them to be in more individual sports, where they can set their own pace and do it themselves, rather than being run by some kind of mob action. And also, my older son is so distressed when he gets injured—and he gets injured a lot.

No, athletics hasn't played much of a role in my son's life. Fortunately, he went to a progressive school where it didn't make any difference; anywhere else he would have been forced. What caused him problems was that he was short, and he's also not very well coordinated; that's probably why he didn't do athletics. A jock! God forbid!

I *know* sports have been important for them. Brian was a baseball player from the day he was able to walk. We have a picture of him when he was twenty-one months old with a little baseball uniform, catching a ball with a mitt. He played ball all through high school and into college, but now he's been injured, and can't play ball anymore. It was really a very sad story because this was our ballplayer. This was his *life*. Jeff, on the other hand, was not a great ballplayer, but hockey was his love; if anything, hockey made the masculinity in Jeff.

Well, he loves sports. But he's so young it's hard to say how important it will be. He hasn't been brought up by parents who sit in front of the television and watch athletics. We've never put any emphasis on it, and there's no emphasis at school. He loves baseball but he's afraid to join the Little League. He's very coordinated; he's a terrific player. My parents are dying to send him to some macho camp, but I put my foot down. He loves to compete, just loves it; he'd excel. I'd like him to be a good tennis player. I'd like him to learn all those things, just not that *way*, exactly. And I'd hate to see him give up his love of nature; he's happy collecting bugs and butterflies.

Oh, shit, yeah, they were all into sports, and I didn't like it. I mean when they were little I really didn't want them to get into sports. I wanted them to be healthy and fit, but . . . But they did it, thank god, and I've changed my mind. It does fill a gap of time and interest. Had Ernie not gotten so involved with baseball, I don't know what the hell he would have been doing with himself. And the same seems true with the other boys: they are terribly into baseball. They read about it, they think about it, they talk about it. It occupies their minds. They play it all the time. It would have been nice if they were playing the violin, but they're not, and they have to have something to do. Their father plays with them all the time; I don't. It just came from the American culture. It's so cheap, they can go all the time; there's always a game. It's funny I don't play baseball, but I don't. I feel like I'm off the hook. I don't have to play baseball, thank god.

No, he wasn't an athlete. The only thing was, he felt that he was letting his father down. I don't think he was angry at his father for wanting him to be something that he didn't want to be, no. He never thought of it in that light. He was just sorry that he couldn't do what his father wanted. No, I don't think so. But then, I don't know what he really and truly thought. He never expressed himself on that point.

I think Francis feels bad; he's got some sense that men ought to do that —be in sports. That his body ought to be in better shape. His father rides him. I don't think his father wants him to be more athletic, but wants him to be in tune with his body. Some of his team experiences have been bad: being on a team and not being terrific at it made him feel bad.

Robert knows his father likes it and is interested in it, so I suppose he sees sports as having value. He does have coordination problems. I perceive that as more of a problem for a boy. And he's real little; that's more of a problem for a boy too. That's the thing of it, you know, whether it's right or wrong, that is the way it is. Not a goddamned thing I can do about it.

Those last four mothers have all linked sports to the father/son relationship, and though it seems there is good cause to do so, this is not always the case, as in the next quotations. Instead, the issue seems to be coming together with other boys, being accepted as a boy—even when the boy isn't really interested in playing the game, as in the very last of these.

Well, he's, you know, joining the club of male compatriots; that's what it really is. He plays baseball, he says he loves football. He probably would be a nervous wreck if he got out there with a uniform on and was getting bashed around, but he swears he loves to watch it and these fucking boring baseball games too. Matt never takes him out and plays ball or any of those things, but we finally had to beg him to take Gabe out and teach him to ride the two-wheeler. Gabe was convinced—he was just crying for a week—that he was a sissy because he couldn't ride his two-wheeler, blah, blah, blah. And I couldn't do it because of my hip injury. So now he's on his bike and he hasn't gotten off for a week. He's on it all the time. Mostly, though, with sports, it's what it all *means:* he can talk baseball with his friends.

Both boys, they live and breathe sports. Season to season—baseball, football, basketball. It became the bond with male friends; that's one reason they don't have female friends, because the girls aren't in the sports stuff. Frank is getting concerned about his figure; he's been real chubby. He's constantly doing sit-ups, and jogging in the morning. It's very important to his young male ego.

All three sons, well, yes. First of all, they had to play. You had to play, that's it. You had to have one thing or, better, to have football in the fall and baseball in the summer, that showed you were really doing it. The other sports weren't important because no one expects you to ride a horse or roller-skate or play tennis, because at school no one does those things. My daughters had no problems with sports because they never felt like they had to be doing it. The boys—they just had to be number one, had to be on the winning team, absolutely. Now with Simon, it's still a natural thing. He feels, "I like that baseball, like to throw that ball, like to catch it with my mitt." He's not talking about being number one. He's young; maybe that part comes later. Joey, he doesn't talk too much about it, maybe because they don't want him on the team; he's lousy. I'm not too sure how he feels about that.

Joseph is very wary; he's wary of any physical activity. He talks about baseball, and thinks about the Cubs, and wears a Cub hat, and wants to know if they won. But he doesn't do sports. It's a combination of a few things. His coordination has never been good, and he's stocky. He doesn't move real easily in his body, and he's pretty pigeon-toed. He doesn't feel comfortable about it with the other kids.

There were many mothers whose feelings about sports and their own sons' involvement in them were far less critical than the preceding group. Some regret that their sons haven't had enough athletic opportunity/experience in their lives.

Athletics is very important, plays a big role. It's what he does when he's down. Two or three years ago, when he'd feel a migraine coming on, he'd play basketball and work out the tension that way. He's an excellent player and takes tremendous delight in it. He refused to play on the team because it was too competitive. He really enjoys the game, and didn't want to have to do it on demand; he wanted to do it out of joy. He's always played exuberantly. He plans to play basketball forever and ever. He was talking with me and some other folks about going into business, and we told him he wasn't going to get a chance to play basketball. He said, "Oh, no, I'll simply say, 'I have to go to a meeting now,' and close the door and go play basketball."

I wish he had more interest and opportunity for sports activities. He never joined a team. The school he went to had no teams, and the roughness of the neighborhood kids has kept him away. He will take out a basketball now and shoot baskets. He loves sports as a spectator. I would like him to do something in the way of sports. He admires athletes very much; he looks up to their excellence. I taught him how to pass a football; I enjoyed it. When he was younger we used to get out and play in the street.

Not enough. I really resent that in New York City's school system there is an incredible lack of athletic programs. They have no team sports. I used to resent that where I went to school we *had* to do all those sports every single day, and I hated it. But here there's nothing at all. And that's absolutely appalling. It's completely unrealistic. We have not been able to afford to send them to classes privately for all these sports that boys should know. That's what our friends would say to do. We just don't have these outlets available to us. So it's a question of hoping they'll be interested enough to go ice skating in the park, or play football with friends.

Obviously, mothers cannot be described as antisports. Mothers are not especially outspoken in the criticisms they do have; many appear to have accepted the athletic requirement on the list. As a group, the interview mothers do not seem to have made connections between the universal training of male children and youths in competitive sports and the behavior of "most men." Few of these women discussed violence, the team mentality, the overriding goal of winning, or even the exclusion of women, and none defined these as serious dangers at the core of the huge national and international athletic networks. Whether they appreciate the value of play and exercise to human health or consider the activity to be proof of their sons' success in the world or have come to value athletics because women have been shut out of the P.E. department until very recently, most women want their sons to be active in sports. Perhaps this *is* because mothers have been excluded, and haven't the familiarity with sports to make the kind of indictment men can make.

Referring to football and baseball as metaphors for "the American way of life" has become cliché, despite the fact that they can only be metaphors for *males*—who are slightly less than half of the population now living the American way. Not only sociologists and psychologists but also players, managers, and announcers have begun to study—and deplore—"fan violence"—the hateful, negative responses of enormous crowds of predominantly male spectators to baseball, basketball, football, soccer, or boxing. The Chicago *Sun-Times* ran a series in 1981 called "Fan Violence: Sports' Great Threat." Several players interviewed for the series connected violence within the games to the violence in the stands, explaining that the crowds were the same as the teams except for the uniforms, and comparing contemporary sports to gladiatorial contests, in terms of the crowds' desire to witness bloodletting and violent death.

Robert Kennedy, whose death by assassination was as American as apple pie, said: "Except for war, there is nothing in American life —nothing—which trains a boy better for life than football"; and indeed, sports do serve as a training ground for men.[15] Competition is the basis and the justification for male athletics, and the competition is not just for status but to prove masculinity. Hence the deliberate exclusion of females: "If women can play, then, by definition, participation does not prove anything about masculinity."[16] Moreover, sports talk and the watching of sports on TV have gained a hallowed place in contemporary male culture. The prize here is less obvious than, but as eagerly sought as, masculinity. The prize is male friendship, defined as acceptance into the fraternity, and that is the reward for memorizing major-league standings, players' histories, and the rosters of All-Star teams. Moreover, given their cultural inclination, most men would much rather talk about batting averages than their own thoughts or feelings—to other men.

Ultimately, "because the subtler, personal rewards and pleasures of sports are played down, in fact often destroyed . . . one's sense of achievement depends entirely on winning. Absolute team loyalty, unquestioned obedience to authority, respectful fear and hatred of the opposition, disregard of individual injury and suffering —all justified in the name of victory—these are the axioms of the sports system."[17] The pursuit and glorification of masculinity through competition has provided a model and metaphor for business and government, especially for the design of foreign policy and the action and uses of the military. Though Teddy Roosevelt, John Kennedy, and Richard Nixon are blatant examples, many American presidents have worked to promote sports-inspired masculinity— their own and that of the nation. The country itself, as a political entity, has been assigned a masculine character. Within a month after Japan attacked Pearl Harbor, the United States was joyfully labeled "magnificently male again. . . . Men again fighting in the crudest man terms."[18] Through the last thirty years and more it has been essential for presidents, senators, and congressmen never to appear "soft on communism." Or soft at all, for that matter; the eternal erection has become policy—wielded like a baseball bat. Sports "supplies a language and rationale for men to use in nonsports situations . . . which reduces the more complex real-life problems of choosing objectives and weighing human costs to the simplistic imperatives of a competitive game."[19]

Many professional athletes have given us insight to the world of professional sports, that intersection of male athletics and business where play is work. Their books examine the lives of men in sports, and reveal—deliberately or not—the single-minded desperation that permeates American athletics, from Little League to the majors, from sandlot to Olympics.

Jerry Kramer's diary of the 1967 season describes the experiences of a man who sees the widening split between who he is and what he does—but accepts the necessity of that split in the lives of men who "play" pro football: "September 17—Before I left the house . . . my oldest child, Tony, who's nine, asked me who my man'd be in the game. I told him Karras. . . . Alex had a good day. I don't know yet how many times he got to the passer, how many times he rushed past me . . . [He] started beating me to the outside, and one time . . . I was so frustrated I reached out and grabbed a big handful of his jersey and just pulled him to the ground. Nobody saw it, and Alex got up calling me every name he could think of. I'm sure that he's been held by about 90 percent of the guys he plays against, but he didn't expect it from me. I was desperate. . . . When I came out from the locker room, my insides all torn up, and climbed into my car, my son Tony looked at me and said, 'Daddy, do you like Alex Karras? I don't mean as a football player. I mean as a person.' 'Shut up, I said.'

"November 19—I started off the day determined to get mean and serious for the game. . . . I tried to work up a good hate for the 49ers, for Charlie Krueger in particular. . . . When I want to hate an individual, I make it a point not to look at the other team before the game, not to see the man I'm going to face. I feel if I don't see him, I can hate him a little more.

"This afternoon, I deliberately didn't look at the 49ers. I didn't look at Charlie Krueger. I convinced myself I hated him. I hated him for trying to make me look bad. I hated him for trying to beat me. I hated him for trying to take money out of my pocket. I hated him for trying to tackle Bart Starr. I worked up my hatred when we did our calisthenics, and I still hated him when we started back to the dressing room to put on our shoulder pads and helmets before the kickoff. I rushed through the tunnel, started up the stairs, concentrating on my hate, concentrating on getting mad, and as I reached the top step, I heard a voice behind me saying, 'Is Gerald Kramer thayuh?' It had to be Charlie. I laughed and turned around, and he stood there laughing too. 'How you doin', Jerry?' he said. He completely ruined my train of hate. . . ."

On December 17, Kramer recorded his realization that the men are being destroyed: "They bruised Donny Anderson and banged up Ben Wilson and Steve Wright cracked a rib. And Allen Brown almost died . . . two broken ribs and a punctured kidney. . . . I don't really realize how brutal the game is until the off-season, when I go out to banquets and watch movies of our games. Then I see guys turned upside-down and backwards and hit from all angles, and I flinch. I'm amazed by how violent the game is, and I wonder about playing it myself. . . ."[20]

It is more difficult for us to believe that men are destroyed—injured or even killed—in sport than in war. But the same inability to see, to acknowledge both horror and terror, occurs in the cultural blurring of war's reality.

Men have glazed and gilded the degradation, fear, and brutality of war by presenting it in literature as a theater of glory and excitement, even beauty. It's tough—war is hell—and stimulating in its glamour and power; indeed, they have made war a media institution which first, in the war movies of the forties and fifties, taught that war was about bravery (personal insensitivity and mindless aggression) and patriotism (willingness to die and kill for the political goals of governments), and which now, through the last two decades, has presented war as a rollicking comedy—the buffoonery of "Hogan's Heroes" and the sarcasms of "M*A*S*H." Nazis are clowns and the reality of fascism has faded away. The Korean War, less delightful, has just about disappeared from public memory, and the Vietnam War—unacceptable even as historical fact, to say nothing of its entertainment value—is being excused or obliterated in history books.[21]

As with sport, the reality is obscured; lamed and blinded men, paraplegic and mad men, broken and blasted corpses—this truth is lost or hidden, forgotten over and over, romanticized and justified as "the price we pay for freedom." Though such voices as those in the shocking poems of Siegfried Sassoon and Wilfred Owen or the prose of Dalton Trumbo, revealing painfully the anguish of men in war, may still be heard by a minority of politically or intellectually oriented men, they carry little cultural power to mitigate against the combined forces of the Little League, network TV, and the ghost of John Wayne. Indeed, the acceptance of war is so carefully taught, and so well learned, that even many mothers believe that our sons should kill, should die, in war.

The poet Alta, petitioning for ERA in a California supermarket parking lot, met such a mother. Asked to sign Alta's petition, she replied, "That law would take away our benefits and privileges." "Name two," Alta countered. "I don't want my daughter to go into the Army," she said. Alta asserted that the draft was illegal; "And besides, would you want your *son* to go into the Army?" The mother's answer? "That's what sons are for."

She is perhaps unusual in the force of her assertion, but not unusual enough. Men who've written books about war have taught us: mothers are to be praised for bravery, fortitude, steadfastness; to be encouraged in loyalty to father-kings and father-gods, encouraged to send sons to war.

> *"Ah, Mrs. McGrath," the sergeant said—*
> *"Would you like to make a soldier out of your son Ted?*
> *With a scarlet coat, and a big cocked hat—*
> *Now, Mrs. McGrath, wouldn't you like that?"*[22]

In the Apocrypha is the story of the mother with seven sons. She encouraged them to be tortured and killed rather than succumb to their enemy. "The mother was especially admirable and worthy of honorable memory. Though she saw her seven sons perish within a single day, she bore it with good courage because of her hope in the Lord." (2 Maccabees 7:20) In the end, that mother was lucky, for she too was killed by the Greek governor; she died for one father at the hands of another, having sacrificed to them both all the sons of her body, all the children of her life.

In the film *Hearts and Minds,* a documentary about the United States in Vietnam, a mother and father speak of the death of their son in the war. She stands still, listening to her husband say that he thinks the American system is "superb." She hesitantly touches a model airplane—her son's—as the father speaks. Her face filled with pain, she touches the model and says that she has forgotten her pain.[23]

In another scene in that film, an American veteran, a recently released POW, speaks to a school-auditorium audience of mothers. His point of view is that the United States involvement and military escalation has been just and appropriate, and that his imprisonment, along with the death and mutilation of thousands of other young men, is justifiable. He says to those mothers, "I am what you made me." The camera scans the audience, searches their faces for agreement, acceptance, pride—a sign that the mothers feel he is right, that he is what they have made. None of them nod, none of them smile. None laugh as he chuckles in recognition of his "tribute" to them. Their faces are mostly blank, though some are puzzled. They look as if they are wondering—especially those with sons who are dead, or broken, or missing in action still, or living in Canada, or in jail—they're wondering, is that true? Am I responsible for this? For my son's condition? For this war? Their faces mirror the faces of women who clutch the flags off military coffins, with hands that don't yet know they cannot touch their boys again.

> Then up comes Ted, without any legs,
> And in their place, two wooden pegs.
> She kissed him a dozen times or two,
> Saying, "Holy Moses, 'tisn't you—"

Tran Thi Bich, a Vietnamese mother of five sons, is a woman who hated the war five times over. Her "eldest, who was thirty-two, was wounded in a mortar attack. Part of his face was missing and his left hand was useless. He could not find work, perhaps it was because of the horrible new face he had, but then, many veterans had no work. The next . . . a thirty-year-old son who had become a madman who could do nothing for himself. 'A bright child, a nervous child, a good son,' . . . he was the one she had loved the most. The third son was a lieutenant on active duty. A fourth son, a twenty-three-year-old soldier, had been missing 'for a long time,' . . . last . . . was the youngest boy, a deserter from the army and in hiding."

Interviewed by Gloria Emerson, she spoke again and again of the son who was mad. "He became strange after a battle, a fierce battle—and he came home two years ago with this look on his face. He wouldn't eat anything I cooked for him. He sat there and wept. Then we wept with him. A friend of his told me that my son saw too many men die, and that for three days and three nights he was unable to move away from the corpses." She took her son to a huge military hospital, but found that once he was inside, she "was not allowed to visit him, to talk to him, to hold him, to bring him food." There was a regular visiting day, like in a prison, when visitors, "nearly always women," moved along a line of barbed wire, stopping "not quite a minute" to see the men they had come to visit.

"He would try and come to me, but that was not possible. He would stand there, his eyes always on my face, calling out to me."

Tran Thi Bich remembers and remembers her second son, "who kept calling out Mother, Mother, until the guards hauled him away. She always heard his voice. . . . the second son who wanted to put his head in her lap and not be afraid of night any more."[24]

> *"Ah, Teddy me boy!" the widow cried,*
> *"Your two fine legs were your mammy's pride;*
> *Them stumps of a tree wouldn't do at all—*
> *Why didn't you run from the cannon ball?"*

> *"For I'd rather my Ted as he used to be,*
> *"Than the king and church and their damn na-vee!"*

Louise Ransom is an American mother of six sons, five of whom did not go to Vietnam and die there.* The death of her firstborn caused "not just . . . huge grief . . . but . . . anger. . . . People would come up to say, 'Isn't it satisfying that he died for his country?' " The June after her son's death in May of 1968, Louise Ransom had occasion to hear the Reverend William Sloane Coffin, Jr., speak of "how much he wished the mothers in America would object to the war, and risk arrest." In July, Mrs. Ransom began, by "chaining herself to a draft resister at an antiwar demonstration." She returned the two medals posthumously awarded her son by the government of South Vietnam. In 1973, she helped to form Americans for Amnesty, continuing to work so that people would know "that my son did not die in Vietnam because [others] deserted, he died because of the policy of his own government, and it is important that you understand this. . . ."[25]

And it is important that we understand this: to the extent that mothers of sons *do not* criticize and work against the standard socialization of our children, we will be accepting, we will be supporting, those qualities and actions that we abhor in "most men," those policies and attitudes in the culture at large that keep our sons—and ourselves—from full humanity. We cannot freely assume, if we live with them, if we are married to them, or even if we love them, that

---

* One son failed his physical; one was a C.O.; one registered but wasn't called; and the youngest two were exempted after the fall of 1971, because their brother had been "a casualty."

our best interests—and those of our sons—will be served by an alliance with "most men." Indeed, even if they could be served so, such an alliance does not exist. Women and men, mothers and fathers, have not got a common set of interests and goals; the roles of the sexes diverge widely in the raising of sons, in the making of men.

4

Fathers

The world will not change until fathers can love their sons. I think it's inhuman to ask a woman oppressed by her husband to love and raise a boy child.

—ALTA[1]

she would have his son. he would pay for it and for her. each year she would have a certain amount of money for herself. he would supervise the upbringing and education of his son. he would make the decisions for his son. she would take care of his son in his home. if she wanted to leave, she would not take his son with her.

—ANDREA DWORKIN[2]

Contrast the ideal parental roles: the idealized mother is a woman who is, both physically and spiritually, boundlessly giving and endlessly available. She is truly present to her son. The idealized father is practically invisible; he is almost never available, rarely giving; his sparse favor and scarce presence to his son become miraculous and precious when they do appear. He is like the unknowable Judaeo-Christian father-god, who is the epitome of this ideal. The dictates of the list require that cold and demanding behavior and a distant and critical stance should have become the paternal ideal. Obviously, though unfortunately, there is a strong element of that ideal to be found in the real.

Sons compare fathers to mothers, and describe their fathers' "duties" as parents:

My father was the disciplinarian: "When your father gets back from the office—such and such will happen." And it did. My mother made a lot of the decisions about how things were to be done—let's say around school stuff. And my father would be the person to carry out the action, to do what needed to be done. My father gladly shouldered that task, I suppose.

Even though my mother worked, my father paid for everything. I don't know how they worked it out with the money; I've never understood that. But no matter what came into the house we were always to thank my father for it. My mother would say that. If she had taken me shopping and bought me a pair of pants, she'd say, "When you get home, you thank your father for these." Oh. "Thanks, Dad." He'd say, "For what?"

Mom was always the one I wanted to go to; you know, when something happened to me, she was the one I turned to. Mother's the one you always go to for comfort. Motherly love—that's really important for the child. You can't get it from the father. The father should participate, you know; he's got his duties, but the mother is the most important factor for the child's feelings. You know, he wants to see me do well; his main objective is to see me do better than he did in his lifetime. And my mother, her main objective is to give me all the love I'll ever need, you know.

He took me on a camping trip once and told me in a real half-assed way what I already knew—about the birds and the bees. It was real uncomfortable for him, whereas my mother, even if it wasn't easy for her, she never made it hard for us. He took each of us boys on one of those camping trips; she felt that it was his duty to do it, even if we talked to her more often, you see. As I got older, and this happened with the other kids, I would tell them, "Don't wait for Dad; just say whatever it is; ask me or ask Mom; don't bother asking him." She would swallow her pride or nervousness and just do it, just say it.

These next two sons see their fathers in terms of the power they wielded in the family; despite the fact that these fathers must have had specific attitudes about morals and behavior, ethics and actions, it is for their power in enforcing these that they are remembered by their sons.

My father just doesn't seem to care. We didn't make that much difference to him, other than that we obeyed him when he spoke. He just let my mother have us. Oh, we obeyed him; we were frightened of him, emotionally afraid. He used to beat up my older brother. He never beat any of the other kids, but we were afraid of his booming voice. I'll tell you, he didn't seem to care about us, and he didn't seem to care about her either. I have never seen any affection between my mother and father, ever.

In a lot of households, the mother may not have much power. For example, my mother had nothing to say about what anybody did. Yet she was an influence, because of the kind of person she is—sincere, not at all dogmatic or moralistic about how you were to act. And my father was just the opposite. Naturally, he controlled my life as far as what I could do and everything, but he's had very little influence on my personality, my values. I'm very, very much like my mother—and have worked at being nothing like him.

Men do long for fathers who are warm, receptive, physically affectionate and comforting, open and honest about their feelings, and approving and accepting of their sons despite those sons' failures relative to the list. Most sons—almost all—are perpetually disappointed. They go to their fathers in search of a response of the spirit, a response of the heart—and they come back disappointed: the connection isn't made; the spark doesn't strike fire. They crave the kind of cherishing that men learn not to give.

Whatever is said about the contemporary father/son relationship by the experts—the psychology, sociology, religion, and philosophy men—is, in effect, being said by *fathers*—men who, whether they are biological parents or not, are *fathers*—owners and leaders, wielders and definers of power in male culture. But the expectations and judgments of sons and mothers are necessary for an understanding of the behavior and attitudes of fathers, the father/son relationship, and the mother-son-father triangle.

When sons are poets, filmmakers, and novelists, they cry and scream and wail and whine—or brag and eulogize. For better or worse, most of them embrace the father/son romance. But when sons aren't choosing their words for an audience, when they're just talking, just saying what they first think to say about Dad—having been asked—they speak in fits and starts; they say, "You know?" a lot. Unused to talking about their feelings, often uncomfortable with the task of discussing their fathers, sons nonetheless spoke many words about these men.

The sons interviewed, like the mothers, are a diverse lot. They range in age from fifteen to seventy-one; they're Black, white, Asian, and Latin; they're gay and straight; they're high school students, mobile-home salesmen, sculptors, and lawyers; they're possessed of many levels and styles of personal and political consciousness.

Most of them described troubled relations with their fathers; many had angry, sad, and painful stories to tell. Men are filled with passion when they speak of their fathers. Their criticism and rejection, their bitterness and denial, are comparable to the attitudes of most daughters about their mothers. In both cases, the child is steeped in emotion directed at and centering around the same-sex parent. Both women and men are required to be—for themselves, for the world, for their children—models of the roles assigned to them. Fathers must fulfill the requirements of the list for their own manhood—and must serve thus as a hero, protector, comrade, and teacher for their sons. Sons learn to *expect* their fathers to be John Wayne, but to *accept* their fathers as much smaller, much weaker men. Just as no mother can be the Virgin/Madonna of perfection, no father can be a god of masculinity. Ironically, if a man did fulfill the requirements of the list—paying with his humanity in the attempt to do so—he could never give his son the tenderness and caring that boys and men want from their fathers.

About 1 percent of the interview sons described only good relations with their fathers.

He used to call the four boys his four million dollars. He was very affectionate; he liked to take us places. Our relationship was close and loving. I thought of him as being strong. He was strong—muscular. We would work together in the house. He enjoyed that. We'd go for walks occasionally, on Sundays. We would talk; my father had a good sense of humor; he had a tendency to tell stories. I could joke with him a little bit.

A real father could not possibly have been any better to me than my stepfather was. When he found out that I wanted to shoot pool, he bought me a cue stick. He was just like that. And, when he found out I'd been keeping his car out all night—the guy at the garage told him—he says to the guy, "Well, he's my son and that's my car. Whenever he wants it he can have it." But he was waiting on me when I came in that evening, and he told me, "Don't take that car no more." All he had to do was tell me don't do something and I respected him to the extent that I wouldn't do it. He respected me too, never tried to run me.

The following sons explain that there is something good, something appealing, about Dad; something desirable and valuable that exists between them and their fathers. This desirable quality, this positive value, is hard won, and that winning requires that a son also acknowledge what is lost.

I argue a lot with my father, 'cause we have very different opinions on a lot of things, like what I should be doing. He wanted me to get involved with a lot of clubs at school 'cause it looks good on your college recommendation. But I wasn't ready for it; I didn't feel like it. I needed to work on the schoolwork, getting my grades up higher. We argued a lot about that. And we—we argue about lots of other things too. But I'd say generally that I have a pretty good relationship with him. I don't know; he seems to feel left out when I'm talking to my uncle, who's a sports buff like me. We talk about football and the playoffs and everything, and my father sort of feels left out. We try to get him into the conversation, but he can't because it doesn't interest him, and he doesn't know, right; he doesn't know the stuff. Like I remember when I was little, he knew nothing about baseball. He didn't even know how to play. But he made the effort, he bought me a bat and a glove and everything, and he took me out to the park and he tried to play, you know; he pitched to me, and he tried. I think we have a good relationship.

That son was still a boy, actively wanting a better day-to-day relationship with his father. He wants so much for it to be better than it is that though he says they have not much in common and that they argue a lot, he gives his father credit for effort, and concludes that they *do* have a good relationship, a "pretty good relationship." This next man, in his mid-thirties, is also charitable, but he has lowered his expectations considerably over the years.

I remember real well the young time; I didn't want to be around him because it was always a real hard, hard time—real unpleasant. I made a conscious effort to be out, to be away from him. I'd try to be in bed before he got home. As I got older, I became more independent, I didn't have to be home so much, I didn't have to deal with him so much. He seems to have mellowed out a little bit lately, like I'll hear from him; he'll ask about my work, the music. What he asks is, "How are you gonna make a buck out of this?" But he does seem to have real concern. I wonder whether the concern is because he knows that there are other people, one man his age, who've taken an interest in my career and boosted me, supported me. My father, on the one hand, thought this was really wonderful, but on the other hand I could tell that he felt this maybe was something *he* should be doing. But he's always made me feel

real conscious of anything I've ever gotten from him, even money for
college—like I've *taken* it from him. So I worked full time after the first
year. He's got a lot of money now, much more than he used to have. If it
ever comes to me or to my daughter, wonderful; but I'm not going out of
my way to get my father's cash. I'm more interested in my mother being
taken care of.

Very strained. Strained relationship. Both of us feel regretful that we're
not closer, but also extremely self-conscious in terms of communicating
to each other. I would like to see him be . . . I wish that he were a more
vital person than he is. At the same time there's lots of qualities that I've
incorporated that I can see are from him. Such as his capacity for
warmth and gentleness, his storytelling ability; and he's not phony—I appreciate that. But we're almost incapable of giving each other direct support, and both of us feel resentful and bitter and each blames the other
one for it.

Expressed here again and again are the need, the desire, of sons
to have a piece of father, to take something of him, to get from him
that token, that gift, that sign of connection that will stand for proof
of their bond.

When I was a kid the governing force in my social life was sports. The
most focused element, most associated with hopes and fears, was sports.
He supported that to some degree. My dad was a golfer; he was a really
good golfer. By the time I was old enough to go with him he had to back
away from it some just 'cause he didn't have the time. You want to be a
good golfer, you got to play a lot. When he was in college, he was very
fine. He never really wanted me to play. He'd take me with him and all
that, but he never really taught me how. He couldn't find a way to get
me to keep my head down. He never tried. I didn't realize that fully until
just recently. I would often reflect on the fact that he'd been so good and
I never was any good. There was a period of time when I would go off
with him to the golf course, but he stopped short of making sure that I
learned how to play. The same thing went for the other stuff. As a kid, I
was in baseball, football, baseball mostly. I was okay, but I wasn't really
one of the good ones. I was passable but not outstanding—at anything.
Evidently there was no help he could give me in that either, even though
for most of that period it meant a lot to me. So if he'd have really known
where I was at, he'd have known that. . . . Sports were really superim-
portant to me, everything was geared to it, and so there was frustration
in not being the star. I think he was to some degree indifferent to

that. . . . Now we're pretty close—in a personal sense. We're not very close in respect to ideology, and we have a sort of—excuse the expression —"gentleman's agreement," not to get into it too much anymore. At some point he had to stop telling me what to think. He had to accept not only that I thought different, but that if we pursued it there was going to be conflict—which, of course, he don't want.

I really love the person. I think just lately he's understanding me and accepting me. I have no gripes or ill feelings. He probably made some mistakes but he didn't honestly know, I think, that he was making them. He was a manipulator. He wanted to give me more money to go to school but couldn't, so now he's slipping me a ten here and there, because he feels he has to make up for that, and now he can do it. I'd like to sit down and have a beer with him, but I kind of know it wouldn't be the conversation I have in mind. He wants to do more, but he doesn't know how; you know what I mean? I mean, he touched me, he spanked me, he loved me, and yet, I don't think he ever felt it was enough. Did I think it was enough? Yeah . . . Well, not really what I expected—it was just what was there.

I would have to ask him if he would hit some baseballs to me. And he would. We would go out on the big parkway in front of his house. It would be a 90-degree day and he would hit the ball for four hours. And when I was done, thanks, Dad. I never asked him much anymore because his idea of play like that was really work. I mean it's not just play. And if I asked my father to take me for a drive around Pittsburgh, he would say okay. He'd take me on a tour of the poorest neighborhoods. And being a real impressionable little kid, I wouldn't ask again. It was the same as with hitting me the baseballs; he'd just say, go down to the ghetto if you want to see what it's like. I was just appalled at the poverty; living out in the suburbs like we were, I was dumbfounded. Okay. I wouldn't ask again. I got the picture. But now, I'd say he has a better sense of me than anyone else in the family. Especially since my parents separated, he's been more at ease with himself. He's improved his mental outlook significantly. Now there's no one in the house besides himself, no one can botch up, leave things in a mess—which used to really bother him. See, I don't like to be told what to do, and my father and I are alike in that way. He won't bother me about the things my mother and sisters bother me about. We both, my father and I, know that there are things that are pointless in saying.

Well, my relationship with my father is pretty good, or very good, considering he lives two thousand miles away, and I see him once a year or so. It took him until I was thirty-five to really acknowledge me as an adult and to relax a little. He's always had what my older brother calls "secret agendas"—stuff going on that he doesn't want to bring out. He's not an emotional person and he's not a direct person, and he had a lot of anger, and he projected a lot of bullshit onto his kids. Also, he did something which I consider weak, and unworthy of him—although it's classic. He married the housekeeper when my mother died, which radically changed his relationship with all of us, his kids. Another thing is that he used to basically relate to me through money, and two or three years after my mother died, he said, "I've decided to conserve my dough, and I'm tired of thinking that you guys are relating to me about my money, so there isn't going to be any more." Just like that. That was a good step, and a positive one, but perhaps he should have done it from the git-go or something. That relationship was not correct.

All of the following sons speak of terrible relations with their fathers. They recall their boyhood complaints and come to adulthood with the clear understanding that the damage is real; even the youngest of them see that Dad isn't going to "get better," come closer, become loving or supportive—or they finally see that he never was that way.

The father/son power struggle is central to this youth's situation:

He's my father so I shouldn't be saying bad things about him, but he treats me—he treats—he says I treat people like everybody's a fool, and I don't, I don't. *He* takes an attitude like he knows everything, and I don't think he does, but I can't say what I think, because then he cuts out all my—you know, free time, money—I don't get that much anyway, but if he wants something from me and I don't want to do it, he'll take things away to punish me. And he likes to embarrass me. He does embarrass me; he shouts in front of my friends; it's very embarrassing; it gives my friends a bad impression.

This man understands that the pressure his father put on him was born in the father's desire that his son should achieve what he did not.

I never went into the competitive sports thing; I know he wanted me to. I just could not. He didn't show me how. Other dads were showing their sons how to play ball, how to play what the other boys play. And I was skinny. I was uncoordinated. I can smile about it now, but ooh, I just got a chill from the memory—the most awful time of my life. I was made fun of by the other boys. Called a sissy. All the derogatory terms. One of the last ones picked—always. Even in high school I used to dread walking into that gym. I knew I wasn't going to take fucking ROTC. I wasn't going to swing to that side. But it was the worst, the absolute worst. Dad really failed me there. I'm wondering if he didn't know how to do it; he never used to take and throw a ball for me, for crying out loud! Yet he wanted *me* to go out there and do it. And, much later, again, he wanted me to do something he hadn't, or couldn't—he wanted me to be a dentist. I remember how scared I was after my second year of college, to tell him I didn't want to be a dentist. I said, "Dad, I don't want to do this."

This man has called a halt to his efforts to please Dad; he has come to see that no matter what he does, the father will not respond as he wishes.

Well, there was a little bit of difficulty between me and my father. Expectations—his of me. He badgered me about why my math grade wasn't A plus (he was a CPA)—why couldn't I get A's in math. Well, it didn't make any sense to me, that's why. That's his ball game, not mine. He pushed me into the Boy Scouts. I'd always wanted to be a Cub Scout, but he would not let me be a Cub Scout. "Wait till you're old enough to be a Boy Scout." So when I grew old enough to be a Boy Scout, I had to be an *Eagle* Scout; I couldn't just be a Boy Scout. I couldn't have a good time; I had to get a medal. There was a lot of expectation, prodding, pushing. Also, there was a thing of my father's taking over any project I started. If I were painting a picture, he would come in and show me how to paint it; he'd finish it for me, and I'd leave the room and he'd be doing it, perfecting it. These things began to wear on me. I felt I couldn't try anything, I couldn't do anything. I don't feel close to him. He has never acknowledged my work. I wanted him to come to Los Angeles very badly, to visit me, to see me in a show I was in. It was good, it was a big show, it ran almost a year. I wanted him to see it, and he wouldn't come. I kept asking him and he kept making excuses. Generally he'd say his wife was sick, or she couldn't come, or she wanted to go somewhere else. So I really felt rejected. Just before the show closed, I delivered an ultimatum; I was really pissed. I wasn't going to see him until he came to the show. So he said that they'd checked the airline prices and they couldn't afford it right now. "But when are you coming to see us?" Or, "Be in a show on Broadway, then I'll come see you." Then his wife died, and he said, "Now I can come see you, can't I?" I said, "Sure, anytime you want, you're always welcome." So he started making other excuses. He got married a third time, and they flew to Austria for their honeymoon; they were going to stop off to see me before or after, but they

FATHERS 149

changed their plans. So I've made a promise to myself that I won't go see him. This is fooling around. The relationship is very shaky now, you see; I don't like it this way; I don't feel comfortable. I can't always be the one who goes to see him.

This man had taken in his father's criticism for more than twenty-five years, believing that there was something really "wrong" with him.

I remember one outing with my father. It was the night he bet a lot of money on the Kentucky Derby and won. I had also done a real big job at home, and was feeling proud of myself. I was thirteen or so. (I didn't do it of my own free will; my mother made me do it.) He came home, and saw those walls had all been done, that he wouldn't have to do it, and he was glad to have won the Derby, so we went out to a bar. He gave me twenty dollars, and I had a Coke and he had a drink. I have no idea what we talked about, but we must have passed the time, just the two of us. We didn't do things together usually, though, he preferred not to. When he'd first taken up golf, he wanted me to do it too; to this day I have a chip on my shoulder and will not play the game. I caddied for him in a tournament, his first tournament. He wasn't doing very well with me being there. I kept dropping clubs and making noises. He gave me a dollar at the end and said, "I lost because of you. You would have gotten more money if I had won. And next time I ask you to caddy for me, say no." So it was straight up. That was it, fine and dandy. He had gone through the motions—taking me into the back yard, "teaching" me to swing a club. I could never swing it good enough for him. He's very precise. Everything has to be perfect. If it's not, it makes him nuts, and he doesn't have the patience for anybody who doesn't have this whatever-it-is of perfection. Now I internalized all this when I was growing up: "My god, I can't do this and I can't do that." It would drive me crazy. It was only about four or five years ago that I had a discussion with my sister and she's had these same feelings all this time too. I don't want you to think he's an awful man; he's not a mean, vicious person or anything. I'm sure he has the best of intentions. But learning that it wasn't *me*, that he'd done it to me, and that there's nothing wrong with *me*—that just made such a difference.

Here is a son whose father and stepfather both disappointed him.

I would characterize my father's relationship to me as a lack of love—really. We started seeing each other again in the last few years, and he told me that he hadn't deserted my sister and me, but that he left us for my mother's sake, which I always said was bullshit. By the time I was thirteen I had become pretty hard-nosed about him. We lacked the American ideal—him playing ball with me and that sort of thing, you know. Now with my stepfather, I'd say that jealousy was at the heart of our relationship. At the time of the divorce I was forced into being an adult, the man of the house, yes. So when he showed up, for a long time I hated his guts. He was just another obnoxious guy as far as I was concerned, and he really did a lot of damage to my sister. He and I had several altercations, physical altercations, but finally I decided that I didn't really hate him. I just felt sorry for him; he didn't know how to express love. He was jealous of me, that was obvious. And he didn't understand that I had been an adult for some time before he came along and tried to push me back into being a child again—which I refused to accept. When my mother wasn't there, we actually communicated relatively well. When she was there, they did a lot of stuff together that didn't include me, like target shooting, sailing, and stuff, and I was aware of their sexual interaction too, because the door was locked all the time. I don't even remember being aware of that with my father. Anyway, my relationship with my father is nonexistent now. When I went back to New Orleans last Christmas, I thought about going to see him and decided there was no point as far as I was concerned.

The deepest analyses of some of the most painful relationships here are spoken by men who are able to have sympathy and compassion for the fathers who hurt and disappointed them. These, unlike many others, have questioned the romantic ideal of patriarchy and try to live with the truth. Other men, equally realistic, eschew compassion, preferring, like the last son in this group, to simply acknowledge that what's done is done.

This son has struggled for years to understand the emotional dynamics of his family.

To begin with, my father hadn't wanted a male child when my mother was pregnant with me. In fact, the first thing I can remember my father saying to me when I was three or four was that he was so disappointed. He said, "You know, when the nurse told me it was another boy, I was so disappointed because I already had a son, and I thought I could never love two boys." Pause. "But then you come home from the hospital and I saw that everything was fine." Now, in retrospect, as I look over the history of the family, I can see that he perceived himself to be a failure as a father. He was really an outsider in the home. He felt that very acutely, of course. His only way of dealing with that was to retreat, to pull away, into the alcohol, which pushed me away even farther. I, too, saw him as a failure and an unnecessary appendage to life, and also as a kind of buffoon, because the drinking had been sort of masqueraded as a clown act. Partly, too, the relationship with my father was an authoritarian one. I knew that there was a sense in which I could push him to a limit, but after that he would not be flexible. I sought his approval, and never got it. I also thought he was mocking me, as I came to homosexual consciousness. I went through the emotional gymnastics of thinking women are attracted to men; I'm attracted to men, therefore I must be a woman. So my behavior at nine, ten, and eleven was effeminate, actually. I was shy and retiring, got excuses from gym class all the time—and my father mocked me for that; that was his way of responding to what was happening with me.

This next son has realized that the gulf between him and his father was made of his own fear; perhaps his father's fear as well. Though he cannot get from his father what he wanted all the years of his boyhood, he can understand who the man has been, and who he himself may be.

My father emigrated two and one-half years before the rest of the family, so I mostly remember not having a father for a while. When we did get back together, my father was always distant; my father was always removed; my father was always the disciplinarian, physically. My father never spoke of his life; my father never spoke of his past and very rarely did he say anything that he had experienced, telling me in a story fashion. When he was angry I would hear it, but it would be rage that would come out. As I was growing up, there was no communication between us; it was frustrating for me to try to relate to my father. There was no understanding; there was no sympathy; there was no love expressed toward me; there was basically fear. I broke through that feeling of fear when I was twenty-nine; I did it by changing myself, by working on myself, reviewing my history and reviewing my father's life, and getting a better understanding of his experience.

The father/son relationship seems to have dissolved for this next man, simply disappeared.

For the first seven years of my life, I was scared of him. I wasn't close to him, or able to talk to him. My father was mad all the time. He was unapproachable, very irritable. After years went by, he moved to the United States. The few times he wrote to me, he did it because he needed something that I could get for him, that I could send him. At that point I was old enough to recognize that and instead of being scared I was angry. I rejected him. Then, for the few years when I first came here and he was still here, our relationship was just one man to another; I never respected him as a father. As a matter of fact, on two occasions I told him that. Our relationship was a business relationship, not even friends, just two people.

Like the last two men, this next son speaks of fear. He has never satisfied himself; he still doesn't know just why his father behaved as he did to his son.

In the early years I respected and feared my father. In later years I no longer feared him—and I really can't even say that I respected him. I honored him, in the sense that he was my father; I gave him the proper rite. There was a period of time when I think that I absolutely could have killed him, when I was working with him. In my early college years I worked in the restaurants for him and upon graduation I went in to work with my dad. At one point I heard him tell another man that the only reason he kept the place open was that his son could not earn a living on the outside. At that point I knew I had to leave. I wasn't able to stay with my dad. He had a tendency to be destructive. He would make promises that he wouldn't keep. He was absolutely cruel—but he couldn't perceive this at all. Even when I was a young boy, when we would rent a cottage up in Wisconsin, he'd take me out in the boat with him, "to keep him company." I wasn't allowed to talk, I wouldn't have a fishing pole. I was a prisoner on this little rowboat for five, six hours. To this day I don't know whether he wanted me away from my mother, or he really wanted company. He may have been punishing me for my mother's being so devoted to me. Maybe he thought that the mere fact that I was in the boat would be fun for me.

Fear is the central theme in this son's narrative, too; yet there are other components, not the least of which is the son's compassion for the father's inability to be a mensch.

My father directed and dominated us all, all four boys; we feared him. He used to take us to buy clothes at Buddy Lee's, and dress us up in clothes that had little to do with us but a lot to do with him—with what he wanted us to wear. If there was any defiance, it was drowned out. I

don't even recall any. Once—and this is the fondest memory I have of
him—I came home and told my dad that someone had pushed me or insulted me or something like that, and my father went down and challenged the guy to a fight. I was between eleven and thirteen. It's so out of
character for my father—because he's not physical, and because he never
had anything to do with us; he never cared. But I have this vivid memory
of him with a headlock on this guy, and punching him in the face, in a
dirt lot. As those things are wont to do, I felt a fatherly thing there—I
felt I had a father. I was glad, even though that kind of thing frightened
me tremendously. I'm not kidding when I tell you that the two main
feelings—no, the only feelings—we had, my brothers and I, about that
man, were hate and terror. Or terror followed by hate. We all shared the
feeling. I can recall an incident where my oldest brother and I were
home, and as soon as Dad came home he started yelling and screaming—
which he would do all the time. I got a knife and my brother got a knife
and we went into the bedroom in the dark, and we were practicing stab-
bing him. We didn't do it, but I can remember my brother and me with
knives, punching at the air with knives. This was how we felt about him
but we never did anything, never acted out. Now that I'm no longer subject to his whims, I can feel compassion for the person. I feel that, when
I reflect on the life he led, and how he was treated, I feel that he did the
best he could and the best he could was absolutely terrible. He was, I
know, a very unhappy man. But I feel compassion for him. He fathered
me, so I have some responsibility for him. I even have some feelings of
tenderness, but when I sit down to spend some time with him, within a
few minutes I've got to go. He's totally preoccupied with himself, and he
starts reverting to his old behavior real soon. I don't react with the same
anger; I react with, oh, I guess it's resignation. I've tried a couple of
times, knowing that this guy is going to die relatively soon, trying to talk
to him before he's dead, but he won't listen. He shuts out the words. So
the difference is that while I don't like him any more than I did before, I
have compassion for him and wish the person well. No closeness, no in-
crease in liking, just that.

The next son, like so many of the others in this group, admits
that he'd make another try for love with his father if he could ever
believe that his father would change. To be the kind of man he
wants to be, he's had to reject his father as a person as well as a
model.

I can remember almost consciously rejecting my father because he was
such a mess, such a raving lunatic most of the time—honestly. I mean,

you don't have to be very old to realize that somebody is just crazed. Anytime I had contact with him, from the earliest age, was unpleasant. And he was the one determining what I would do and what I couldn't do —mainly prohibiting; he was very prohibitive and very punitive, so I don't share any of his values as an adult. But there's always a void, always an unhappiness about it, that my relationship with him was so bad. If I thought there was some way to construct a good relationship with him, I'd probably do it even now—but I don't think there is because he's not willing to admit he has any problems. He's drinking a whole lot now. There doesn't seem to be any hope. My brothers and sisters, except for one brother, have real bad relations with him too. I mean, there are times when my father seems very personable, he has moments of calm. And I think then that maybe . . . everything feels so wonderful and warm, maybe it'll just go on like this. But the next day all hell breaks loose again for no good reason; it's all within him. So I have tried to be just the opposite kind of person. My father is the kind of man who is constantly at odds with the world around him, with everyone, just about everyone. He spends his whole life seething with rage over the "injustices" that happened to him, and what bad luck he has, and how people take advantage of him—and this is *all* the time. So I—well, I probably let too many things just go by. I won't start a fight; I won't get into a fight if I can possibly avoid it. I saw so much strife, for so long, so much yelling and screaming from him and so much misery that wasn't necessary, that I decided, even twenty years ago—even younger than that—that I would not spend my life that way.

This last statement is very clear.

Oh, I don't hate him anymore. I felt guilty for a long time that I was so happy at his funeral. I got over the guilt. Well, he treated me badly; why shouldn't I be happy? At least I didn't show my feelings to my mother and all the relatives, and make them feel strange. It's not so I even think about it anymore at all. I don't any longer wish, "Oh, if he were here I'd strangle him." The man abused me verbally and physically; he made my life miserable. It's just gone; I don't feel bad about it; it's over.

A sizable group explained that, while their relations with their fathers had not been—and were not—consistently warm, close, or happy, they—the sons—had found that the situation improved as they grew older. In retrospect, viewed through accumulated experience, the old man hadn't been so bad. As the sons aged, their fathers became acceptable to them. They believe, or seem to believe, or make themselves believe, that the relationship is satisfactory. They want it to be so, and they wanted me to find it so.

Nonetheless, they were all able to articulate what had actually been wrong between them and their fathers, especially in the first ten to twenty years of their lives. Many sons explain that *distance,* both emotional and geographical, was a major feature of the relationship. The element of distance is obvious in situations where the father and son have lived separately.

My father had nothing to do with my growing up; it was my mother and my brother who raised me. I can count the days I've actually seen him on my fingers and my toes. Hardly even knew him. I know where he is, I hear about him. Whenever anyone in the family moves, we all hear about it. Whenever I did see him, there was always this tiny bit of fear, that this is my old man, who with one hand could knock me down. I don't still feel like that, but I have to respect him. Mom wanted that more than anything. My mom would say, "He's your father, you've got to love him." I'm saying, "It's not cool the way he did us," but she says, "That ain't nothing; we made it this far, we'll keep going. You've got to love him and respect him." So if I see him on the street, I'll stop and talk to him; he's my old man.

The following sons are among those men who recognize that, even though they lived with their fathers, they had almost no intercourse with them. (One well-known research study, done in 1974, showed a group of middle-class fathers who spent an average of *one minute per day* with their infant children.[8]) Whether the father works very long hours or, as one son says, simply "misses connections," it is by his absence, not his presence, that he makes an impact on his growing son.

The first son in this group introduces the theme of male bonding around traditionally male activities; the father isn't present until the son can enter his sphere—in this case, athletics—and then disappears again when the son leaves that sphere.

My earliest memories of him are really vague. I don't remember him as being that influential. For a long time. He was just not around—even though he was there all the time. And then one day he showed me where the basketball hoop was, and "Here's the ball and here's the way we're going to do it." And that's where things started changing. "Here's the fireplace we're going to build, there's the bricks, you move those over here." And so all of a sudden, bang—he was right there, and then it was pretty intense between the two of us, yeah. We were pretty intense. See, in high school he was my coach. So I played football for him. That's pretty intense—being on the old man's team. I didn't get too much grief out of the whole affair, because we won the state championship and I was All-American. Nobody in town could say this, that, or the other. When I went to college it ended almost as abruptly as it began. I continued in athletics a couple of years, but I was on my own and I was me. He wasn't my coach. I was far away from home; since then we don't even . . . He doesn't think what I'm doing is very intelligent—living in San Francisco. "That's where the crazies go," he says. There's a distance between us; it's mutual.

Well, it was distant. I had a lot of respect for my father because of the kind of job he had, and the kind of responsibility he had, and people would come to see him for help in different kinds of ways. Immigrant miners and farmers would ask him for help with their papers and so forth. People who had businesses would come to him to get their books audited. He was a very competent person in many ways, and I had a lot of respect for him. I wasn't close to him; in spite of all that, I wasn't very close to him. As I grew older I became closer to him as a person. And got bigger than he, of course. My father was not very tall. When I was a child I looked up to him geographically. As I grew older, I was able to look down on him, geographically. And that makes a big difference. I became more affectionate to him as someone who was physically smaller than I. Of course, when I was a child, he was a giant.

    This next man sees his father's power in relation to other aspects—including tenderness and generosity—of the relationship between them.

First of all, he was not there much of the time; he worked much of the time. He was emotional and came across with his feelings sometimes, when I was very young. Or he would put himself out there, like singing me lullabies at night. It was real clear that in those instances he was doing for me what his mother had done for him. And then there was that other side where he just wasn't there, or was the disciplinarian. He sort of came home, read the paper, and worked, just like that. He was not into the activities that I was; he was not an athlete in any sense of the word. I suppose he taught me to throw, but . . . There's an incredible disparity between the man who sang those lullabies and the man who was capable of great rage and anger. Of course, I see that in myself, and in many men. I never felt close to him, but I always feel that he cared for me. There were times he preferred my brother; he preferred him as the first son, and often did things with my brother because he was the first son. I felt that, and I was hurt by it. But one of the things that I've always sensed with my father, and to this day feel, is that he will be there for me, and has—sometimes to my astonishment—done for me whatever he could or whatever he felt was necessary. Not that he wouldn't be angry sometimes, and put off, and find it hard to do, but he would be there. Much of the way he dealt with me, of course, was through money, through supporting me. But I guess in the past couple of years I've felt a lot better about our relationship. I'm willing to leave it where it is. There are many things I really don't like about him, but I have a greater regard for him now. Also, my attitude about what he *does* has changed. Particularly as a man, what he is, what he was to my mother, or to other men, or to things in the world. Basically, he is a pretty good person.

Well, he always worked. He worked hard, but the times we did get to spend together were real nice. Like he would take me with him on his day off. I would go out with him in the morning when I was a little boy; we'd walk around the neighborhood. I always remember him taking me to get my haircuts, with his friends. But he wasn't the sort who'd take me to the ball game, take me here, take me there—no, not really. He would play with me with my trains, and talk to me a lot. When I got older he advised me about what to do. He told me about women, about not getting married young and to keep going to school. My mother always told me that my father really loved me a lot; she told me that a lot as I got older, because sometimes we had differences, me and my father. He grew up in Mexico; I guess I was more influenced by the American way of life. We ran into a lot of conflicts for a while. I hurt his feelings a few times. I guess I was embarrassed to walk with him 'cause where we were living there were very few Mexican people. My father looked real Mexican. That's an awful thing to say. He had greasy hair, stuff like that. Now look, *I* got greasy hair.

Yes, they said I was my father's favorite when we were all growing up. I'm the only son he had which bears his name. But understand this: I didn't have any of my father's time. I mean, if my momma was going to whup me, my father might say, "Oh, come on, leave him alone, give him another chance." That's what was considered favoritism in my family.

The next two men, the first one raised in the middle class, the second raised in the working class, describe fathers who would seem to have little in common—and yet the sons somehow wind up rather sadly saying very much the same kind of thing as they conclude their statements.

It's very hard to say. I don't feel like I know my father very well. I'm very interested in that relationship. I chose to write part of my dissertation on fathers and sons in literature, and it's something I dream about too. When I was a boy probably we did sports things together to some extent. He took me to ball games. He's not a particularly rabid sports fan. I think he enjoys it enough and thought that was a good thing to do with his son. I can't recall that we did much together. Maybe I helped him cut the lawn. I can tell you an anecdote which is kind of interesting to me. When I was in school we were asked to write about what we did with our fathers—in fourth grade, I think—and I wrote that he and I made model planes together, which was a lie; we never did. I must have thought that the teacher expected that kind of answer. He got hold of this and tried to make model planes with me for a while. He was terrible at it. We both were, neither of us liked it. Also, he had a picture of me as he wanted me to be, and I didn't turn out particularly the way he wanted me to be. He wanted me to go into business. He was disappointed when I went to graduate school in English. But he didn't stand in my way. He paid for it. He paid for a lot of it, in fact. I don't think he's unhappy with the way I turned out—but he's made a little uneasy about it. My father may feel that I think he is a kind of Babbitt character. When in fact he's not; he's very bright. Pretty well read and I trust his judgment and opinion on a lot of things. Somewhere along the line, I'm suggesting, we missed connections. I'm a little disappointed by him and he's a little disappointed by me. Mostly I feel like I don't know him very well.

I never really had very much to do with my father when we were younger, but I always liked my father. I also knew that he never had enough time for us. But I knew that his working schedule was incredible; he was a very hardworking man. He went out at three o'clock in the morning and wouldn't get home until five in the evening, and he'd go to bed at seven-thirty at night. And then he would always go down on Saturdays at six o'clock in the morning till around two, and then on Sunday morning again. I respect him for that, but as I grew older I realized that as much work as he put in was not necessary. You know what I mean? To a certain degree his work came before his family. I started looking at that when I was around thirteen years old. I started working for him then. I was very proud of him then; everybody knew him; he was one of the best-liked guys down at the market. But at the same time, there was no closeness at all between us. I mean, I could never talk to him. There would be nothing at all I could ever talk to him about. When I was in high school, he never attended one thing, not any kind of benefits or honor things, like when I was on the football team and they had father-and-son banquets. That never really bothered me. I must say, it never bothered me at all. I guess I just kind of . . . I was on my own enough not to have it bother me. I imagine it bothered me enough to remember it. I got in a little bit of trouble with him later on, when he wanted me to go to a large university on a football scholarship. But I knew we would end up that way eventually anyway, that I would probably leave the house and not have to do anything that he wanted. After I was sixteen years old, the way I thought about him was just that he never really knew me very well.

Maybe because of this wistful affection, this wishful yearning, many men belittle or ignore their fathers' shortcomings and flaws; they speak in obvious euphemisms, or ignore and cover up problems in the relationship. This has been easy for men to do in terms of the ideal; the father/son relation requires no more, existing as it does between two males who live by the list and expect no more of each other. Unlike the expectations both sons and daughters have of mothers, fathers are expected to actually do—and be—very little *as people* for their children, even for their sons. Much of what is expected of fathers is that they be models, that they stand for masculinity and fatherhood, that they be larger-than-life heroic symbols.[4]

Yet, sons have felt the pain, the loss and the lack; and they've had to deny these feelings—along with most others—and pretend that the standard father/son arrangement was just fine. They didn't mind not seeing Dad; they didn't miss him—he wasn't supposed to be there anyway; they didn't feel that his discipline was too harsh, his demands uncompromising—that's what a father is *for*—to hold that list before his son's eyes, to *be* that list, incarnate.

But the pain doesn't just disappear because its existence is sociopolitically incorrect. Boys and men bury it, cover it up, and bluff like crazy. They come to Mama with their grief; they take it out on their own sons and men with less power; they keep a hidden collection of grievances-turned-weapons, and use these weapons to act out violent abuse of children and women—as they deny their need for Daddy's love and support.

We mothers watch young boys go from expecting to be cherished and nurtured by their fathers, to demanding that behavior from their fathers, to the sullen and bitter understanding that Dad will not come across. And then, so powerful is society's sanction of that "ideal" paternal behavior and character, we see our sons come to an acceptance so complete that they will defend their fathers even against the criticism and anger they've expressed themselves. And all along, the boy will not—or cannot—confront his father. Young sons will not push their fathers the way they'll push their mothers; they learn early that Dad's affection, such as it is, is tenuous and conditional. Most boys understand all this before they are twelve or thirteen years old.

Sons are unrealistic to hope for spiritual presence and emotional nurturance from their fathers. Men are not trained to care for children—or for adults, really—and they are not part of daily family life, so that even those men who are, as one mother has said, "misfits"—men who ignore the list—are hard pressed to spend enough time with their families to give and get loving.

Fathers have no models or patterns to follow if they want to relate to their children as mothers do. They cannot sit in the sandbox and share their problems with other fathers who are mothering:

> I don't get to talk about my feelings as a father with other men very much. Even the fathers I feel closest to seem far away in terms of how they relate to their kids. . . . I have heard other men talk about the joys of fatherhood, and appreciating their children, but not about the fears and the uncertainties. . . . everyone wants to project a positive, confident image. . . . Maybe other men don't feel those things as strongly as I do. Maybe their kids are less central to their lives. Maybe I should pull back from being so intimately tied to [my son]. . . .[5]

Mothers, having been raised as women, trained to respond to the emotional needs of others, are keenly aware of the poor relations between fathers and sons. We are attuned to the needs and desires of both man and boy, and whether we've studied the theories of the experts or not, we are generally critical in our analyses. Most mothers are saddened or angered by what we see. Even those mothers who remain loyal to the father (i.e., when he is the mother's lover or spouse) can see injustice and inequality in the father's treatment of their sons, particularly during the years of boyhood and adolescence. Moreover, part of our training as women, part of what we've learned to *need* to do, is to take it all personally, and to want to "make it better."

Some mothers in the interview group, a minority, saw mostly positive relations between sons and fathers. While they did not claim the best of all possible worlds, these mothers did describe good father/son interactions.

His father has been quite—really important in his life. Norm, his stepfather, has lived with him fourteen years now, since he was three. Their relationship is off again, on again. Sometimes there's a gap between them; they just don't seem to get together. And then other times they get kind of buddy-buddy. He gets something from Norm that he doesn't get from his father. He loves movies, and Francis does too, so they love to talk about film and the movies. There's a kind of camaraderie. His stepfather's gay, and Francis gets a real leavening from that; I notice his gentleness. His father's also gentle—but real sexist, and real homophobic. So it's nice that he gets from Norm the possibility of brotherhood among men—at least in his head.

My relationship with his father is very, very difficult still, but I support him in dealing with Frank because he and Frank have a great deal in common. It's a good relationship and he has a lot to offer. Last summer Frank went down to Alabama to stay with him. His father's a poet, and he had Frank writing, really doing it. I was impressed; Frank's stuff was fantastic. He is influenced by his father, but he really thinks for himself; I loved it. With Vince, the father/son relationship was incredibly important. Having a stepfather who was supportive made it possible for Vince to let out all the anger he'd been saving up, all that pain. One night he was sitting on Ray's lap, and he began to hit him. He was talking about his real father, hitting Ray on the chest. During those moments, Ray became his real father, and let him do it, let him beat on him. *I* was horrified—much too young to understand anything like that anyway. He sat there and supported that, and took it for two or three hours, until Vince had screamed himself into exhaustion. He cuddled him, kissed him. Then he carried him off to bed, came into the kitchen, and passed out. He was black and blue from his neck to his waist. He was very much the teacher and the guide.

A second group of mothers talked about both good and bad aspects of the father/son relation, weighing them against each other, trying to find a balance.

These three mothers make their comparisons between and among sons, talking about the different relations the father has with his various sons.

They're good friends. But my older son has a lot of anger toward his dad. A lot of times he hits and "accidentally" bumps into him. He's not as close as my second son, the little one. The little one is very close; he'll come over to José, lay his head on his lap, share his food with him. My first son, he was born early in the marriage, and he saw all the fighting and the hitting, so he has a different idea of his father than the baby has.

Their relationships are changing, changing because Earl has changed the way he's dealing with them in the last eight months. He was quite an authoritarian type—though I don't know where the fuck that came from. But he decided, "I will not be the bad guy." So now he is being very warm and very, very supportive no matter what the hell they want. I mean, he still gets exasperated—Ernie is fifteen, and fifteen is, oh god, a difficult time—and he forgets his resolve with Ernie most often. They get into it about this, that, and the other. And his motive is trying to reduce "shoulds." So it's "I should not have any shoulds." On a practical level, that's difficult because no one will put their shoes on. But with the generosity of time Earl is giving the boys, you can see them blossoming.

The older boy is close to his father, cares about him a lot, and is protective toward him. He likes to spend time with him. He is favored, I think, over his younger brother, probably because he's older, more mature. I don't know. It's strange, because Paul thinks a lot of his younger son, feels that Tommy's going to be a great musician. So he respects him a lot, but he treats Michael better. Well, Michael behaves better; he's not as cuckoo.

Another group of mothers describes, often in detail, the same sadness that is common to the sons' stories related earlier. Several of these women have sons under eighteen, and are still close to the process; they still live in the battleground—so they are speaking of their daily experience.

Those boys are really all he has at this point. Since the marriage and his business all broke up, he's kind of looking around for what it is he's going to do for himself, and till he finds out, he really is emotionally dependent on his relationship with the boys. He feels very close and attached and he feels like he *needs* to take care of them—and they are becoming real careful of his feelings, watching out for his needs. Like when there's a plan for a possible outing, Edward will say, "Do you think it'll be okay with my dad?" You know, when his dad has nothing to do with it. Both of the boys use the expression "my dad." They never just say "Dad." There are times when I feel that Stanley is sort of promoting them to take care of him—by feeling really bad; he would just feel so *awful*, and they would have to make him feel good. If they want to go off and stay overnight with a friend, and he's planned to be with them, he makes them feel that they shouldn't go; they should stay with him. There's this feeling that they somehow have to take care of him.

Frank played the macho father image—stern, strong, absolutely confident —played it to the hilt. He didn't play *with* the boy a whole lot, but he would play *that*. He postured magnificently. He never hit him, but he would do things like pick him up and say to him, "You stop bothering me, or I will throw you through that window," and then laugh. Now the relationship is in the nature of "Hi, son, how've you been doing, do you need any money? Yes, I'll get you something." Of course, now we all know he won't come through, but that's what the pose is.

These next sons, whose fathers care so much about athletics, are an interesting contrast to the sons who complained that their fathers didn't, wouldn't, or couldn't, play ball.

My husband was a little disappointed, because he had been a ballplayer all his life. Even as an adult, came the spring and he would buy a dozen baseballs and half a dozen bats and on his day off he would go to the playground. He had a bunch of kids he would coach. But Irving was not a ballplayer. Of course, when he was coaching, Irving was too small. But through the years he was not a ballplayer, and his father was disappointed. He wasn't extremely close to him, but he had an average relationship with his father. His father was never home. By the time he got out of the business, by the time he got sick, and stayed home, Irving was already married.

My husband had ambitions to be a great sportsman, a sports figure. He was a Golden Gloves champion, and a very famous baseball player in the minors; he almost became a pro. He would like to have enforced his sports regime on the child. My son wasn't able to sympathize or even understand my husband's feelings about sports, so they fought bitterly over it. He would abuse the child, hit him. He'd throw a baseball and hit him in the stomach with it. Or aim for the head. And a professional pitcher has quite a bit of strength there. He may have been slightly brain-damaged from the boxing—throwing a baseball to maim a child!

My husband was a very powerful man who enjoyed beating the kids at tennis. He was a magnificent athlete. He'd take them on drop shots and make them cry. I remember him having Lucas in the backyard when he was five, and insisting that he learn to play ball, and throwing balls at him too hard to catch. I mean it was necessary for him to beat small people. Now their relationship is very difficult, rather tacky from time to time. My husband is an alcoholic and makes long-distance phone calls at night and that kind of stuff. Lucas has become the adjudicator, the one who facilitates the relationships in the family; so he does that for his father.

This next woman has three sons, and all of them, starting with the oldest, whose trouble with his father is just beginning to surface, have been in some way disappointed or grieved by the relationship.

Our first son feels real close and real loyal. He's got the first-son thing of identifying with the father, feeling almost that he has to be for him in the world where he's not. Yet I sense a growing difficulty with it, a tension. He's having to face up to who he is as a person—and look at what his dad is, and he's not ready to face that. They haven't yet gone through their personal hell with each other. The second son—because in the last several years their father has been in some ways somewhat distant, not real attentive—has a deep love for his father. But he is almost totally independent of him. I don't think he counts on him for much. He pretty much runs his own life and ends up giving to his father in the relationship, not receiving. He doesn't expect a whole bunch. The third one has been fighting for a relationship with his father. He has felt quite abandoned and real despondent. He feels that he needs his father and he doesn't trust that his father will be there for him.

This mother has taken on some guilt along with a greater sense of what her role might have been when her son was younger.

My feeling now is that I should have intervened before, but I wasn't able to. I was getting information from outside the family that my husband's way of handling his son was much too rigid and authoritarian, but I couldn't hear it at the time and would not have been able to cope with it if I had. My husband is not a man who could relate to the kids in personal, intimate kinds of ways. Not at all a hugger—which is not to say that I was so hot in that department myself, but certainly much more so than he. One thing he would do which I just found horrendous, was this: The kid wouldn't do something he was supposed to do—a chore or something—and my husband would get him up at eleven at night, one in the morning, if that's when he happened to come in and discover it—and perhaps spank him, and force him to do it. So there was always interrupted sleep, and the horror of this thing going on. And that was one of the more—well, that's one of the things I remember vividly. At this point, he's struggling to try to come to some sort of understanding with his father. Very often, when they see each other, it'll be about work that they talk. They are just starting to be able to talk to each other. At one time they weren't able to; there were just horrendous fights; they'd end up screaming at each other. [Laughs.] Now they can say things like, "Help me with the car," "I've got to do some electrical work." And my son is in his late twenties!

The next two mothers both have two teenage sons. Their thoughtful and explicit replies enlighten the complex process that is just beginning to begin with Daniel and me.

I frequently tell my husband that he has become so involved with thinking what they should be doing that he doesn't have any fun with them. They'll walk in and say, "Oh, Daddy, I want to tell you this or that or the other," and he says, "Have you had your bath?" or something like that. It puts a tremendous distance between himself and his sons. I wish he could be more relaxed as a father. He and our older boy clash constantly. I think it would take a psychiatrist to say exactly why. Some of it has to do with my husband's relationship with his father—which wasn't a very warm, open kind of relationship. He's made a terrific effort with the children; he loves them so much. But he's not very articulate with them. He will tell them to do something but he won't tell them why. And we'll all ask him, "Why, why are you saying this?" and he won't say. Later he will say it to me in the bedroom; he'll tell me why. And it will be a very good reason that everyone would have felt very comfortable with, but in the meantime a terrific confrontation of wills has occurred, and since there's no reason given, nobody really understands why. It's not that he's an inarticulate person, but he's inclined not to articulate certain things. I really don't know why. With the second son, there are the same things, but the relationship is pretty good. Jules is very hard on both boys, but Daniel is an extrovert, while Jules and Kenny are both introverts and they get into it less. But there will be a clash—I feel instinctively it's going to come. They have the same kind of strength, but Kenny seems able to work around it. So far he seems able to jolly his father out of the anger. And where Daniel always seems to be asking, demanding, Kenny never wants us to give to him; he's wanting to give back. And Kenny is very neat and studious, and Daniel extremely concerned with his friends; his clothes are strewn about, and get torn and so on. And these things act as a perpetual irritant to his father, less so with me; I'm easier-going.

My older son has had a very difficult relationship with my husband. Jean is just obsessed with his work. I've told him he's a workaholic. I didn't have the perception or the guts to say that when our boys were preschool and early school age, but it's clear to me now that that's what he's been; he was just always loaded up with work. But I'd say that within the last several years some bonds have formed. They are bonds I don't understand; I characterize them as a kind of intellectual repartee. They're both bright, very sharp people. There is a deep feeling there that I just don't understand. I see Jean reach out with his arm and bring the boy to his chest. There's very rarely that physical connection, though. So now the older boy is an overachiever, just like his father, and that's where the bad vibes come up in the relationship. René can never do enough to please Jean; he's too critical. He pushes René too hard. René has begun to be able to say that to his father, just lately; that's been good. Some of what he does makes the boy angry—and I think justifiably so. A lot of their conflict now is around René starting to drive the car. He's fifteen; it's a big deal; he has a learner's permit. It's one of those rites of passage for a male child in this culture—to be the driver of a car. And his father goes out in that car with him, and they are awful together. What they do to each other I don't know, but it's awful—and the boy is under such strain from the way his father "teaches" him. It must take an incredible amount of guts to come up against your father. God, yes. Jean is beginning to understand what this all is; he's a man who knows that it's all going to come around someday. The second boy, Dirk, is not going to put himself on an intellectual track with his father; he's all sports. He's put his heart and soul into being a sports person. He has a lot of resentment to his father. At some level he can let his father's criticism roll right off, but the resentment is there. He's said a lot of times, "I'm not going to be like Dad. You won't catch me working that hard." He sees that workaholic syndrome and he doesn't want any part of it. And he removes himself emotionally from his father. I see it as a kind of punishment: "You're not very nice, so I'm not close to you. I don't want to be around you." I see that a lot. He resents the expectations and he resents the emotional vibes that go with them, that he feels coming from his father to him. Jean asks him to shape up, to conform to his personal expectations. My husband has just begun to try to understand all this, and is making a move toward trying to change who he is with the boys, and with me. With himself, really.

Mothers' views, like sons', come out of their particular angle of the mother-son-father triangle. Both have needs, frustrations, and angers born of this three-way stretch—as do the fathers. But what the mothers say generally reinforces and repeats what the sons have said; they bring up the same issues: especially difficult and intense relations between the oldest son and his father; the absence or distance of the father; sports as a source of anger, fear, and disappointment; and so on.

It would seem, then, that many boys have their mother's sympathy as they struggle through life with their father.

Even when she doesn't know what I'm doing, see, my mother doesn't let anything wrong touch me. See, I had a federal marijuana bust in '52, and I told my mother about it, and she gave me money to pay for my case, and said, "Don't tell him about it." And once, while she was having a club meeting—she was in that early group of Black women who became "society"—you know what I'm saying?—and they met to plan their parties and dances—they gave fabulous dinners— while she's doin' that, I'm goofing around over on Wabash Avenue. And I came home right in the middle of her meeting—like she's having all these ladies, right, and they're really, really hooked up—and I came to the back door with this undershirt wrapped around my head full of blood. And she stopped what she was doing and took me to the doctor. And we came home and my old man said, "What's the matter with him?" She says, "He had an accident." "How did it happen?" "He slipped and fell." And that was all of that. He never questioned me.

When he did come into the family picture, and that wasn't very often, he had to have everything done his way. Like around the guitar lessons for my older brother and sister: they had to deal with a lot of beatings, but my mother sheltered me from that. No, I didn't get beat, even though all the rest of them, including her, did get beaten all the time. Actually my mother was very clever. She did it in very clever ways. She talked me out of violin lessons so I wouldn't be in the position to make him want to beat me. There would never be any intervening—her stepping in between if my father went for me—she couldn't do it. There was nothing like that. But she protected me from him in these clever ways.

There was some conflict. My mother would tend to take my side in a situation where I would be in conflict with my father. He would be telling me, "Don't take the car," don't do this, don't do that . . . and all that kind of stuff, and I would be on the opposite side, of course, and my mother would back me up in those situations. She'd say, yeah, "Leave him alone." Sometimes we fall into that scene still, and she'll say to him, "Well, he's grown up; he's thirty-three years old now."

There are several reasons for this maternal sympathy. First of all, the basic family unit is, both historically and in actual practice, comprised of mother and children. The father is a culturally late arrival and, according to sons and mothers, he doesn't arrive often or stay long. Secondly, while fathers are aloof and non-nurturant, woman's role in this culture is to devote her energies to both children and males; our sons derive double benefits from this arrangement. Third, motherhood is still the occupation that provides greatest approval for women, and producing male children is still considered an achievement.

Mother's position in the triangle may generate empathy for sons as well as sympathy, for mothers are also subject to the power of fathers. Women and children alike are the property of men, under male control. Furthermore, an alliance with a son is an alliance to a rising star, a possible source of power. Sons may take care of their mothers; they might even protect them from father-husbands.

This son, now over forty, despite his admiration for his father's power—the same power used to abuse his mother—made an alliance with his mother, a spiritual bond of protection for them both.

I never had a sense that they were working together as parents. It was like he set the tone and everyone else followed it. My mother wasn't any better than the rest of us most of the time. Because when she stepped out of line, he would beat her. So in that sense, we all felt close to her because she was one of us. It was his decision to send us to church; it was his decision what kind of food would be served at dinnertime; it was his decision who would do what in the house when he was home. My mother chose me as an ally; I was the one she talked to. I was never the kind of male that my father wanted, because I never wanted to go and be a truckdriver. I wanted to read books; I wanted to go to school. My father resented the fact that we were allies. I said and showed my disapproval of the fact that he beat her, in small ways, when I thought I could get away with it. I noticed we often got beatings on the same days. I mean, like for two months he used to come home and beat us—just come home and *beat* us. Every single day, yeah. She gave me all the affection; she resisted him in the only way she could, by holding back sexually. For the most part, my mother has the same image of masculinity that my father has. She admired his strength and his life force, the fact that he was able to provide a living for us. I mean, during World War II, when people were needing very much, he always found a way to get us fresh fruits and vegetables and meat. And all of us had the feeling that if we were in a depression or the end of the world or something, he would find a way. No doubt at all that he would have cracked the world in half to make sure we had something to eat. That part of him—that part with the strength and masculinity thing, I admired. But she always was very secure that whatever it was, I would never move away from her.

These sons took to heart their father's threats against their mother, and acted to protect her. The man speaking is forty-four.

All four of us sons were terrified of the threat that if we didn't pay attention to him, he'd take it out on my mother. We used to talk it over among ourselves, but we couldn't really do anything because the burden of responsibility was not on us. We could handle it in some ways, but we knew he'd do things to my mother. We didn't know how to deal with that situation. What he did was, he would yell at her—no beating—but we were all just terrified of his yelling and screaming. He did that all the time, and threatened to not give her any money. My mother used to say the same thing—for us not to speak up to him because he'd take it out on her. She'd say that right in front of him. He would say it out in public, about the money.

When this man was a boy, he saw himself as his mother's protector, fairytale fashion; now, in his early thirties, he recalls his feelings:

Mom and Dad used to compete for my affection and my attention. I was very angry because Dad wasn't giving me what I wanted, and on behalf of my mother as well. I was in between them. Mom and I had a unique relationship; we were close. And I knew he couldn't interfere with that. They rarely yelled, but he would yell at her once in a while and she got scared and acted helpless, and kind of like, though she didn't say it, she was thinking, You beast. I used to get furious when he would yell at her. I would have all kinds of fantasies of defending her.

Here is a son whose father tried to turn him against his mother, but failed. At fifty-three, he passionately holds some of the anger and resentment he felt as a boy.

My father told me the delivery was very difficult, so much so that he didn't even want to see me at birth because he felt that my mother was in such pain. Then, immediately thereafter, my father was threatened by me because my mother began to love me and my father felt left out. My father finally felt that my mother and I were a team, or possibly a conspiracy against him. My dad could never come to me and tell me about my mother—to the point that I would believe him. He knew that I would not believe him. He did this at times, he complained to me about her, and I felt that it was totally unbased. Now I was prejudiced in favor of my mother and against my father. I felt that he was not acting as a man. I didn't think that he was acting with any dignity in his role as man and father, by coming to me, or by relating to my mother as he did.

The following three sons are similar to the last because they recognize that rivalry exists between them and their fathers.

My father used to accuse my mother of favoring me over the other kids. Maybe she did; I don't think that's true. I think that what it was was that I had this good relationship with my mother and this awful relationship with him, and he was jealous of the fact that we got along so well and shared things, and that I talked to her and I didn't to him. In a way he wanted all those kinds of things from me without putting out anything. You know? He was the kind of person who expected me to assume his personal interests. Of course, I didn't, because naturally I wouldn't have been interested in anything that brought me into contact with him, unfortunately. So he was always real pissed off about that, that I wasn't interested in what he was interested in, and yet he never, ever, considered that he might take an interest in something I was interested in doing, you know?

My parents decided to stay together until I was through with high school. That didn't work out. At the time of that decision, my mother and I, I guess because my father and I were having this tension start to build between us, my mother and I sat down and wrote up a list of grievances we wanted met. There was a feeling of camaraderie between us. At that time there was competition between them for me, just around the time of the divorce. Suddenly there was separate gift giving; it wasn't from Mommy and Daddy; it was from Mommy and from Daddy. I wound up living with her.

Because my father didn't live with us, when he came home it always caused a major upheaval in the house. My mother would always be getting ready, getting the house ready and cleaned. It was ironic, because we always waited like that for him to come, and were excited about it, but when he came, he usually arrived drunk, which caused a scene right away. So we witnessed a lot of friction between my parents. Nothing ever physical, but a sense of anger. I know my mother was angry at him, coming home that way. And he would keep me back when the others went to bed at night, because he would want to talk to me with my mother. I remember feeling very awkward about those situations because generally my father was pretty drunk. He was setting up a situation for me and my mother, for me to take care of her because I was the oldest, to be stronger and more in control. And he would then just forget about it in the morning. But he had almost no influence on me anyway; he was away so much that it was as if he wasn't a father. When he came home I had the sense that he was an outsider. If she told him about something we'd done wrong and he took a disciplinary move, we would look at him like, "Wait a minute, who are you?" I felt he had no authority over me at all.

Some mothers choose their sons as favorites; some choose their sons as confidants; some choose their sons in preference to their husbands, either for their taste and style or for their power. These mothers preferred the sons to the fathers *as men;* that is, the mothers seemed to think the sons were better men than the fathers. Often this situation is described as pathological, and considered a cause of homosexuality in the son. In this group, however, there are both straight and gay men who had such relationships with their mothers.

When mothers are blamed for their sons' homosexuality, the line runs like this: The mother depended on the son; she was overprotective, she sissified him, etc. So he grew up resenting her, hating her—and therefore hating all women, turning to male lovers as a way of ridding himself of her stifling influence and presence in his life. If we were to insist on blaming male homosexuality on parents, we might consider the possibility that fathers should carry that weight; it could easily be construed that the fathers' bad behavior and attitudes presented such poor models that the sons chose to deviate from the male pattern so they wouldn't grow up like them.

But placing blame anywhere assumes that heterosexual male behavior patterns are *good* and that deviation from them is *bad*. Instead, it seems clear that it is the patterns themselves which are dangerous and damaging.

Homosexuality, while no longer necessarily considered an evil or a sickness, is still no good in the eyes of most people (including some homosexuals). The psychologists and psychiatrists have taught us that when a mother is "dominant and aggressive," or has chosen her son as her "protector" or "surrogate lover," her son's homosexuality is the result. This is common knowledge, a staple in the routines of comedians, and a stock situation in the theater—like the boy whose story opens the movie *Fame*. He is (tragically) gay because his mother doesn't give him love or attention, is concerned with her career, etc. A classic case of damned if you do and damned if you don't; the blaming of mothers for male homosexuality is all-encompassing. If the mother is loving and nurturant, she is labeled seductive or smothering. If she is aloof and distant, she is castrating. In popular opinion, fathers—absent or present, friendly or cold, brutal or noncommittal—are almost irrelevant to, and are excused from responsibility for, their sons' sexual destinies, except insofar as they, too, are considered victims of mothers.

Since many straight men have lived in similar family circumstances, application of the theory of simple cause and effect is obviously incorrect. Sexual orientation and identification and the choice of sexual partners are extraordinarily complex matters, incapable of such reduction.

In any case, or perhaps in every case, the sources of maternal sympathy and empathy are rarely present in the conscious minds of mothers as they step between fathers and sons. And there are more triangular possibilities and configurations than the teaming up of mother and son against father. Another common alliance is between mother and father, to the exclusion of the son.

Even many women who have opposed fathers to plead or promote the cause of their sons may—either repeatedly in confrontational situations, or when the boys grow to adolescence and adulthood—drop their sons' cause and bond into a tight heterosexual couple, moving out of the mother-and-child family. Many suppose that this choice is made out of fear or an overdeveloped sense of propriety—which in this case suggests the mother's need or desire, for the safety of her own position, to uphold the rules of patriarchy.

If there's anything I resent my mother for, and I do resent her for this, it's the fact that out of fear or insecurity she put him ahead of us. Consistently. I mean, there were big knock-down drag-out showdowns and she betrayed us every time. I felt she should have stuck up for my sisters —and what my sisters went through! My mother still lives that way. And when we come back now, she still expects us to cater to his every whim like she has, and bend over backward to meet all his ridiculous requirements. I've told her—the very last time I saw her, I said, "You can do that for the rest of your life if you want to, but I will not compromise myself in order to satisfy him in some way that is absolutely unnecessary." I mean—he's hit her. I know one time he ripped her clothes off her, out of sexual jealousy. I don't think that if she had put herself on a par with him, we—the kids—would have suffered. If she had held out for the things she wanted, it would have included us a lot; she sold out herself as well as us.

My mother lived in constant fear of this ogre coming home. That's how the house was. We would be playing around and messing around, and she would say, "Dad is coming in fifteen minutes." And the place became like an army camp. "Put this away, do this, look good, don't talk about what we were talking about." This went on for years. It was incredible. Once, when I was eleven or twelve, I went by myself for a haircut for the first time. I was very proud of myself, and got it just the way I wanted it. I came home and my father said, "I thought you went for a haircut; that's not a haircut." I went to my mother and I was crying and telling her that I liked my hair like this. And she liked it too, but she said I had to do what he said; it would grow back; but I had to do it; there was nothing else to do. That was the kind of instance where my mother would usually take my side, saying, "Yes, I understand, you're right; but, son, you've got to obey your dad." It was out of fear. It wasn't because you're supposed to respect the man of the house or your dad. It was just out of fear. Everybody knew that.

It continues to play itself out. When my father and I came into a conflict in late adolescence or early adulthood, my mother made a switch in allegiance. Whatever my father said or did, no matter how unreasonable, she had to support him against me. And she would say that he's wrong, he's being unreasonable, but he's my husband so I have to support him— which I found very interesting, to say nothing of surprising. She was say-

ing, "You may be right, but I'm with him." I feel some resentment toward him that he gets—that she will always be supporting him.

But this alliance is a hazardous one for mothers. Later, the father and son may well bond together against the mother, shutting
her out of both relationships. This latter is the solution to family
problems currently being projected in the movies; the "new" trend in
mother-blaming, a modern variation on an ancient theme.

In the culture of male supremacy, a mother need not have attempted to juggle her loyalties and failed, in order to lose her son to
the fathers—or lose her position, such as it is. In the old testament,
"Rachel travailed, and she had hard labor. And it came to pass,
when she was in hard labor, that the midwife said unto her: 'Fear
not, for this . . . is a son for thee.' And it came to pass, as her soul
was departing—for she died—that she called his name Ben-oni [son
of my sorrow] but his father called him Benjamin [son of the right
hand]." (Genesis 35:16, 17, 18) Rachel could not name her son,
and thus define him, in terms of her contribution to his being. The
fact that Benjamin's birth was his mother's death would not be his
mark; rather, he would bear a statement of his inheritance of father-
right.

Moreover, there are a great many mothers who choose not one
side but both, spending their energy as peacemakers, desperately trying to bring father and son together. If these mothers favor one of
the combatants, they work against their own preference, treading
stormy waters, pouring their blood out over the waves to calm them.
If they seem to favor their sons, they are only taking up the side of
the underdog, for the son is the smaller, the weaker, the younger in
this contest. But the motive is not to advance one or the other
against his adversary; such a mother desires only peace; she wants
them to love each other. She loves them both; their rage and fear of
each other torment her.

> *In the old guerrilla war*
> *between father and son*
> *I am the no man's land.*
> *When the moon shows*
> *over my scorched breast*
> *they fire across me.*

> *If a bullet ricochets*
> *and I bleed,*
> *they say it is my time*
> *of month.*
> *Sometimes I iron*
> *handkerchiefs*
> *into flags of truce,*
> *hide them in pockets;*
> *or humming, I roll socks*
> *instead of bandages.*
> *Then we sit down together*
> *breaking only bread.*
> *The family tree*
> *shades us, the snipers*
> *waiting in its branches*
> *sleep between green leaves.*

Out of the raw material of her love, the mother creates hope.

> *Only survive long enough;*
> *the triggers*
> *will rust into rings*
> *around both their fingers.*
> *I will be a field*
> *where all the flowers*
> *on my housedress*
> *bloom at once.*[6]

The mother who takes this position, who makes herself a two-sided shield between father and son, is in jeopardy—and not just because she stands upon a battlefield. She also risks direct attack, in a critical form of mother-blaming. One of the late Marilyn Monroe's husbands, Arthur Miller, has written two plays that treat the father/son relationship and examine the mother-father-son triangle. They are *All My Sons* and *Death of a Salesman*. Written and first acted in the late 1940s, the plays are products of the cultural/intellectual environment that justified and codified mother-blaming as a psychological rule.

In both plays, the mother becomes that dual shield, or, rather, a lightning rod, catching and holding the electric heat of the father/son confrontation. But ultimately, we see that both Kate Keller and

Linda Loman have taken the side of the father *against* the son. These mothers are such devoted patriarchal wives that they deny their children for their husbands. Both Kate and Linda struggle to protect their mates, to save them from their sons, and from their own inclinations. Miller writes so that we will consider the presence or intervention of the mothers as an obstacle, preventing connection between father and son; the mother is an interloper. Miller's scripts direct us to understand that the women have undermined the men's integrity; Willy Loman and Joe Keller are seen to have made their major life decisions *for* their wives, *because of* the women's influence.

In both plays, the morality of the mothers is different from that of the male characters; the women's highest good is preservation of peace of mind for their husbands. They operate on the premise of the sanctity of the father-family, the sacred husband/wife bond born in patriarchy. But the men do not. Instead, the romance of an idealized male bond is invoked by them. Joe Keller is "a man among men," Miller tells us. And Chris Keller, Joe's son, speaks earnestly of his wartime discovery of "the love a man can have for a man." Willy Loman's great romantic passion is for his firstborn son; Willy is in love with Biff. Willy rejects Linda's care and his neighbor Charley's kindness, turning instead to idolization of his older brother and idealization of his older son. Though mother-blaming was being promoted in the culture as these plays were being written and first performed, it is only the last three decades that have seen the open destruction and banishment of mothers in theater.

Mother-blaming by sons in real life is much like mother-blaming in the theater, of course; it frequently takes place within the mother-father-son triangle. The three-way construct is elastic; time and pressure change its shape. Since a good number of men speak of coming to understand and accepting their fathers at a certain point in adulthood—even though they have had virtually no close relations with their fathers for twenty or thirty years, we have to ask where this change comes from. Is it prompted by the deep longing for paternal love, finally forcing its way up, demanding recognition? Certainly that longing is there, and well buried. But the change is more complex, more modern, than a primal eruption of tormented love.

As they age, men begin to understand and accept the confines and privileges of the male role, and so may begin to understand and accept their fathers. When they realize that what they feel is what he must feel, what he must have felt *at their age,* then they can allow themselves to know that they are like their fathers,[7] and that, because of that likeness, they may be able to know their fathers. They have *become* the fathers; they are adult males in the culture of male supremacy—and they have that position in common with their own fathers. Previously, they suffered the oppression of children; they were members of the women's class. Crown princes kept from the throne as long as possible, they resented the fathers' power for most of their lives—before this change.

This process is not openly described or defined in terms of the need for father's love or the recognition of similarity. Rather, as explained by the experts—and as practiced by sons—this psychic coming of age, this realization by sons that they, too, are fathers, is quickly perverted into severe mother-blaming. In order to learn to love Dad, to relate to him, to make a serious bid for that love so long denied, and take his place as a *man,* a son must deny his mother.

In the following chapter, we will see how mythology and legend have been used as justification for the psychoanalytical advice to "kill the mother." Psychological theory has equated the father with masculinity. To suit up, to make the team, to be a contender, sons have to align with the fathers. But they cannot just embrace them, go to them and speak of their feelings, spend time with them and bring them into their lives so that, together, father and son can come to an understanding of what they've done and been to each other. No; the list—and the experts' advice—preclude such action. Instead, they must get rid of the mothers; the men form an alliance by excluding women. The power of masculinity makes this transition relatively easy. Being close to mother is like playing with girls; it's unsuitable behavior. It verges on the neurotic, and it casts doubt on a man's heterosexuality—which is equated with masculinity, of course.

Basically, the argument runs like this: The son's real memories of no father, or distant father, or abusive father are moved aside, explained away, and lessened by comparison with the mother's alleged sins. What you thought was a problem with your father really wasn't —see how he loved you but didn't know how to express it; he must be forgiven his inadequacy. In fact, *she* kept you from knowing him; by being nurturant, and by criticizing his lack of caring, by protecting you from him, or from the pain of your missing him, she turned you against him. What you thought was a problem with the old man turns out to be nothing compared to the problems you've had with *her*—and so on.

The son goes through a mental process like this:

"As I was growing up, I was very close to, preferred, shared interests with, spent time with, and really respected my mother. My father was rarely (or never) in our home, distant, an alcoholic, brutal, and harsh and insensitive to my mother and/or me. But now I realize that I have a lot in common with my father, resent my mother's guidance and the work and time she put in. *She makes me feel guilty* and now I realize that I admired her or loved her or enjoyed her only because she tricked me into it, one way or another, that I was too close to my mother, and that I have to get away from my mother, geographically and emotionally.

"So, I will now move closer to my father."

This blaming of mothers is necessarily matched with the excusing of fathers. "He was never around; he had to be always working." "He's pretty inarticulate, but I knew he loved me." "He never touches me, but I know he has very warm feelings for me."[8]

Look, I'm sitting here in a defensive arm position while we talk. My father, he—I communicate with him now. We have something to talk about. I understand him more than I ever did. I had to just get out of the picture to view the picture. And I did it. His emotions, for instance, are kept within him. It's there, but it takes a person to search for it. You can see it, but it takes searching. It's not something which is obvious. In the process of the searching I've learned to feel a sense of warmness when I talk to him, even though it's not like he'll . . . I mean, inside I can feel that *he's* feeling, "That's my son." He won't say it; he never will: "I love you, son." He won't say this, but he has felt this way. I can see this.

Here is a situation wherein a brother actually got the affection this son desired, but the father is still excused:

My father made some attempt at talking to me, trying to be available. He was *much* more available to my brother. His attempts were sporadic, and in between he was mocking, or distant, or he retreated into drinking. My estimation is that he was just tremendously frightened by fatherhood, and unable to get in touch with that. Of course, I didn't know that then.

Some sons have the notion that the very presence of love may be the cause for the lack of expression: " 'It's hard to sit down and really talk about how difficult it is to be his son. He knows. We love each other very much and, I think partly as a result of that, sometimes we had a hard time communicating about serious things. . . .' He broke off abruptly."[9]

Some of the interview sons talked about how they came to change their minds about their mothers through therapy—direct intervention of the professionals.

Until I took therapy, I never knew there was anything wrong with my relationship with my mother. I always loved her, and really felt grateful to her, that she stayed and worked a hard job to raise me and my sister when my father left us. I admired her a lot. In therapy, I came to see how I had idolized her all out of proportion. I mean, she put a tremendous responsibility on my back. She let me know that I had to be my sister's brother, her companion, her father, my mother's keeper—so I never thought of me; I always thought of them. And all because I was male, and because they were divorced, so she expected to get all the love and affection from me that she didn't get from my father.

Well, I was very close to my mother. I was the eldest, and she depended on me, more than any of the other six kids, and especially with my father hardly ever at home. She related to me very well, sometimes too well. As I was growing up, I felt proud that she could count on me—even though I gave her trouble; I was *very* wild—but now I can look at it and recognize that there were things about our relationship that were not what I would term healthy. There was a lot of tension. I feel now that she used me almost as a surrogate husband, or lover. She had nobody to talk to, and so she talked to me a lot. Her husband wasn't there; she wasn't close to his family; she had all these kids, and she was a very delicate woman, not bred to be doin' all this work with all these kids—and when her husband shows up, he's drunk half the time. I was all on her side in those days.

Well, my father was the stern disciplinarian; he was a brooding, depressed sort of person, only home on the weekends. Counterbalanced with that was my mother, who was very close to me, sort of a pal; we'd joke around together. So there was this thing about Mom and me in cahoots against father. Now, as a father of teenage people, I find myself repeating a lot of my father's actions, and bearing the brunt of the bad-guy label. My father accepted that role, so my mother had the other role, but I don't want it. I have become aware that I wanted to get closer to my father, and in order to get closer to my father it was necessary for me to somehow change my relationship with my mother. It seemed necessary to interrupt that kind of buddy-buddy, adolescent play that my mother and I did, so in the most recent past, I've really almost rejected my mother, in order to get closer to my father. It was conscious, yes; it's been necessary. In my early childhood I was friends with Mother, and Father was the bad guy. I'm trying to even it out, right. I made the decision when I was at a point in my life where I was becoming more like my father. I realized that I had been stuck at a certain sort of developmental level. I wanted to grow beyond that level, and in order to do that I had to put Mother aside, get rid of Mother, let her go. It was painful for her because she didn't understand everything that was going on. Now, this was the result of pretty intense psychotherapy that I was going to for three and a half years, twice a week.

If fathers follow the list, they may not only be excused but rewarded with the affection and admiration of their sons:

He didn't kiss me goodnight or anything. I think his attitude was probably that you don't want the child to get this growing dependence that at the end of the day someone's got to put you at ease or something. So he never did. My mother did it all the time, of course, but when he put me to bed, or once, I remember, when he gave me a bath and dried me in a big towel, I felt more secure than when she did it.

Equating harshness, or even brutality, with manhood, men learn to make a virtue of their father's inexcusable behavior:

When I was younger, I wanted to be like my father in many ways. Later on, I still admired him, but I didn't want to be like him. I didn't want to do what he did for a living; I didn't want to be what he was as a father —I didn't want to beat my children—I didn't want to be what he was as a husband because I didn't like that at all. The funny thing is that I didn't want to be anything like him—except that I wanted that strength, I wanted that size, and I wanted that powerful life force, because I felt that somehow that would give me the edge to deal with life, to overcome whatever intrusions might come in. More than anything else, I probably set out to do everything better than he did—and I've only just realized that in the last few weeks. He was more than anyone else I have ever seen. I had been aware of why I was trying to be like my father, but I was not aware of the fact that I was trying to outdo him. I mean, I only became aware of that two weeks ago. But that's what I was trying to do. And that's not something that I was particularly happy about. You know, you spend a good chunk of your life trying to outdo somebody that you don't even like very well; that means there's something pretty mixed up in the whole thing.

Men have decided to love their fathers, and think that to love them they must excuse them. But this excuse constitutes acceptance of behavior that is inexcusable. Grown sons think they need to excuse their fathers, so that they can love them, and want to excuse them so that they, as men themselves, may be excused. Instead, sons ought to again demand of their fathers *and themselves* the kind of behavior and attitudes they wanted when they were little boys. The loving, the spiritual connection, the nurturance and trust—these must be both the method and the goal when grown sons approach their fathers to affirm their bond.

As the mother of a son, I resent the existence of that bond. It seems so undeserved; they don't do right, the fathers; they don't give —and yet they get. But, as the daughter of my mother, I can recognize the passion born of that deep connection—like bodies, like circumstances, and shared life experience.

For men to deny their mothers, following the current cinematic flash of superficial father-and-son union, is to abandon their original source of energy, inspiration, and love. Fathers and sons can learn from mothers, can take strength from the examples of women. Sons must learn to love their fathers; but to excuse or ignore the sins committed in the name of the list can never foster affection or trust.

Men must learn to love their fathers without casting off the mother/son relationship. They cannot hope to gain the kind of exchange they want with their fathers by abandoning their mothers. That mistake is where patriarchy began.

5

Origins

*Anasuya, "woman among women," cursed the three gods
Shiva, Vishnu and Brahma for their violent attack upon
her. "Calling them 'the Phallus', 'the Head', and 'the Two
Feet', she warned them that all worshippers would laugh
at them unless they realized that they were as sons to her,
as to any mortal woman. With wisdom, she explained that
their uncontrolled desires grew from their ignorance at
not recognizing that they were but children to her, and if
they desired to be revered as worthy holy beings, they
must learn to know her as their mother."*

—MERLIN STONE[1]

*The god is a son truly born "of a Virgin mother. He is
a model of male power that is free from father-son rivalry
or oedipal conflicts. He has no father; He is his own
father. As He grows and passes through his changes on
the Wheel, He remains in relationship to the prime nurturing force. His power is drawn directly from the Goddess: He participates in Her."*

—STARHAWK[2]

Confronted with the need to know what a mother is, what a son is,
and what they may be to each other, we must realize that much of
what we feel and imagine these to be comes to us out of literature.
The feelings and beliefs of the human race are reflected—indeed,
they are catalogued—in our literature. Though we tend to call the
religion we don't believe *mythology,* and label the stories we do not
deem true *fairytales,* it is within such myth and legend, tales and
dreams, that we find the epic of the human family, turning out
behind us on the wheel of time.

In this christian culture, the most common image of the mother/
son pair is that of Mary and Jesus. We may also conjure up Eve and
her ill-fated boys, though in the twentieth century, we usually go

directly to Freud's defamation of the tragic Theban queen Jocasta and her son Oedipus—with an occasional reference to Shakespeare's Gertrude and Hamlet.

But behind what is felt and imagined through these, there is illumination, a light that casts these relatively recent images into shadow. Seen in this light, reclaimed and restored, ancient signs and symbols constitute a revelation. These signs and symbols were born in the time out of mind, the once upon a time, the time beyond time—the time *before* what we have learned to call the beginning.

Ancient accounts and images of the beginning of time, the creation of heaven and earth and the making of human beings, were told and written long before the old testament's seven days/Garden of Eden version.

From Egypt:

> *The Lady of Flame,*
> *The Lady of the Flaming Waters,*
> *The Lady who shed Her skin*
> *to be born again and again and again,*
> *for Ua Zit had existed before Egypt was born,*
> *had existed before the Creation.*[3]

From India:

> *She who holds the Universe in Her womb,*
> *source of all creative energies,*
> *Maha Devi who conceives*
> *and bears and nourishes*
> *all that exists—*
>
> *. . .*
>
> *For it is Shakti who is the ultimate source,*
> *the infinite Cosmic Energy of all that occurs,*
> *Maha Devi of the thousand petalled lotus.*[4]

From Sumer:

> *Ama Tu An Ki—*
> *Mother who gave birth*
> *to heaven and earth*
> *Primordial Creator of the Universe*
> *who oversees the fashioning of life*
> *and to each decrees their fate,*
> *Oldest of the Old. . . .*[5]

From Greece:

> *Her black wings sheltering her nest,*
> *Nikta brought forth the Egg in the Wind,*
> *The egg from which Erotic love, Eros,*
> *come into the world at the beginning of time—*
> *so that the race of mortals might begin.*[6]

From North America:

In the beginning there was nothing but Spider Woman, She who was called Sussistanako, Thinking Woman, Thought Woman. . . . In the dark purple light that glowed at the Dawn of Being, Spider Woman spun a fine line from East to West. . . . From North to South. . . . And then She sat by these threads that stretched to the four horizons, . . . and sang in a voice that was exceptionally deep and sweet. As She sang, two daughters came forth: Ut Set, who became the mother of the Pueblo people, Nau Ut Set, who became the mother of all others.[7]

From Britain:

Goddess whose spirit lives in the mighty waters that flow from snow capped Alpen mountains into the darkness of the Black Sea. . . . She brought the dawn of being for those who dwelled upon Her banks so that they understood it was Danu who gave them sustenance and life.[8]

From Babylon:

> *Aruru, Oldest of the Old*
> *Creator of Life,*
> *Mami, Divine Mother of All,*
> *Womb that created all humankind*
> *and still creates all destiny. . . .*
> *. . .*
> *it was She who made all life*
> *by pinching off the fourteen pieces of clay—*
> *and laying a brick between them,*
> *She made seven women*
> *whom She placed to the left,*
> *She made seven men*
> *whom She placed to the right,*
> *Forming them into people*
> *She then placed them on the earth.*[9]

From China:

To the valleys of the wide flowing Hwang Ho, came the Goddess Nu Kwa and there from the rich golden earth, She fashioned the race of golden people, carefully working the features of each with Her skillful fingers . . . the ancestors of the Chinese people.[10]

Worship of the Great Mother was not simply "the opposite" of current father worship. Nu Kwa, Aruru, Danu, Sussistanako and Nikta, Ama Tu An Ki, Maha Devi, and Ua Zit—these were not imagined as giant women who demanded the subjugation of desire or obedience to specific commandments. The old religion was, rather, a spiritual acceptance of the human presence on earth, a respect for and "inspiration in the movements of the sun, moon, and stars, the flight of birds, the slow growth of trees, and the cycles of the seasons. . . ." Worshipers of the Goddess understood that "life and death were a continuous stream,"[11] and saw the Mother as the source of that stream.

The peoples of the earth also recognized the existence of the male principle; so the son of the Goddess emerged from their imagination to join her. Alone, they say, She created him. They say She has taken him out of herself, given birth to him—so that together they might represent the fertilization of all things. He carried the seed and impregnated the Mother through sacred sexual rites. (Eve names no daughters; even in Genesis, the [hidden] assumption is that the Mother mates with Her sons to create humankind.) He personified in his own birth and death the full cycle for all the natural world. In the thousands of years preceding the destruction of Mother worship, religious belief included these stories:

From Panama:

In the days before the world began, Mu gave birth to the sun, and taking the sun as Her lover, She gave birth to the moon. Mating with Her grandson Moon, She brought forth the stars, so many that they filled the heavens. Then mating with the stars, the sacred womb of Mu once again stirred with life, so that in this way She brought forth all the animals and plants.[12]

From Zaire:

> *First there was The Mother*
> *fertile nurturing Mboze.*
>
> . . .
>
> *Taking Her son Makanga as Her lover*
> *Mboze swelled with new life.*[13]

From Borneo:

. . . *The woman and the infant survived the great flood . . . the waters grew lower, as the infant that became a young man grew higher, until the time that the flood finally subsided, and the woman and her grown son wandered back to the land she had once known. . . . Thus it was that Fire Woman took her son as her husband, and along the now calm waters of the Dyak they raised children. . . .*[14]

From Colombia:

> *From the clear blue waters*
> . . .
> *emerged Mother Bachue*
> . . .
> *and with Her came Her son of three years,*
> *holding tightly to Her hand. . . .*
> *She raised the lad to manhood*
> *until the time She took him as a husband*
> *to bring forth all who live.*[15]

From Greece:

Primeval Prophetess, most ancient Earth, came before all else and brought world into being. Alone, She created the heaven, and naming him Uranus She took him as a lover—thus giving birth to the deities of heaven. Alone, She created the sea, and naming him Pontus She took him as a lover—thus creating the deities of the sea.[16]

These mothers and sons came long before the father-god and trinity of the Judaeo-Christian era in the West. Faded versions of their ancient worship are found in classical Greece and Rome, the cultures we have learned to consider the "cradle" of this culture. As schoolchildren we learned to revere the "democracy" of Athens—in which men owned slaves and women were denied citizenship—and to rejoice at the European "Renaissance," rightly described by Sir James Frazer as a period in which "manlier views of the world" held sway.[17]

If we read the old and new testaments critically, we see the fervor and violence employed to destroy the old religion, and the accommodation and adaptation that followed. Of course it was not only in those "biblical" lands surrounding the Red, the Dead, the Black and the Aegean, the Caspian and the Mediterranean seas that the Mother and Her son were worshiped. As the rites of the father and son now flourish around the world, so once the worship of the Great Mother and Her son. Heroes and kings everywhere—even some in the early stages of patriarchal woman-hating—acknowledged that they were born of woman, and revered the Mother's body and spirit.

The old testament explains in detail how the priests of Yahweh, the father god, attempted to eradicate the old religion and customs of the Near East and the Mideast, and how they created a new morality based on father right and the concept of women and their children as property, to strengthen male lines of descent. Phyllis Chesler, in her notes on Michelangelo's and William Blake's paintings of the male god creating Adam, remarks that nowadays "no one ever wonders: 'How can a child be born without a woman. . . . where is that male God's mother?"[18]

Judaism, beginning at a time and in a place where the old religion had already begun to change, originated in a convenant between a son and his father-god, and rejected utterly the worship of the Mother. Four mothers, ironically called "the matriarchs," served in Genesis to beget sons "in the name of the Lord": Sarah, Rebekah, Leah, and Rachel. All but Leah, who is undesired and unloved, are described as "barren" until "the Lord" sees fit to open their wombs, to produce male children in keeping with his covenant with the husbands, the patriarchs: Abraham, Isaac, and Jacob. The bodies of these women are owned by men and their pregnancies are quickened by god. They have no fertility of their own: "And the Lord remembered Sarah as He had said, and the Lord did unto Sarah as He had spoken. And Sarah conceived, and bore Abraham a son. . . ." (Genesis 21:1, 2) Their very femaleness is inconsequential, for "it had ceased to be with Sarah after the manner of women." (Genesis 18:11) These women are vessels—like their spiritual daughter and blood-descendant, the Virgin Mary—carrying god's seed for men.

Less powerful even than these were the concubines, slave women who also bore sons toward the wealth of their masters. Hagar is the mother of Ishmael, Abraham's firstborn son; Bilhah and Zilpah each bore two sons to Jacob, helping to found the twelve tribes of Israel. Bilhah also suffered being raped by Reuben, her master's firstborn son. The men who wrote this book also use the bearing of sons as a lever to keep the women apart, fostering jealousy and hatred among the wives and concubines.

In the next four books of the old testament the position and purpose of mothers is explained. Marriage is required for women, and in the book of Numbers we learn that the choice of mate is prescribed: Every woman must marry "one of the family of the tribe of her father, that the children of Israel may possess every *man* the inheritance of *his fathers.*" (Numbers 36:8; my italics.) Readers are reminded repeatedly of the dangers and temptations the "promised land" presented to the new nation. The danger for the priests of the new father god was that all those Philistines and Amalekites—and the earlier Hebrews as well—were her people, who had, since Neolithic times, worshiped the Great Goddess in groves, on hills, and in temples garnished with images of the Great Mother and her son. We must remind ourselves as we read: *people lived there;* the land of milk and honey was not empty. Like the Americas before European conquest, that land was rich with cultures many thousands of years old. And they, too, had begun to abandon the Mother.

As the worship of the father god struggled for predominance in the Mideast, pagan religions were advancing the son god (often, literally, the sun god). The rise of christianity out of Judaism runs parallel to and blends with the rise of male influence in the old religion itself. This blending is very clear, for instance, in the Book of Esther: Ahasuerus is a king who has great power (very early patriarchal) though his queen, Vashti, still in her separate palace, will not obey him. He overturns the (obviously weak) power she retains by deposing and banishing her. Then he takes a new wife—several dozens actually—though he chooses a favorite. The new wife-queen, Esther, is a Jew, worshiper of the father god, and chattel of her kinsman, Mordechai.

The "Mother of the Gods brought with her the worship of her

youthful lover or son to her new home in the West."[19] Descriptions of rituals and beliefs from the time of the change present the increasing importance of the young god and the lessening importance of the Mother. Indeed, he becomes He, and takes on Her attributes:

The nativity of the Sun, as celebrated in Egypt and Syria: The celebrants retired into certain inner shrines, from which at midnight they issued with a loud cry, *"The Virgin has brought forth! The* light is waxing!" The Egyptians even represented the new-born sun by *the image of an infant which on his birthday,* the winter solstice, they brought forth and exhibited to his worshippers. No doubt the Virgin who thus conceived and bore a son on the twenty-fifth of December was the great Oriental goddess whom Semites called the Heavenly Virgin or simply the Heavenly Goddess. . . .[20]

The sacrifice of Her son in Egypt: The people celebrate Isis, the corn mother, and Her son, who "produced corn from himself; *he gave his body to feed the people; he died that they might live."*[21]

The resurrection of Attis, in Assyria, Babylonia, Arabia, and Phoenicia: "For suddenly a light shone in the darkness: *the tomb was opened: the god had risen from the dead;* . . . the priest . . . softly whispered . . . the *glad tidings of salvation. The resurrection of the god was hailed by his disciples* as a promise that they too would issue triumphant from the corruption of the grave."[22]

The mystic baptism as practiced in Rome: The worshiper emerges "as one who had been *born again to eternal life* and had *washed away his sins in the blood* of the bull. . . . At Rome the new birth and the remission of sins by the shedding of bull's blood appear to have been carried out at the sanctuary of the Phrygian goddess on the Vatican Hill, at or near the spot where the great basilica of St. Peter's now stands; for many inscriptions relating to the rites were found when the church was being enlarged in 1608 or 1609."[23] (All italics mine.)

Contemporary christianity is obviously the outgrowth of that blend—evolving pagan worship of the son who becomes the father, and old testament worship of the father who begets sons in his image. The second, "new," testament had to adapt the old trinity of the goddess, the three-faced Hecate of the triple crossroad (Maiden, Mother, and Crone), into three male personalities to cover all the manifestations of the new male god, and consolidate his worship.

(Though even the three bears would know that the third corner of the triangle is hers; Father, Son, and Holy Ghost: the dove, long a symbol of the Goddess, represents the spirit among the three.) This blend was suited to the needs of the changing social order, both reflecting and creating new attitudes about women and men, mothers and sons.

It would be foolish to assume that the story of the conception and birth of Jesus, his death, resurrection, and subsequent godhead are *coincidentally similar* to previous practices, in the same part of the world, by virtually the same people. Such a notion is easily rejected, not only through common sense but through the words and deeds of early christians themselves. The writers and elders of the new "church" understood well the compelling aspects of their rival and the strength of its long history. They frankly admitted that their feast days were lifted from the pagan calendar, adjusting the dates for the birth, death, and resurrection of their christ.[24] Mary was honored with the titles Queen of Heaven and Mother of God (at the Council of Ephesus in A.D. 431) because the people who'd been worshiping the Goddess with those titles for thousands of centuries would then be automatically—instantaneously—converted.* The people thus didn't have to be convinced; they need only go on as they had done year after year, marking the harvest, the planting, and the turning of the seasons through the ancient worship of the Mother and her son. The Queen of Heaven continues to be worshiped as Madonna—but today, it is *only* as the mother of god that she maintains importance. Beginning again in the twelfth, thirteenth, and fourteenth centuries, in great cathedrals raised to *her* glory, men hanged effigies of her dead son. In the twentieth century, her aura yet compels us, and we stand gazing at painted and sculpted images of the Lady holding her son, an infant or a dead man, in her arms. By now, of course, all the erotic and passionate aspects of the relationship have been dissipated. The sacred,

---

* In *The Sexual Life of Savages in Northwestern Melanesia* (Harcourt Brace, 1929, pp. 186–87), the anthropologist Bronislaw Malinowski suggests that we "realize that the cardinal dogma of God the Father and God the Son, the sacrifice of the only Son and the filial love of man to his Maker would completely misfire in a matrilineal society, where the relation between father and son is decreed by tribal law to be that of two strangers, where all personal unity between them is denied, and where all family obligations are associated with mother-line. We cannot wonder that Paternity must be among the principal truths to be inculcated by proselytizing Christians."

the holy, and the glorious have lost all their blood and flesh, and the dominant patriarchal religions aspire to "purity." Virginity, for instance, especially in women, no longer means integrity, but refers to heterosexual chastity.

It is not enough for us to learn and understand the mythic history of the relationship of mother and son; we must also acknowledge that these beliefs and tales are present in our own lives. We human mothers are not goddesses; we do not mate with our sons; we do not kill, mourn, and resurrect them to keep the earth alive. But our sons grow into an unearthly power, a power long abhorred by us. Sacrificed to or by their fathers, they grow up to *be* the fathers, to rule and dominate the sons to come—and the mothers and daughters as well.[25]

To have come to this, there must have been a time when the sons broke with their mothers, refused to gain power through their mothers and rule with them. They must have superseded the mothers, overthrown them. Early on, men could not have known that their semen contained sperm, nor that sperm was necessary to make people. Later, when the women shared their knowledge and power, men accepted the duality of sexual reproduction and celebrated women and men as mates. But then, men denied the natural order, ignored it, and began to speak of male gods creating alone, out of themselves. Not only was it written that these new gods made the heavens and earth, but they gave birth. Greek men taught that Zeus bore Athena out of his forehead, Dionysus from his thigh; any bizarre and desperate story was acceptable, apparently, when the sons destroyed the mothers, became the fathers, and designed the worship of the male as sole procreator—in opposition to Nature Herself, the Primordial Goddess.[26]

This process, the evolution of religious practice, may be easily followed in mythic literature. Once imagined, the youth was deified, naturally partaking of his mother's divinity. The mother and son loved each other, the mother often bestowing gifts of great value on her beloved boy, the son pledging faith to her. So we find that Hina and her mother and daughter gave Maui tools and magic with which to capture the sun in Hawaii. And Spider Old Woman kicked the sun up into the North American sky for the Kiowa braves who could find no place high enough for it. Scandinavian Frigga traveled the earth seeking immortality for her frail son Balder, and Hera gave Hephaistos the power of Greece's volcanoes, the source of fire.

Soon, though, came stories that told of the boy's laziness, or his sullen refusal to do his chores. Thus the Divine Ancestress Hanna Hanna in Anatolia gave her grandson Zaskhapuna the honor of making storms, to bring rain to the crops. But he, seeing his responsibility only as a chore, gave the job to his son, who fell asleep hidden beneath a tree, leaving the earth to parch and burn—until Hanna Hanna found the sleeping boy.

A slow, subtle change, raising the son first to a position of prominence, then to predominance, may be traced through legends in which the hero (son) mocks, challenges, sometimes rapes, and finally kills the mother, who is queen, priestess, and goddess.

We begin to find young men who lack respect for the Great Mother—some of them trying to gain her wisdom or her love by trickery, as in the story Merlin Stone tells of Mother Somagalags, whose people, the Bella Coola, live along the sea in British Columbia. In this tale, the mother is deceived by her four sons into taking care of them as if they were helpless cubs—when they really are strong young men. When she discovers the hoax, she beats them with her digging stick until they admit that they have "wronged their mother." They promise to "pay her back for all that she" has done for them if she will teach them her secrets: how to find the clams, how to choose the straightest cedars and fell them, which trees to use to carve the sacred totem, and "how to carve the totem form of Somagalags, First Mother of the Clan. . . ."[27] (This particular story is important not only within the history of the mother/son relationship, but as one of the tellings of how men gained knowledge to make human culture—from women.)

The classic disrespectful son is well represented by Awe, a braggart who boasted to the other people of Dahomey that his magic was mightier than the power of Mawu, the Mother of all life. He climbed to heaven to challenge Mawu, failed, and returned to earth to die, having eaten death at Mawu's table. Another foolish fellow was the Irish lad Crunnchu, who won the love of the Mighty Macha, who came to live with him in the forest. In his weakness, he exploited the power of the Goddess, betting the men of Ulster that his pregnant wife could outrun the king's horses. Naturally, she did, and, delivering herself of lusty twins, stood in the road and darkly cursed all the men who'd relished the race, giving no thought to the mother and her babes.

Other sons went beyond disrespect; Apollo in the Aegean islands and Huitzilpochtli in Mexico turned to violence against their mothers. Apollo attacked and killed the Python, ancient consort and oracle of Lato, taking the Mother's Pythian shrine for his own, forcing the priestesses forever after to *his* will at Delphi. Huitzilpochtli attacked and killed Mother Coatlicue's older children, the sun, the moon, and the stars, severing their heads from their bodies, plunging the Mother into grief.

In Hawaii, Maui determined to murder his mother, Hina, so that her life's years might be added to his own. One version of this story is that he tried to reenter her vagina, to pass through her body and emerge from her mouth. He would have killed her and reversed his own birth; but she crushed him between her thighs. This story, an attempted rape, reveals the sexual violence employed by men in their usurpation and destruction of women's power. (It also demonstrates the value of fighting back.) Some similar elements are present in the tale of Cerridwen, in Britain, who brewed great magic for her son, only to have it stolen by Gwion. Ultimately Gwion became a grain of wheat, which Cerridwen, in the form of a hen, devoured. Gwion grew inside of her for nine months and was reborn a son of the enchantress—to be cast into the waters for his evil.

Other young men, who may never have cherished hostility toward their own mothers, have become legendary in their quest to destroy the worship of the Mother. These sons are responsible in myth for insulting and rejecting the Goddess, breaking down the ancient practices of her worship and replacing them or co-opting them with early patriarchal ideas. Among the Celts we find the story of the time that the Daughter of Eternity, the Morrigan, lusted for CuChulainn, and asked him to lie with her. He refused, and made the greater mistake of rejecting her aid in battle, denigrating her strength. This—to the Goddess who, in the form of a great raven, shrieked her war cry and swept the fields of the enemy with her powerful wings! In her wrath, she humiliated CuChulainn, and filled him with dread.

In Sumer, another young man rejected the advances of the Goddess, but was not put down like his Celtic brother. Gilgamesh, whose beauty stirred Ishtar, was invited to marry her. He refused, recalling that the youth Tammuz had died of that honor. Moreover, he insulted the Goddess, killed her sacred bull, and led an army against her worshipers, taking the throne by force. From that time, the Sumerian kings, who continued to call themselves Beloved of Ishtar, did not die with the coming of the winter months, but went through a brief period of mourning and lamentation merely to symbolize the death of the crops. Such stories show the growing reluctance among men to accept sexual initiation and initiative from women, and the advance of rape as a technique of subduing women.

In Greece, Theseus took the part of Gilgamesh. His journey to seek his father led him on a tour of destruction of Goddess worship. He passed through Eleusis, holy city to Mother Demeter and her daughter Persephone, and though he killed the young king there and took his place, he broke the tradition and established a patrilineal monarchy. When he arrived at his father's palace in Athens, he drove out Medea, a priestess of the Goddess who had been his father's guest and adviser. He then journeyed to Knossos in Crete, where he killed the Minotaur in the labyrinth, bringing down a matrilineal royal house and stealing its priestess, the Goddess-on-Earth, Ariadne, whom he then abandoned. Theseus even brought down in battle, raped, and took to wife the warrior queen Hippolyta, priestess among the Amazons, and raised her son to be his heir.

The Goddess Aphrodite took her revenge on Theseus, for the prince Hippolytus was a fervent worshiper of the Mother all his brief life. She caused his father to destroy him, and then took the youth into her heart, leaving the high king of Athens with no (patrilineal) heir—a tragic circumstance for a man of the new order. He kept his hand in the game by later assisting Orestes and Oedipus, but Theseus' spirit was broken, destroyed by the retaliation of the Mother. He was, however, one of the last men to suffer defeat so clearly linked to his spiritual transgression and antiwoman violence.

Ultimately, these sons *did* kill their Mother, giving rise to that new order—the patriarchy—and paving the way for countless gods and sons of gods, male rulers justifying further degradation of the power of women everywhere. Their will be done, on earth as it is in heaven. So Marduk, a bold and exploitive usurper, killed Tiamat in Mesopotamia, climbed upon her throne and gleefully recounted the murder, claiming to have created heaven and earth from the two halves of the torn body of the Mother. Thus Rama, in India, cut off his mother's head with an ax.

These stories go a long way toward explaining the emotional motive—generally self-defense—for the mother's killing of her son, and her subsequent suffering. The mothers' mourning of the sons' deaths has remained one of the classical episodes in this history. The lamentation of the Goddess at the loss of the fruit of her body is deeply felt and tragically expressed in myth and legend. The mighty Ishtar regretted the loss of her lover—radiant and beautiful; the loss of her consort—who sat beside her and helped to guide the people; the loss of her son—the babe who nursed at her breast. "Oh, my child!" she cried, "at his vanishing away."[28] So the Mother mourned —"as Inanna grieved when Damuzi died, as Ashtart grieved when Tammuz died, as Isis grieved when Osiris died, as Kybele grieved when Attis died, as Anat grieved when Baal died. . . ."[29]

In some mother-and-son myths we can find evidence of the very earliest kinship systems—systems in which the only recognized blood relation was *mother's* blood.[30] Tragic consequences arose with the coming of the social role of father and the recognition of the biology of fatherhood. The mythical killing, by mothers, of sons whose allegiance had become—or threatened to become—patriarchal, was not only emotionally understandable but often politically astute.

Among the clearest examples of these legends are those that have come down to us from or through the early patriarchal period in Greece. For example, Procne, wife to Tereus of Thrace, discovered that Tereus had abducted, raped, and cut out the tongue of her beloved sister, Philomela. In her rage, Procne murdered his son, the young Itys and, to further punish Tereus, fed the boy's body to him at a feast. (It may be that in an earlier story Tereus not only raped the sister but ate the baby; such cannibalism is scattered here and there in Greek myths, relics of the *really* old days.) Procne and Philomela changed into birds to escape from Thrace, and Procne became a nightingale, whose song forever mourns the loss of her child. Althea, the mother of Meleager, also destroyed her son in the confusion of cross-blood kinship struggle. The Fates had told her that Meleager's life thread was tied to a log—which she then carefully kept from the flames, knowing that if it should burn, her son would die. But when she heard that Meleager had publicly dishonored his uncles—her brothers—she rushed to the woodbox and threw the log onto the fire.

Notorious Medea killed her two young sons just before she escaped from her husband—to prevent their becoming slaves in a land which regarded her as a barbarian witch and the boys as *her* kin. She understood that this murder was also the appropriate revenge on Jason, who had abused, dishonored, and abandoned her after she had willingly betrayed and destroyed her blood alliances for him.

Queen Mother Agave was priestess of the old religion in Thebes, but her son Pentheus ruled there, a sign that the old order was much changed. When Pentheus refused to recognize the holiness of the women in their sacred frenzy, and was caught as he spied on them, they tore his body to pieces, led by his own mother. When the queen returned to consciousness, she was horror-stricken and overcome by the murder of her son.

Young king Pentheus embodies one of the most common themes in mythical accounts of struggle between mother and son: male arrogance that allows for no understanding or respect for the old ways—the ways of the mothers. And his is a story from the very end of matriarchal time; the women no longer worship the Goddess, but the Young God, Dionysus. By the time the old religion had become thus degraded, there had also arisen in Greece the now-fabled House of Atreus: fathers, sons, and brothers who committed murderous atrocities against each other through several generations, leading up to a man who serves well as the true culture hero for the patriarchy: Orestes. It is in the story of this son that we find the crux, that moment in cultural history when the sons chose to align themselves with their fathers, and throw over their long alliance with the power of their mothers.

Orestes is the fourth generation of the House of Atreus in popular mythology, born to suffer torture and to benefit *man*kind through his suffering. His story marks a great and terrible moment in the history of the mother/son relationship. Both of the major classical sources[31] for this story are devotedly patriarchal, promoting marriage and obedience in women. Though Euripides is harsher than Aeschylus, both writers make a point of belittling women, including sarcastic lines unrelated to plot or character development. Aeschylus makes much of the concept of blood kin, but more of the (new) sanctity of marriage. He even cites the rape-marriage of Hera to Zeus as a symbol of the holiness of the vow of matrimony. Despite this sharp bias, we can still find traces of the older beliefs, often twisted and corrupted to suit the needs of father right and king rule.

Agamemnon, the father of Orestes, was the high king of Argos, helping his brother Menelaus to recapture his wife, Helen, who had been abducted and taken off to Troy. The two brothers mustered an army but were unable to sail because there was no wind. The brother generals had angered Artemis, protector of woodland creatures, by wantonly slaying a pregnant hare just as she was about to deliver her young. The fleet's lack of wind was explained as a punishment of the Goddess.

Artemis is portrayed by a male priest as demanding the death of Agamemnon's daughter, the princess Iphigenia, as reparation for the crime of killing the hare. This demand is incomprehensible coming from the Great Virgin, of whom maidens were beloved and devoted followers. Nonetheless, the tale has been told this way by men since the fifth century. So, convincing his wife that their daughter is to be married, Agamemnon insists that the princess come to his seaside encampment. He then slaughters Iphigenia on the altar and sails for Troy.

Ten years later, Agamemnon returns from the Trojan War. In his absence, Clytemnestra, the mother of Iphigenia—a priestess-queen who keeps the old religion and allegiance in her heart—has ruled Argos with her consort. She has also nurtured her desire for vengeance—and the day Agamemnon returns, she kills him. Standing over his body, she tells the assembled citizens, "This is my work, and I claim it. . . . I am jubilant."[32] When the crowd responds with anger and recriminations, she shouts, "He was the one you should have driven from Argos; he, marked with his daughter's blood, ripe for punishment." Grieving for her daughter, she recalls, "When he by guile uprooted the tender plant he gave me, and made the house accurst, when on my virgin daughter his savage sword descended,* my tears in rivers ran. . . ." As to Agamemnon's burial, Clytemnestra tells the citizens with bitter sarcasm, "I felled him; I despatched him; and I will earth his bones. . . . But, as is fit, his daughter shall meet him near the porchway of those who perished young; his loved Iphigenia with loving arms shall greet him, and gagged and silent tongue."

In the ten years of her husband's absence, Clytemnestra had been virtually childless. Her young son, Orestes, had been sent to the home of a distant friend, so that the boy might not fall prey to the allies of Troy, and her second daughter, Electra, was no comfort

---

* This line carries the symbolic suggestion of incest-rape, perhaps harking back to an older version of the story.

to her for the loss of Iphigenia. Despite the fact that she is a woman born only a few generations from the time when "marriage and paternal ties counted for little compared to matrilineal 'blood kinship' ties,"[33] Electra is the prototype of all women grown faithful to patriarchy. Her father, her brother, and her future husband all come first in her mind and heart, come between her and her mother, her aunt Helen, her cousin Hermione,[34] and her slain sister; she is Daddy's girl to the core. When she prays, she asks, "For myself, a pure heart and clean hands, and ways and thoughts unlike my mother's."

When Orestes returns to Argos to punish the murderer of his father, he slowly comes to realize the task before him. He hesitates briefly, the former sanctity of his mother's blood recalled to him. But Orestes is no Hamlet, and his hesitation is brief indeed. Urged by his sister, who cannot wait to see her mother dead, and strengthened by his companion Pylades, who serves as a goading reminder for the god Apollo, Orestes recalls the words of that god: "Shed blood for blood, your face set like a flint. . . ."

The night before her son murders her, Clytemnestra is visited by a dream of terror. She dreams that she gives birth to a snake, which she covers "in shawls, and lulled . . . to rest like a little child. . . . She gave it her breast to suck . . . [but] with her milk the creature drew forth clots of blood." She has dreamed a parable for all mothers here, for the serpent was honored as the symbolic consort of the Goddess many thousands of years before christian and Hebrew patriarchs changed its wisdom to evil, or Greek priests sent Apollo to kill the Python.[35] Giving birth to a snake is not the fearful sign. It is that the snake—her own son and companion—then turns on her; *that* is the nightmare.

Orestes recognizes himself in his mother's dream, and prays "that the dream's meaning may be . . . fulfilled. . . ." He even recognizes that he must be a monster to commit the matricide he plans: "it means that she who nursed this obscene beast must die by violence; *I* must transmute my nature, be viperous in heart and act! . . . I am her destined murderer." He understands that what he is about to do is an act against nature.

Nevertheless, his resolve remains strong, and he only pauses a moment when she bares her breast to him, reminding him that his head lay there while he slept or sucked sweet milk. He asks, "Pylades, what shall I do? To kill a mother is terrible. Shall I show mercy?"—but merely three lines from his companion serve to put

down such tender consideration, and after an interchange with Clytemnestra in which her part has been made passionless, Orestes
slaughters his mother.

His immediate response to his act is a long speech justifying the
murder, in which he says that Clytemnestra has profaned the sanctity of the marriage bond by killing Agamemnon. But that speech,
delivered in shock, gives way to rising hysteria. In that state, Orestes
has no idea that he stands on the shifting ground of an earthquake
in the kinship system. He is caught in that upheaval in which " 'marriage . . . cuts across the most strongly institutionalized social
bond. . . .' the matrilineal blood bond which is shared not by man
and wife but by the woman and her kin."[36]

He quickly begins to lose his senses: "My wits chafe at the rein
under my weakened grip, and carry me off the course." He an-
nounces that killing his mother was "no sin" because she was guilty
of his father's murder and, therefore, "unclean." With this procla-
mation, he severs his alliance to his mother, to the bloodline of her
people, and to matriarchal culture and history.

He tells the assembled people that Apollo has promised him
that he'll be "clear of blame," and calls them to witness his departure for the shrine of the god who'll cleanse him. Even as the Ar-
give people (the eternally ignorant Greek chorus, who name him
"most loyal of sons") try to calm him, he cries out at the approach
of the Erinyes, the primal Furies, who've come in response to Clytemnestra's death curse. The Furies rage around Orestes, whipping
him with serpents; they drive him from the city and scourge him
over the countryside until he reaches the shrine of Apollo, where,
still reeking with his mother's blood, crazed and exhausted with guilt
and terror, he falls on the altar. Apollo appears to him and sends
him to Athens, where Theseus, destroyer of the worship of the
Mother, is king, and Athena, faithful daughter of the father god, is
protector of the city. At Clytemnestra's ghost's urging the Furies
pursue him to Athens, where they track him to Athena's temple.

Before his trial, we learn both that Orestes has bribed Zeus,
Apollo, and Athena with the promise of the loyalty of all Argos and
a political alliance between Argos and Athens, and that Apollo has
promised—in advance of the jury's deliberations—to save Orestes
from punishment and restore him to honor. The presence of Athena,
whose stated allegiance is to men, further renders the trial a sham.
Only the Furies (who have become the chorus in this play) are

fooled by the appearance of due process—trial by a jury of men in a city where women have no political power. As the hearing moves toward its obvious conclusion, the Furies stand amazed and say, "Now true and false must change their names, old law and justice be reversed," and rightly predict that mothers' blood will be spilled again and again in years to come, as a result of this decision.

A more blatant fix would be hard to imagine: Here are the Furies to represent the right of the Mother; they are presented as bestial and disgusting, foul and loathsome. Here is Apollo, so-called god of light, who has destroyed his own Mother's shrine, raped and abducted Her priestesses, and murdered Her consort; he is the counsel for the defense. Here is Athena—the judge who casts the tie-breaking vote—who describes herself thus: "No mother gave me birth. Therefore the father's claim and male supremacy in all things . . . wins my whole heart's loyalty." (She is exempt from marriage, however, a choice not available to the women who populate "her" city of Athens. Both Aeschylus and Euripides, in telling of Clytemnestra's defeat, make clear to the audience of Athenian women that the marriage bond must supersede all other connections.)

The Furies make what they consider one of their strongest arguments when they say that Agamemnon was not a blood relation to Clytemnestra. At that point, Orestes actually asks if he must consider himself blood kin to his mother, and a discussion of kinship leads to Apollo's famous speech about motherhood: "The mother is not the true parent of the child which is called hers. She is a nurse who tends the growth of the young seed planted by its true parent, the male. . . . she keeps it, as one might keep for some friend a growing plant." With such a rationale, Orestes' crime against his mother is reduced to a misdemeanor, for which he has already been punished too much.

At the conclusion of this painful miscarriage, Apollo and Orestes leave the temple together, and Athena, the original token woman, argues with the Furies, convincing them not to contest or attempt to overturn the verdict—or even to regret it. She urges them to accept the new order, calling the proceedings a "fair trial, fair judgment, ended in an even vote." She says, "You call on Justice [the Goddess Themis], I rely on Zeus," making it clear that she understands the distinction as well as the Furies do—but that she has given up justice for law. She offers them "a home, and bright thrones in a holy cavern," where they will be honored by the citizens of Athens. The Furies accept her offer, submitting to a comfortable, though powerless, new role for the mother in the new world of the father.

By the time of the infamous decision to free Orestes, the patriarchy had already made monsters of the primal creative powers, and the Furies—like the Gorgons, the Sphinx, the Hydra, the Harpies, and the Chimaera—were male-designed personifications (called female and despised as such) of the deepest fear, rage, and illness of the human spirit. In the new male scheme of things, moral recrimination, outpourings of conscience, and ravings spurred by overwhelming guilt are considered brutes of the deepest dark, creatures of the night to be exorcised, destroyed, and buried in the cave of dread female power, repressed and cut off from the surface, the light, and the day.

The agony Orestes experienced, hounded by the Furies in his travels toward paternal blessing, is wholly appropriate to a man who has murdered his mother. The denial of his father's crime against his sister, and the ultimate expiation of his guilt in the name of the patriarchy are a greater horror than the just and righteous fury of the Mother that torments Orestes' soul. And the taming of the Furies is a major step in the suppression of the life force of Mother/Woman; the raging Daughters of Night are subdued and domesticated. The Furies lose their power, their position, and their purpose; they are given in exchange a quiet home and the veneration of the people—a clear metaphor for the ideal of patriarchal motherhood.

When Orestes took the false guidance of Apollo and accepted the traitorous counsel of Athena, he did so believing his torture would cease, his guilt would be put to rest, and his tainted soul would be cleansed. But the sons who came after Orestes have not only left their mothers, they have lost their fathers as well. Men have not reaped what Orestes thought he sowed; patriarchy has failed to satisfy the human spirit.

We see that, for most of the history of humankind, there were no fathers. That is to say, the father, either as a family member or as a biological parent, originally was unacknowledged, mythically or otherwise[37]: "instead of the creative force of a father, the [earliest] myths revealed the spontaneous procreative powers of the ancestral mother . . . nor is there any other role in which the father appears. In fact, he is never mentioned, and does not exist in any part of the mythological world. . . . the primeval woman is always imagined to bear children without the intervention of a husband or of any other male partner. . . ."[38]

Patriarchy began as the sons gave over their connection to the power and lineage of the mothers and aligned themselves instead with the growing social force of paternity, *becoming* fathers themselves. Whether they sired children or not, men began to organize themselves in terms of male lineage and allegiance.

The mother would bear, nurse and nurture the child, love him and care for him. Then, at the paternally ordained time—by decree or on demand, she would give the boy a token, a symbol or a gift, and send him out to find his father, who would test and instruct him in the rights and powers of manhood. So it was with Theseus, one of the first sons of the patriarchy in Greece; his father left a sword and sandals under a stone, with the admonition that when the boy could move the stone, wear the sandals, and wield the sword, he should come to the palace at Athens to claim his heritage.

Sometimes in the legends, the boy leaves too soon, like Phaeton, whose story is told by the Latin poet Ovid. Phaeton is anxious and eager to show himself a man, desperate to prove that the sun god Helios is his father. He claims as proof the right to drive the chariot of the sun, but, too light to steady the car, frightened by the vast sky, and ignorant of the fierce horses, he perishes. Phaeton falls through flames, foreshadowing Satan, another arrogant son who challenged his father-god.

Often sons in the myths had to struggle to be acknowledged, to be named true heirs, to be claimed by their fathers, for the core of patriarchy is a man's ownership of his children, especially his male children. Fathers have to "own up" to paternity of their sons; sons fight not to be "disowned." A man can be a bastard only in patriarchy. Only in a system in which the father's name and claim are *required* for legitimacy or social acceptance, could the concept of bastardy exist—and be an *insult* defaming both mother and son.

Early in the mythic history of men, sons fought against reluctant fathers for their lives. Dozens of myths have come down to us of men and gods who learned from the oracles that their sons would overthrow them, would be greater than they—or would kill their fathers. The later belief that young heroes were the sons of gods may have sprung from the fears of fathers who, worried lest their sons should overtake them, chose to believe that the youths were not theirs, but seed of the gods, who were thus responsible for the strength, beauty, and ambition reflected in those princely boys.

Oedipus was one of these—cast out by a father who feared death at his son's hands. Only the intervention of his mother, Jocasta, made Oedipus a foundling instead of a victim of paternal infanticide. Perseus was another; his grandfather Acrisius had tried to prevent his conception, but failed to account for Zeus's rape of his daughter, Danae. So Acrisius cast his daughter and infant grandson out upon the sea in a great casket, in the futile hope that the boy would starve or drown, rather than grow to fulfill the oracle by killing his grandfather.

Zeus himself, patriarch of the Olympian gods, narrowly escaped being eaten by his own father, Cronos. Rhea, Zeus's mother, gave her mate a stone to swallow instead of the baby, and hid Zeus until he was grown, whereupon he returned and forced his father to spit up his siblings, who had all been devoured before Zeus's birth. In the war that followed, Zeus and his allies defeated Cronos, much as Cronos had destroyed his own father, Ouranos. In response to his mother's plea, Cronos attacked and castrated Ouranos, who had buried alive the eldest of his mate's children.

The mythology of the father/son relationship began in this violence—fear, rebellion, castration, cannibalism, and murder. By the time the Greeks gave over to christianity, though traditional father/son violence remained, the form had been altered; the son had become the father's sacrificial victim, sometimes dying in place of the father, sometimes dying so that the father might satisfy his father god.[89]

In the old testament, Noah cursed his grandson Canaan into eternal slavery; Abraham banished his firstborn son, Ishmael, and willingly bound his favorite son Isaac on the altar, ready to commit him to the blade and the flame by god's demand; Isaac and Jacob divided their sons by loving and honoring one over the others; the law demands that "the firstborn of thy sons thou shalt give unto me," and decrees that "rebellious sons" be stoned to death; Saul cursed his son Jonathan, whose soul "was knit with the soul of David"—but left his throne to that same David at his god's command, and the vainglorious prince Absalom died leading an army against David, who is *his* father. Finally, the new testament has, *in*

its heart and as its very purpose, the story of the sacrifice of the father god's "only begotten" son, Jesus.

The killing of sons by fathers has profoundly influenced this
culture—not least of all through the work of Freud, who suggested
that both the son's fear of his father and the father's desire to kill or
castrate his son were elements in the consummation of his theoretical "Oedipus complex." As in patriarchal mythology, patriarchal
psychology's resolution of father/son violence has been for the sons
to become fathers themselves—saving their lives and their manhood
while perpetuating the cruel power struggle.

Therapists and academic psychologists, many of whom seem to
be twentieth-century supporters of Orestes' crime, have likewise continued to assert that men must kill their mothers. Wolfgang Lederer,
one of those "experts," says that "the separation from mother must
be accomplished, if a boy is to become a man . . . he must also slay
his mother. . . ."[40] Lederer also cites his colleague Joseph Rhein-
gold, who has suggested that sons' primary dissatisfaction with their
fathers is that they don't help boys escape from their mothers.[41]

Another male expert in the interpretation of mythology is Erich
Neumann, who has addressed himself specifically to the story of
Orestes, and says, "Here, identification with the father is so complete
that the maternal principle can be killed even when it appears . . .
as the real mother."[42] He understands that the roles of father and
mother are *in opposition* to each other—since it is his "identification
with the father" that enables a son to kill his mother. Neumann has
also understood that "the slaying of the mother and identification
with the father-god go together." Indeed, he has looked over much
of the same scene that we are now surveying, but, like his colleagues, his point of view is a problem. Neumann views the male
ego, as personified by Orestes, as "heroic." He can speak of mother
rape as "active incest," and call it bravery.[43]

Basically, Neumann says that the son rapes and kills the mother
to overcome his fear that she might castrate/kill him—and he says
that's not only a healthy response, it's heroic! He defines "victory
over the mother, frequently taking the form of actual entry into
her," as action that produces "a transformation of personality which
alone makes the hero a hero, that is, a higher and ideal representative of *man*kind." (Italics mine.) Neumann also admires the
"more powerfully developed masculinity" of Gilgamesh, whom he

calls "a real hero"—no doubt because that son succeeded in both raping and murdering the mother.

Neumann says that the stronger the male ego/consciousness, the more a man comes to recognize what he calls the "emasculating, bewitching, deadly and stupefying nature of the Great Goddess." We have to remind ourselves that this man is speaking of relations between adolescent sons and their mothers. He goes on to say: "For the . . . male, the female is synonymous with the unconscious and the nonego, hence with darkness, nothingness, the void, the bottomless pit. . . . Mother, womb, the pit and hell are all identical."[44] So much for apple pie.

And Lederer, getting carried away to the point of the confessional, tells his readers this: "I can still vividly recall something . . . about old women . . . their smell. Perhaps it is something about post-menopausal chemistry; more likely it had to do with a certain physical neglect once physical charms were past. . . . with modern hygiene and modern perfume, I have not noticed it lately; when I still noticed it . . . during my medical internship—I could not get away from it fast enough."[45] Heedless of the effect of his disgust on his unfortunate patients and not in the least reticent to publish it, Lederer goes on: "Not only old age smells. Menstruation may smell and so may sexual excitement and so, of course, does vaginal discharge. Men have always reacted with hostile apprehension to these organic odors." Here, he suddenly generalizes: *all* men *always* share his response to the smell of women, and, apparently, not to their own. His personal revulsion becomes completely generic by the end of his book, when he tells us that, "For men, there has often seemed to be something excessively physical about women—too many secretions and smelly fluids. . . ."[46]

The words of these men, their feelings and opinions, are representative. They are not unusual, and they are the men who've dispensed both information and therapy to mothers and sons seeking knowledge and assistance for the past century. It is men like this who have been responsible for promoting sex, both "overt" and "sublimated," as the major issue in the mother/son relationship.

Sigmund Freud's famous theory, the Oedipus complex, is a commonplace today, in language and in the consciousness of society. Many people *assume* that sons are sexually attracted to their mothers, that mothers are often seductive with their sons, that son and father compete for the sexual attention of the mother—and that these feelings and actions are organic, natural. The power of Freud's idea cannot be overestimated, despite the many decades since it was first publicized, or the presence of new therapies and "growth groups" which claim no connection to Freudian analysis. The power of male experts to establish their notions and suggestions as fact is very great; the now-widespread belief in the natural existence of such a sexual triangle is proof of that power.

The story of Oedipus begins with Jocasta, a descendant of Agave and the queen who held the throne in the matrilineage of Thebes. She married her cousin Laius, and they had a son. An oracle predicted that this son would kill his father, so Laius chose to kill the child instead. But his wife, who, like Medea, committed a crime against her own blood for the benefit of her husband, protested, and instead sent the infant to be exposed—abandoned in the wild. Just like Snow White, the infant Oedipus was saved by the kindhearted servant entrusted with the cruel task, and given over to a shepherd, who took the boy to the childless queen and king of Corinth, to raise as their own son.

When he became a young man, Oedipus was told by the Delphic oracle that he would kill his father and marry his mother. Though he'd already begun to suspect his adoption, he left the country of his supposed parents and wandered in self-imposed exile, attempting to thwart the Fates. He then met and killed Laius in a brawl (at a triple crossroads—sacred place to the Goddess), never knowing that he was fulfilling half of the prophecy in doing so.

Near Thebes, he encountered the Sphinx, who was challenging male wayfarers with a fatal riddle. Those who could not answer correctly were killed and eaten. She had "devoured man after man" when Oedipus accosted her and answered her riddle. She disappeared and the people of the city of Thebes hailed him as their deliverer.

Since the queen was a widow, Oedipus was crowned king of Thebes—taking, as Laius had done, some of the power from Jocasta and her brother Creon. We must remember that he *had* to marry Jocasta to become king. Vanquishing the Sphinx led him to the throne, but he could not take that throne until he became the consort of the queen—the female holder of the blood right.

They lived happily enough until their four children were grown, when a plague struck Thebes. The oracle proclaimed, "There is an unclean thing . . . which must be driven away." Creon interpreted the oracle to mean that the killer of Laius must be found and banished or killed. Oedipus agreed, and instigated a search which revealed himself to be the "unclean thing." When Jocasta realized that her husband was her son, she hanged herself; Oedipus blinded himself with the golden brooches of her cloak. He was then banished by Creon (now sole ruler of Thebes) and again became a wanderer. This time he is a spiritual leper, polluted and polluting, shunned by all who meet him. Many years later, Theseus shelters Oedipus as he had Orestes, and gives him comfort and safety in which to die. (Theseus' hospitality to men who have been injured in the war against women has come down to us as an example of the humane principles of early patriarchal Greeks.)

The fate of Oedipus belongs to that early phase of the patriarchal revolution, when the failing beliefs, standards, and practices of the matriarchy continued to coexist with those of the new order. Unlike Orestes, or even Theseus, Oedipus could not make the complete break. Though he defeated the Sphinx and tried to countermand the Fates—even mated with his own mother—he accepted the old rule of marriage with the queen as a necessity for his own power. Resenting Creon, he still did not question the right of Jocasta's brother to equal rank, honoring the kinship of sister and brother. A great part of his spirit continued to live in the old ways; he subordinated himself to the matriarchy even as he struggled against it.

In a simple sense, Oedipus was an innocent victim: he must have loved his adopted parents, even to the point of committing hubris—the Greek sin of arrogant pride, an affront to the gods—in trying to escape his destiny, to spare his parents the shame and destruction he was doomed to bring them. Even his defeat of the Sphinx was an accidental meeting; he blundered into heroism. No Theseus, Oedipus never sought confrontation with monsters and villains; he ran away from his fate—only to find it everywhere he ran. Ultimately, Oedipus' "victory" over the Sphinx can be understood to be no victory at all. It was just one more step toward his unavoidable fate.

Freud suggested that young boys have sexual desire for their mothers—mostly unconscious, but obvious under analysis. Not only was his choice of myth inappropriate, but his notion was that this attraction was somehow organic (and different from sexual attraction in general, that any young child might have for another child or an adult) and, therefore, universal—found in young boys the world over, throughout history. Of course this could never be substantiated, but, more important, Freud's theory took no social or political elements into account. If he really did find sexual desire for mothers in young boys, he found it in young boys of middle- and upper-class European nuclear patriarchal families of the late nineteenth and early twentieth centuries. Such findings would have to be studied in terms of the dependence of male children on their mothers, the high social value of male children and resultant status of their mothers, sex-role definitions, the climate of heavily repressed sexuality at the time, and so forth. Moreover, the "finding" itself is open to question and interpretation, especially given Freud's deliberate distortion of his own data about girls who were incest-rape victims (see Florence Rush's *The Best Kept Secret*).

In our time, also, such considerations as emotional dependence and the power dynamics of the family must be analyzed in social and political terms. For instance, the fact that small boys (and small girls, for that matter) have intimate and prolonged physical and emotional relations with mothers rather than fathers is surely explained for the most part by the fact that almost no fathers give care/nurturance to children in this culture. Small boys rarely spend time talking with their fathers, much less touching them, confiding in them, or exchanging ideas with them. Many children hardly know their fathers as actual people until they are ten or twelve years old—if then. Fathers continue to be remote and associated with discipline or impersonal power.

Moreover, in both Freud's day and ours, the image of woman is that of an object, a *thing to be used* by males for the satisfaction of their sexual (and other) needs. At the same time, of course, despite obvious everyday reality, the image of mother is the personification of home and security—a boundless source of love, care, support, admiration, etc. Out of their rapidly developing sense of the masculinity society expects of them, and their own real needs, little boys may turn easily to their mothers—rather than fathers—for warmth of feeling and intimate relationship, only to find, as adults, that this turning has been understood as the "fixation" Freud suggested.

If such a "complex" did exist, it would, in this society, arise out of the constraints of the nuclear family. In this form, the blood tie to the mother is no longer sacred, and the power of the father is imposed by the threat or reality of physical violence. Hostility between fathers and sons certainly exists, and is complex enough without the introduction of the psychological red herring of Freud's Oedipus complex.

(For our own understanding, perhaps the best thing we can do is to recall Freud's own words about mother/son relations—"A mother is only brought unlimited satisfaction by her relation to a son; that is altogether the most perfect, the most free from ambivalence of all human relationships"—and judge his work in the light of those words.)

Mistakenly—and unfortunately—we have looked at the mother/son relationship in terms of the mating of the mother and son, rather than the denunciation and slaying of the mother by the son. That's why Oedipus, not Orestes, has become a household word. Interestingly, Oedipus' murder of his father, though discussed by Freud, was not so much emphasized by him, and has been nearly overlooked in the popularization of this story. So the violent power struggle between fathers and sons is hidden, while the supposedly sexual relation between mothers and sons becomes common knowledge. This emphasis has led to a waste of time and energy in our attempts to understand the mother/son relationship—and interaction between males and females in general.*

Oedipus is the wrong symbol for the son in relation to his mother, because sexual intercourse and/or marriage is not at the center of the mother/son relation. (And because Oedipus' sexual relations with his mother were ignorant—in the course of their liaison, they did not know that they were mother and son.) Moreover, Oedipus' crime is that he killed his father, an unforgivable, though common enough, act in patriarchy—as is the killing of sons by fathers.[48] Orestes is an appropriate symbol because he stands for both the sons' alliance with the father (and the father's power) and the sons' blame and destruction of the mother (and her power).

---

* Muriel Rukeyser, the poet, understanding this error of emphasis, has written "Myth": Long afterward, Oedipus, old and blinded, walked the roads. He smelled a familiar smell. It was the Sphinx. Oedipus said, "I want to ask one question. Why didn't I recognize my mother?" "You gave the wrong answer," said the Sphinx. "But that was what made everything possible," said Oedipus. "No," she said. "When I asked, What walks on four legs in the morning, two at noon, and three in the evening, you answered, Man. You didn't say anything about woman." "When you say Man," said Oedipus, "you include women too. Everyone knows that." She said, "That's what you think."[47]

Both of these young lords suffered grief and terror, but Oedipus, though he was ultimately allowed to die in peace, remained unsuccessful in the changeover to patriarchy. He was honored by the new order in the person of Theseus, *because he made the effort to destroy the matriarchy,* even though he failed. Orestes, by choosing the male line at that time in history when it was the winning side, was triumphant.

Myths are not exact replications of life on earth: Women have had to create systems of taboo to avoid murder, cannibalism, and sex among blood kin, while goddesses mated with and killed their sons, and sons later raped and killed their mothers. Orestes' act is not performed by every mother's son in patriarchy, but his attitudes of fear, blame, and hatred of women are the underpinnings of male supremacy.

Now the old myths did not die, and did not fade away because common knowledge came to absorb Freudian theory. Pushed back into the mother earth with their own roots, the classic tales emerge in this culture in books and stories for young people. The struggle to overthrow or undermine the mother's power and position, the son's fear, hatred, or ignorance of his father, and the "battle of the sexes" are all present there. The action is never so obvious as in the oldest myths, and the stories often carry the weight of more recent attitudes about women, laid down over older forms of patriarchy. Violent battles between fathers and sons are often denied, and the mother/son relationship is sometimes twisted or treated superficially and romantically. Nonetheless, the old themes are basic; the three figures—mother, son, father—appear as their history dictates.

Tom Sawyer, who has no father, and Huckleberry Finn, briefly burdened with his evil Pap, are raised by aunts and widows, whole platoons of mothers—women young and old—who teach, as well as raise, them. But these women are trivialized, their ministrations mocked or supplanted by male authority, and we finish Twain's books with no sense of a strong maternal presence. The dozens of boys mothered by Jo March in *Little Men* and *Jo's Boys* are neglected children or orphans who receive hugs and sweetness and caring advice from her, but "manly" discipline, academics, and vocational instructions from her husband. Jo is strong and smart, but she always gives herself away, denying her power, preferring boys to girls, and forcing herself and the little girls under her care into the constraint of women's roles.

Vexatious little Roo is hilarious, never suffering in his lack of a father. Kanga is mother enough to scold Owl, bathe Piglet, and reprimand Tigger—for she is the only female character in A. A. Milne's Pooh books, and she *only* mothers; she does and thinks of nothing else. Though Peter Rabbit suffers for his transgression, none of his suffering could be linked to his lack of a father. His mother, in her self-sufficiency and competence, comes close to being an admirable female figure, but the focus of the story and illustrations cannot help supporting sexist stereotypes—with Peter in his little blue coat, and his goody-goody sisters in their rose-pink capes.

Peter Pan and his troop of lost boys are obsessed with mothers, but never give any consideration to the use or need for a father. Peter is a chip off the old Greek block, both in his unconscious assumption of the father role and his vision of the mother: Wendy is to be a slave to the needs of Peter and the lost boys. Mowgli's father is virtually nonexistent, and Father Wolf is insignificant, but Mother Wolf—Raksha, the Demon—and the village woman Messua play the roles of nurturer and cherisher in Kipling's *Jungle Book*. Paternal education is covered by Akela, a wolf; Baghoora, a panther; Baloo, a bear; and Kaa, a python. Mowgli respects the Mother, but spends his boy-life in the company of males. In fact, Kipling tells us that but for a sexual desire for women, Mowgli would remain among nonhuman males all his life.

In the folk tale *Anders and the Cap His Mother Made,* bold young Anders is quite fatherless. His loving mother knitted him the cap that stirred envy and desire in everyone he met. Anders' story has recently been redone, and lightened up considerably, but older versions portray the boy with absolute allegiance to his mother; for her, he rejects the ultimate gift of patriarchy: the king's crown. The Chinese boy Aladdin is left fatherless before his story begins, and that is the key to his adventures and riches. His mother functions only as a servant, but he rewards her with wealth and comfort when he becomes a prince. In this tale from the *Arabian Nights,* the role of the mother is a direct descendant of times gone by, when mothers did do the bargaining and arranging for their sons, but at their own will, not at the boy's bidding. And the evil African magician, Aladdin's false uncle, is the substitute for his own father, who, in much earlier days, would have been his enemy.

And all the Prince Charmings, Prince Darlings, and third youngest sons of penniless farmers who ignore and abuse them—these youths manage to find, rescue, riddle, and wed princesses on the advice of their mothers, grandmothers, godmothers, and assorted witches, fairies, and crones, who give the boys food, advice, and courage—and then disappear. In fairytales, which are descendants of the most ancient mythology, fathers are nonexistent or inconsequential or play their old role of villain. All the youthful kings-to-be are *sons,* making their way through a world of magic mothers and maidens.

But one classic children's story portrays openly and unashamedly the pattern of the twentieth-century patriarchal nuclear family and the masculine ethic which young boys learn from grown men: *Bambi.* I read *Bambi,* dimly recalling the movie as the story of a male child and his mother. Written by Felix Salten, translated from the German by Whittaker Chambers, *Bambi* was made popular in a feature-length cartoon by Walt Disney. Though Disney's film is ideologically fuzzy, the original text is a complete primer for the masculinity list.

In *Bambi,* I found a description of an idealized patriarchal father/son relationship so deliberately done that it couldn't have been more clear if Salten had been writing directly about people, rather than deer. This is because he freely applied his analysis of human family and sexual relations to the deer in his story. Perhaps his candor also is a result of the fact that in Germany, in 1929, it was not necessary to obscure the reality of patriarchy.

Bambi's relationship with his mother is sensual; she nurtures him, nourishes him, warms and comforts him with her body. Her smell and the feel of her body are his world. As he grows, her judgment and power are absolute—until he discovers "the fathers." At the sight of them, with their "gleaming antlers . . . stately and beautiful," Bambi is "overcome . . . entranced and silent." Two stags pass by, "honoring no one with so much as a glance." Asked to identify them, a doe says, "solemnly, 'Those were your fathers.'" Though the word is not defined, the fawns understand. After a long silence, Bambi asked his mother, "'Didn't they see us?' His mother understood what he meant and replied, 'Of course, they saw all of us.' . . . 'Why didn't they stay with us?' 'They don't ever stay with us,' his mother answered, 'only at times.' Bambi continued, 'But why didn't they speak to us?' His mother said, 'They don't speak to us now; only at times. We have to wait till they come to us. And we have to wait for them to speak to us. They do it whenever they like.' With a troubled heart, Bambi asked, 'Will my father speak to me?'

" 'Of course he will,' his mother promised. 'When you're grown up he'll speak to you, and you'll have to stay with him sometimes.' " Bambi's "whole mind . . . filled with his father's appearance. 'How handsome he is!' he thought over and over again. 'How handsome he is!' As though his mother could read his thoughts, she said, 'If you live, my son, if you are cunning and don't run into danger, you'll be as strong and handsome as your father is sometime, and you'll have antlers like his, too.' Bambi breathed deeply. His heart swelled with joy and expectancy."[49]

Bambi remains enthralled by the very sight of his father—and "completely dominated by his masterful voice." He wants praise and approval from the older stag, but in his presence, under his criticism, "He was obedient and felt terribly ashamed. . . ."[50] Only in extreme danger do Bambi and his father come together; Bambi is wounded by a hunter, and the old stag comes to him, helping him escape to live to inherit his father's title as Prince of the Forest. Bambi is struck, even in his pain and fear, by the unusual tenderness in the stag's voice, but still cannot rise to follow him. "Then the old stag said hurriedly and anxiously, "Get up! You must get away, my son.' My son! The words seemed to have escaped him. In a flash Bambi was on his feet."[51] Danger and desperation bring them together; Bambi's wound elicits his father's concern, and their mutual victimization and fear create the bond between father and son.

When that moment is past, they continue to have almost no relationship but the tutorial: Bambi is, on rare occasions, taught survival skills by his father. The implied reason for their estrangement is that the rigor of life in the wild keeps them apart. But the old stag does manage, just before he dies, to convey tersely to Bambi the whole of patriarchal hierarchy, making sure he understands that even as the hunters (male humans referred to in capitalized pronouns) deal out death to the forest dwellers, "There is Another who is over us all, over us and over Him." With this passing of the spiritual baton, the old stag leaves Bambi. As he turns away from the younger male, he says, "Good-bye, my son. I loved you dearly."[52] Evidence of that love has been less than sparse, but Bambi is gratified, even satisfied, by this lip service to their almost nonexistent relationship.

When Bambi was young, his mother's world was all the world; the glade in which she bore him, in which they slept and sheltered, was his home. Once he learned of the fathers, he moved toward their domain; the power and freedom of an adult male became his life's goal. His relationship with his father, intimating bondage and discipline as well as sadomasochism, is reminiscent of the relations between fathers and sons in early patriarchal myths and legends. Bambi seeks his father, desiring approval, acceptance, and intimacy, and learns to prove himself in masculine terms: he becomes silent, apparently emotionless, powerful, dominant, and solitary.

Having followed all the rules, he is rewarded as his mother said he'd be—with both the inheritance of his father's position and the words of love he has craved. Though most men live and die waiting to hear those words, and would thrill to hear them, they seem but slight recompense for years of faithful unrequited love, and negligible compared to the affection and comfort they got from their mothers. Yet Bambi cherishes those words; Bambi takes his father's words of love to *be* love.

The father/son relationship as it is lived by most men is rarely the poignant romance Salten describes—though it often contains the implied elements of bondage, discipline, and sadomasochism. Ironically, the romance remains the ideal—but even this ideal falls far short of deep and lasting human intercourse, depending as it does on (rare) symbolic behavior instead of actual interchange, and on the expectations and goals of the list. In this way, the father/son relationship is much like most relations between women and men—based upon illusions of romance and mass-market images of idealized femininity and masculinity, containing elements of sadistic and masochistic behavior, and, most often, falling short of a true exchange of spirit, mind, or body.

6

Women and Men

> Suppose there is no difference between them except the
> power he wields over her. And suppose that in an in-
> stant of feeling himself like her, he lets this power go,
> then would he not become her, in his own body even.
> And some part of him seemed to know what it would be
> to be her in his body, and how he came to know this he
> does not choose to remember. And he went no further
> that way in his thoughts because space closed in on him
> and slowly he had to push it back to give himself room
> to breathe. He had to push space as far as it could go, to
> the outer limits of the universe.
>
> —Susan Griffin[1]

The original mother/son relationship, which serves as the prototype
of relations between males and females, exists between an adult
woman and a boy or a very young man. What is the mother/son
relationship like, how does it work, when the son is full grown?
Myths, legends, and fairytales are little help here: most son-gods did
not live past the bloom of youth. Attis, Adonis, Tammuz—all died
young. As the patriarchy arose, mythical sons began to leave their
mothers at the age when they had previously been wont to die. They
sought their fathers, killing or dying in the encounter. They did not
stay with their mothers, and so do not provide us with models of
men as mothers' sons. Moreover, the mothers of mythology—
Tiamat, Hina, and Eve—were deposed. When Clytemnestra was
killed, the Furies became Benevolent Ones; they became the good
and obedient mothers of male culture, domestic and supportive, content to be left behind by their children, sitting beside the mild
hearthfire that was once their blazing volcano.

In myths and fairytales, young men, especially when faced with
difficult tasks or on dangerous quests, do return to their mothers for

advice and assistance, for the answers to riddles and magic secrets. In legend, the mothers remain a primary source and connection to the life force—though they appear as witches, fairies, sorceresses, seers, or symbolic elemental forces. The world's young gods and heroes turn to these mothers and grandmothers, to the ancient woman who holds up the sky, the queen of the mice and queen of the cats, to the sibyl of the cave and the priestess at Delphi, to White Buffalo Woman and Spider Old Woman. But these sons have become visitors and beggars; they rarely remain close to the mothers.

Judaeo-Christian tradition follows this pattern. After giving birth to their sons, most old testament mothers have little to do with them, and the new testament features a son whose mother comes back into his life only at his death. Jesus, in that old pattern, dies young, a father sacrifice at thirty-three. This is of course the western heritage; in other places, mothers and sons retain a stronger bond. In traditional China, for instance, a mother cherishes her adult sons, for they will live with her, care for her, honor her in her old age, and supply her with daughters-in-law who will function as her servants or slaves. This is an example of the way in which men insist upon a separation of *mothers* from *women*. Chinese society has institutionally degraded women for centuries—but has held mothers of sons to be estimable, and the mother/son relationship to be of great importance.

Similar distinctions can be discerned in tribal West Africa: "Traditionally, the only serious love relationship of the African man's life is that with his mother . . . but there is . . . with most West African tribes, a ritual spurning of the female virtues of peace and gentleness. . . . When a young Ibibio man joins the society of adult males he becomes an apprentice member of a politico-religious underground movement, one of whose chief functions is the subjugation of women both in the home and in society."[2]

The distinction between *mother* and *woman* is present in this culture, though it is not so clearly defined, nor presumed universal. It is not unusual to find, in the United States, that even a man with no respect for women will treat his mother better than the rest, and will claim for her the distinction of being "special," different from other women, even different from other mothers. A contemporary example is Andy Warhol, both as artist and as cultural phenomenon. His reputed exploitation of women drove the feminist/anarchist Valerie Solanas to attempt to assassinate him. But Warhol recently filled a whole room at the Whitney Museum with portraits of his mother.[3]

We have no tradition, no ritual, no cultural sense of what should be happening between mothers and sons when sons are men, not boys. Instead, we have the sense that there should be *no* relationship; a youth should leave his mother—even "kill" her—and strive to become a man under the tutelage of the fathers. This culture has devised a derisive nickname to mock sons who remain physically and emotionally close to their mothers. They are "mamas' boys"—scorned not only for being close to their mothers but for the suspicion of homosexuality which automatically follows.

A similar situation exists between fathers and daughters. We daughters, no longer little girls, are at a loss to relate to our fathers. We no longer require, if we ever did, their protection and support; their expressions of affection often become an embarrassment or a burden. Beyond the general sense that it would be good for adults of both sexes to respect and feel affection for their parents, there is no expectation that, once grown, sons and daughters will relate to their parents in any but semiformal ways, on any but special occasions. We don't expect to be friends to our parents, to spend time with them, to *know* them. There is some notion that same-sex pairs will have superficial bonds; i.e., fathers and sons will watch football games together after Thanksgiving and New Year's Day dinners, while mothers and daughters wash the dishes, exchanging recipes and gossip.

In fact, the sexes have a rather difficult time relating altogether. We live in a culture which separates boys from girls, fostering mutual ignorance and teaching contempt, fear, and disdain for each other, and then—rather insanely, encouraging and expecting them to mate, marry, and spend decades living together. By the time we've grown up, having been conditioned twenty years and more, women and men have little in common and much cause for discontent with each other. It is with this in mind that we must examine the relationships between mothers and adult sons, and relations among women and men in the society at large.

The evolution of the mythical mother/son relationship is reproduced in the personal history of individual mother/son pairs in this culture. Through pregnancy, infancy, and very early childhood, the mother is indeed the Great Mother. She has given life, and she gives sustenance; she nurses and feeds her baby boy. She appears to the boy as lawgiver; her existence is the external center of his world. Her size and apparent capacities contrast with his weakness and ignorance. But as he grows, he learns that his mother's personal and political powers are limited, and that his have only begun to develop, like his body. He grows rebellious—as did the young god —more and more so as he learns that she is a person of little value and less power in the world. She accepts his growing disdain as "typical" and therefore "normal," even though it hurts her deeply. Perhaps he retains affection for her, and gratitude for her nurturance, for the sacrifice and struggles she endured to raise him. Perhaps not.

As he seeks satisfaction in the company of the fathers, he is disappointed; his father does not give him what he wants. His mother continues to take pleasure in him, but sees that he takes none in her. Disappointed by his father, he tries to satisfy himself by taking up the position and supposed advantage of a grown man. He moves to exchange his status as a son for that of a father. He learns that to consummate the transformation, to become a man, he must blame his mother for his fears and needs, deny his former dependence on her, and sever any bonds that remain between them. She learns that her continuing love for him is inappropriate and foolish. She realizes that the role, if any, that she plays in his life is that of an encumbrance, a burden, a problem. She understands that they no longer share love or knowledge. They both come to know that their relationship has been altered to a point just short of extinction. Their interactions—physical, spiritual, or intellectual—are perfunctory and brief. As a man, the son scorns his mother—and all women, who are identified with her in his mind. Thus, each mother and son recapitulate the history of the mother/son relationship.

Boys first learn what women are from their mothers; their earliest sensation, comprehension, and comfort come from a woman's body. This intimate experience of their mothers creates a conflict with what men and male culture later teach them about women. The extent of that conflict varies by the degree to which each son's mother has accepted her assigned role as a woman. If a boy's mother has been passive, submissive, weak, and reactive, he will have little trouble accepting the idea that "woman" is all of those things. But to the extent that his mother has rejected that role and has—to the boy's knowledge and *in his sight*—been active, self-affirming, strong, and an initiator, he will have to make serious adjustments in his acceptance of the roles/rules. He may come to consider his mother an exception—better than most women. A great number of men do this. Or he might realize that women need not be what male culture decrees; fewer men come to that conclusion.

One reason few men come to the latter realization is that, far from being influenced solely by their mothers in even the earliest years, they take in the sense of the fathers' judgments as they grow. From their fathers, boys often get a two-faced picture of their mothers. While fathers may tell boys to "listen to your mother, respect her, and help her out," they also, in their treatment of their wives and lovers, demonstrate disrespect, contempt, disdain, resentment, and ridicule. Even when this duplicity is unconscious in fathers, it is understood and absorbed by sons.

The influence of fathers' view and treatment of mothers is very strong, despite many fathers' frequent absence and minimal attention to their children. Both girls and boys generally understand that they are to take their fathers' opinions as the better informed and more authoritative of the two parents, and to desire a relationship with him that supersedes the maternal bond. Each daughter is supposed, in adulthood, to mate and live with a man—a husband-father—who will protect and support her. Each son is supposed to grow into and become a father himself. So both sexes are raised up to take Father as the symbolic center of family life. The father is acknowledged as primary, despite the obviously greater importance of the mother.

Since most men have a jaundiced view of most women,[4] *including their wives,* the general cultural definition that comes down to sons and daughters is negative, even when cloaked in "humor." Boys and girls learn, often directly from their fathers, that women are weak, silly, ignorant, incompetent, soft, dishonest, lazy, devious, etc. It is interesting to see that many men try to reject application of this definition to their mothers, while accepting it for women or mothers in general. In fact, when I asked them if their mothers were "typical mothers," many men said no and went on to explain how, in this or that way, their mothers were better than, less deserving of blame than, "typical mothers."

When asked to describe their parents as a couple, separate from their roles as mother and father, most of the men whose parents had lived together described troubled relationships. Whether or not the sons were themselves critical of this situation, or noticed that their mothers suffered from lack of power in the dynamics of the couple, their stories reveal mismatched, uncomfortable, dishonest, frustrating, and inequitable alliances. Yes, there were some stories which did not, and there were some sons who seemed to see nothing wrong in the situations thus described. But most took a dim view of a dim scenario.

My parents' relationship was a complete farce. By the time my smallest sister came on the scene they were more or less deliberately shamming a happy relationship, so the kids growing up could enjoy all the benefits of a "happy family." After we got out of school they didn't have to play the game anymore. They separated three years ago. They were totally unsuitable for each other. I never saw my parents touch or kiss each other except when my dad came back from a business trip and my mother picked him up at the airport. My father is an incredible disciplinarian; my mother is not. They didn't have the same friends. My mother always felt inferior to my father; she had never prepared herself to do anything but have babies, so she felt very insecure with him. If she would have to argue with my father, she knew she wasn't going to win.

These men see the unequal power balance in the marriage.

My parents were hardly ever affectionate in front of me and my brother, not particularly emotional. My mother did the cooking, took care of the house; my father often worked six days a week, which I think put a great stress upon the relationship at certain periods. I think there were some times where my parents had a lot of trouble in the marriage. My father still has the expectation that she will take care of all those things, the groceries and so forth, though they both work and are both over seventy. He's also kept from her all the financial business; that was not what she was supposed to know. To a certain extent, he doesn't respect her mind. Maybe he does a little more today, but basically no, not really. He is forced to see it now, but he's so uncomfortable with it he needs to put her down; he can't acknowledge that she's competent. I do think they like each other, yes. But there's still *never* any touching, *never* any kissing.

They aren't overly affectionate. Probably they show less physical affection than the average married couple. When my father comes home from work, it's "required" that they kiss each other once. In fact, if that kiss doesn't happen—if it doesn't take place because my mother's busy or something, or just forgets—that can be grounds for hassling or even argument. And if my father's unhappy about something else, or upset, and in addition to that my mother forgets to kiss him, it can really be bad. [Laughs.] The main thing is that while my father doesn't *beat* my mother, he's not physically brutal to her, she is, on the whole, pretty subservient in just every little thing you can think of that goes on around the house: the preparation of meals, cleaning up, all those sorts of things. My mother's just very subservient to my father.

As a couple they lived more or less separate lives. They're not displeased or unhappy with each other; nor are they pleased. They simply accept their differences. My mother likes to go to shows and plays, and my father does not. He likes to go to the race track. Other than that, he doesn't like to go to anything—and he's got a headache. As a result, they just live together. She has her room; he has his room. They sit and watch television, and they go to sleep. He wakes up in the morning before she does, goes to work, comes home before she does. She wakes up when he's gone, comes home long after he does. Then dinner, and the TV. They're together, but it's not the type of relationship I'd want.

He used to be on the road a lot working, leaving my mom alone at home. She was miserable. Later, she worked in her parents' store, and they were more like partners then, both working. But recently he went out and bought another store, and it isn't doing well at all, and he never even told my mom that he was doing it, she had no say in the matter at all. That's the way my dad does it. He just kind of does something and then says, oh, you'll have to deal with this now. He pulls nasty things. No, they don't touch each other, except maybe a kind of mechanical touching. She was real unhappy in this one period, and she went to a psychologist. That really bothered him; he felt like he was losing his wife to a stranger. And that she was dredging up things that were not good. He says, what good does it do you to figure out that your dad didn't do this or that, and that's why you're angry today?

These next three men see their mothers' emotional dependence on their fathers without understanding its roots.

My father has always put more stock in what his parents, especially his mother, have told him, than he ever put in what my mother says. Even in his will, everything goes to his parents. And I don't know what it is, but she just cannot seem to pull herself together to strike out on her own. We've talked about it, she and I—do you know, she says that if she were to leave, she wouldn't even hold out for her share! She says she wouldn't take anything. And that just slays me. She's got a job; she certainly could have another man—there've been men just wanting to take her away from it all—but she won't go. He treats her no better than he treated any of us children—and I've told you how miserable *that's* been—but she stays. It can only be an incredible insecurity.

I think my mother was attracted to him in the early years, and lost that attraction from his bad temperament and his inability to love. My father was not loving, not a warm, kind man. He never took my mother out to dinner—or even came up with a kind word; he was incapable of it, insensitive to it, and stayed that way up to my mother's death. He was threatened by, and jealous of, my mother's love for her children. He felt she didn't appreciate him. She felt he didn't love her. They had a typical European relationship; he was dominant, the woman was submissive. Not openly loving or sensitive or understanding. Maybe my mother was guilty of giving too much to her children, but she didn't know. It was what she had learned from her own mother. She was a *devoted* mother. Some ten years ago, we all got together and got an attorney, and tried to help my mother divorce him. He was really quite shocked by it. He believed that he could achieve any goals by bulldozing.

She told me this story about when she came home with Joe, who's my oldest brother. She came home to her apartment with this newborn baby, and she walked in the door, and there was nothing in the apartment. He had sold all the furniture. All the jewelry, including the wedding ring, to pay off gambling debts. She decided to leave him, so she went home to her parents. Remember, this was 1938. She went home to her parents with the baby, and they told her that they could keep her for a little while but they didn't have enough for themselves so she couldn't stay long; she'd have to leave. The only other thing she knew that was available was charity. She is a person who doesn't believe in welfare, in taking stuff from the state. Also, she was not a worldly woman, didn't know about child-welfare organizations or things like that. So she felt like she had no resort but to go back to my father. And she did. She went back and stayed with him ever since. She's told me that she wishes he would leave. She won't leave again; I don't know why. I remember her telling us all, "Boys, don't send anniversary cards to us, there's nothing to celebrate. I'm married to this man, but there's no reason to celebrate." My father always told her she was dumb, because she couldn't read English. He used to call her—there's this Jewish word for being dumb—he used to call her that constantly. One of the things he used to say to us, his sons, was that if we didn't straighten up we'd be like my mother, dumb. Years later I found out that she had somehow found the time to go to school to learn to read. And when he's not in the house, she reads, but not when he's there; she can't do it if he's around.

And here are three men whose statements demonstrate that even though their parents were emotionally dependent on each other, their marriage was not a true partnership.

Everybody on the outside thought that my parents were the ideal couple, but I don't think my father spent enough time with my mother. He used to play golf a lot with his cronies—golf all day, and cards all night. And the other time, he'd be working. Though he was monetarily fair with her. He always gave her a new car, which I guess is a good superficial thing, a replacement. But his real time was spent—let's say 70 percent was in the business and another 20 percent was playing golf. So maybe 10 percent was for the rest, you know. But my mother didn't seem to mind. She never complained. Apparently *she* thought it was enough. Maybe my mother wouldn't have liked all that attention. No, they didn't really talk to each other, but then, they rarely argued. She pretty well went along with my dad's decisions. Generally speaking, my dad did pretty well financially, so whatever decision he made, she went along with. She generally went along with whatever he said.

There was very little open display of physical attraction and loving between the two of them in front of us, and particularly anything that had a sexual connotation to it was not apparent. But they're both attractive and they're both kind of normal people, so I can only conclude that they must have had a fairly satisfying sex life. From as early as I can remember, they had separate beds. Sometime in the last five years or so, he's told me something to the effect that what made life worth living for him was living with her. Or that that was the main thing he liked—that gave him joy in life. If I had to think about it, I know damn well that she'd do better than he would without her. She wouldn't be any less wiped out if he died, she's just more able to cope with reality. He might rise to the occasion but he'd have to do a lot of rising based on the kind of life he's used to, and the kind of—excuse the expression—*service* he gets out of her. I don't think he respects her intellectually. He would want to bring her everything that he could muster about his feelings, his experiences—and tell her, like she was his mother. But *not* bring her all the nuances of intellectual problems he encountered in his work, for example. Not expect her to be able to give and take with him about whatever those problems are and help him to find solutions to them. He's not thinking that she carries in her head an understanding of the stuff he dealt with; why should she? On the other hand, what else would there be for her when she's shoved into this role?

It's an odd thing, really. In a perfect world, she would have gone into business and he'd have stayed home. He's a gentle man, a quiet man. He's very shy. She's a dynamo, a fighter. And she's stuck with this ladies' luncheon/hospital volunteer life. So they argued a lot. She wants to be someone. She wants to gain respect; she wants to make herself felt. When they fight, they don't have real arguments, because her need is to assert herself in some way. The arguments aren't about what they're ostensibly about, and that makes them very hard to deal with. But, on the whole, they're very devoted; they've had a good marriage. She would be lost without him and he would especially be lost without her. He thinks of her as a disturber of the peace and there are times when he would really prefer more peace.

Where daughters frequently condemn their mothers, often with no consideration of motive, personal history, or political analysis, many sons examine both motives and history, and take into account their mothers' relatively powerless position in the family and in society.

My mother made lots of mistakes in raising us. But in general, I think she loved us and had our welfare in mind, so the mistakes don't matter that much; the overall intent was what mattered—and we sensed that as kids. My mother had been a farm kid, and she's a very strong person physically. Because she's always had to rely on herself, she has a hard time asking anybody for any kind of help. I mean, I can see how she made the kinds of mistakes she did, considering who she is.

My mother's family was high-class. She was raised to be pampered; she *was* pampered. She never had to do much work. She wasn't very strong physically; she was very, very thin and slight and delicate-looking. She did have a certain inner sense that was strong enough, but the way she was raised could never have prepared her to have five children, to be married, to deal with the kinds of problems we had to deal with in our family. She always seemed not to fit in. She read constantly, and she played the piano a lot. That was her release.

Sons also seem to be more sympathetic than daughters to the fact that so many of their mothers, oppressed as women, led desperate, unsatisfied lives. Though few of the men I interviewed could be said to actively support the women's liberation movement or to be antisexist men, they often expressed an analysis that could lead—if they chose to follow—to a feminist analysis. When these men were asked if they considered their mothers to have led satisfying lives, particularly during the fifteen to twenty years of raising their sons, *80 percent* of the interview group said no. Each of the mothers described below can stand for a group of thousands, hundreds of thousands, of women.

I hardly ever thought my mother was satisfied. Well, I was living there and I saw all this torment going on that my father put her and me through. Even though I was a kid of five, I had the sense of who was right and who was wrong and what was going on. Now I can understand the psychology of his position, but it was still wrong. He wouldn't support us, really, and they had no friends, and they never went out—you know, he spent years at a time in the house, and even when his own relatives came over he was incommunicative. I don't say she made a great show of being dissatisfied, but one could just tell. You don't have to mention it, you just know what's happening.

Absolutely not. She told me. She hated her life. By the end of my father's life, she and my father were just barely tolerating each other. Now that he's dead, she feels that a trick has been played on her—all those years of suffering, and finally she's free to do what she wants—and she doesn't have the physical ability, the health, to do it. I really see her as a tragic figure. She is a truly tragic figure. She has taught me, more than anything else, she has taught me to love and experience life right now, because she never did. She had mountains of clothes and jewelry, and she said, "Well, I'll wait and wear this when I can be who I want to be." As a result of this, her house is filled with things that were being saved—and there's nothing to save them for now.

This man's mother suffered abuse at the hands of father, mother, sister, and husband; her "near"-alcoholism is one result.

My mother's dissatisfaction can be traced all the way back to her childhood; she found very little happiness in her life. She was one of ten children on a farm. There were only two boys in the family. So her father, who was a really evil guy, picked two girls to be boys, to do boys' chores, and my mother was one of them. Her sister, my aunt, though she is married and has kids, is very masculine as a result of this—I mean she could walk into any lesbian bar in Chicago and be overwhelmed by adulation, I am sure. At any rate, my mother was the other picked to be a boy. She drove mule teams, she plowed, she built fences. She's sixty-three and her biceps are still bigger than mine. But even though she did all that work, her parents did not like her. She was no one's favorite. Oh, her life has been so hard. She earned money to go to college to be a teacher. She had to go live with a sister, who treated her like a servant, a maid, and finally kicked her out just before she would have graduated, so my mother couldn't finish school; she had nowhere to live. I'll tell you, I'm glad my mother isn't introspective, because she'd likely be despondent a lot more than she lets herself be—and that's not even counting what happened in the marriage with my father, or the fact that now she's just about an alcoholic! I knew she wasn't satisfied with her life. From the early years my parents always had very loud arguments late at night, and my brother and sister and I would lie in bed and we would hear them screaming and hollering at each other—and it was not something my mother brought on. I think my father had started drinking heavily, that's the thing. And he started abusing me and my mother, and that's what they fought about. They argued about his drinking—I try to remember specific arguments, but I've obviously blocked them. I remember the horrible screaming, but not what they said.

This is a woman who, like so many in this country, has had a breakdown obscured and smoothed over with drugs.

Once, at the lowest point in her menopause, she got the worst possible help. She went to her parish priest. And he told her everything would be all right, and to go home. The worst possible thing—wrong. She did go into the hospital for ten days. I believe the doctor called it acute anxiety. Would that be a term for a nervous breakdown? Anyway, they told her they'd give her some happy pills and she'd be okay. Yes, they gave her very mild drugs, tranquilizers. My mother does take a sedative now, too. And that's because she has developed, about six, seven, maybe eight years ago, the great fear that her throat was closing—while she was falling asleep. She couldn't breathe. So she'd wake up in a panic, gasping and choking. So the family doctor—I talked to him about it—gave her some mild sedatives so she would fall asleep without this choking. If she's still taking the pills or not I don't know. But now she's totally happy with what she's doing. I think she's happy. She's really happy. I think. She's too busy to think about not being happy.

These sons describe the boredom and lack of meaning in the lives of middle-class mothers.

She always felt that she would have liked to see more of my father. There were fights and one of her complaints was that he wasn't around enough. When I got to high school she began to do volunteer work, and did find great satisfaction in that. She's a competent woman. Efficient, terrifically good on details, an amazingly good memory. She probably is an unsatisfied woman. My father's life is one well apart from her; that must be hard for her. She doesn't complain about it but it's apparent between the lines of a lot of what she says. She's very careful, for instance, to tell me how busy she is. It seems to me she wouldn't tell me that unless she wasn't. I mean, she *is* very busy, but she wouldn't insist so much if *she* didn't think she should be doing something else. Or could be doing something else—other than playing golf, going to matinees, bowling, and playing bridge.

She was always slightly unhappy being in Los Angeles; she had had her own life in San Francisco. You know, L.A. in the forties being a slightly sparse kind of scene. While she was very pleased with her children, she was unhappy not to be in San Francisco, working and achieving. She was not into the standard housewife kind of trip. She had what would now be described as rages, but then it was not polite to have rages, so we only spoke of her "headaches." It was her custom to read every night until midnight or two or three in the morning. She never got up in the morning. That was not her thing. She was not the organized housewife. My mother was, in many ways, a very unhappy woman. She drank— not a lot, but at times she was what you would call an alcoholic. She had feelings of guilt about being unable to be happy being a suburban mother. She was in no way suburban, but there we were in the suburbs. And like that.

And here is the heartbreaking desperation of a woman who feels that her life is wrong somehow, but cannot see or say why—or change it. Her vague yearnings and intuitive sense stab through the institutional façade of motherhood.

She explicitly said that she wasn't satisfied, that she wished she had been able to accomplish more, that she wasn't worth anything and so on. I remember asking her, "What would you like to do?" And she would say, "Oh, I don't know; I don't know."

A few men spoke of a changed mother—not the mother who was constrained by institutional motherhood in her son's behalf, not "mother," but simply *herself*, a woman in the world. These men recognize that their mothers were dissatisfied for years, and they speak with pride, pleasure, and relief of the change.

If I think back on it, I probably thought she wasn't totally satisfied. You know, people who are just stuck in this life usually aren't satisfied. But she never said things like Jesus, I wish I wasn't here, or I wish I was doing something else, or that I didn't have any kids around or I wasn't with the old man or something. Sometimes, obviously, that was conveyed by her unhappiness, anger, or anxiety. But she's come to rationalize it to an extent. She accepts the past but she is more satisfied now because my father is more sensitive to where she's coming from. On the other hand, she's remarkable. She went back to school, and went to night school. For eight or nine years after I graduated from college she went to school and she got her degree. She might even have gotten a master's degree; I'm not sure. So now she does some library work, some substitute teaching. And even stuck in that ridiculous urban-school substitution situation, she tries. She goes out there and teaches some pretty progressive stuff. She's really come a long way. Politically, socially—from being a supporter of Eisenhower to supporting the McCarthy/McGovern, antinuclear stuff. When she teaches, she teaches social issues. It takes a lot of courage.

When they moved down to Miami Beach, they moved into what they call the Social Security Section. She found employment. The constant threat my father had over her was money, and she always had to take care of the children. He would always say to her, "I'm not going to give you the money," "If you don't do this, I'm going to take away the money," and a lot of times there wasn't any money. Now she works all the time; she has a source of income that is not dependent on my father but on her own abilities; she seems to have flowered. I find that even in the way she talks; she never would have talked back to him before for fear of all kinds of retribution. Now she'll talk back to him. She seems much more independent, much more secure. She has many friends, many people who admire her and care about her, even men who would like to see her single.

Among the 20 percent who do consider their mothers to have been satisfied, there are several men who simply haven't given the matter much thought, and some who are just unwilling to believe that their mothers really have *suffered* from the constriction and oppression of women's roles. One of these men, who obviously knows something about his mother's situation, said:

She's friendly and personable. She's pretty smart. I'm afraid she's a little wacky of late, but in a way that I associate not so much with getting old but with having been *reduced* under the role of wife, and having therefore had her intellectual capacities stunted, by lack of development, lack of variegation, lack of that which would have resulted in a full development of those capacities in the course of a seventy-year-long life. She has too much energy to be worked out in her small space there, so it overflows. It pushes her into a kind of wackiness. I can't describe it any other way. Like she'll get into an argument and hold a stupid point forever just because she . . . because the important thing that's going on is the contention. It's not common for her to get to do that, to get to exercise those capacities. Those capacities in her are stunted, there's no question about it. Another aspect of it is that she puts a lot of energy into trivialities—for the same reason, I'm sure—'cause the energy's got to go someplace. She's an incredibly energetic person, physically, emotionally, socially, intellectually—and nowhere to put it, really.

But when asked if he considered her to be satisfied with her life, he was still able to say:

For the most part, yes. Because there was no objective basis that I was ever aware of for her to feel dissatisfied. In other words, I would be surprised to hear of any kind of lost hopes, in terms of a life of her own, that she ever had, or any kind of ambitions or wishes that she ever had to be something other than a wife and mother.

He can say this; he can see no objective basis for dissatisfaction because he refuses to really *take in* the certain knowledge expressed by longing and unspoken desire—"I don't know; I don't know!"

Sons apparently do know the truth of their mothers' lives—but choose not to hold that truth in their consciousness, or recognize its meaning. Here are all these men who can see, can even describe and explain, grief in the lives of women. Are they "typical" men? Are they like "most men"?[5] Can we assume that most men appreciate the struggle in their mothers' lives? We already understand several elements in their cultural position that keep them from acting on this information, or even from making an analysis that can lead to action, that can lead to their thinking and doing differently in the world and in their relations with women.

Men actively resist acknowledging the oppression of their mothers. The basic reason for this might well be the false, inflated, and idealized definition of motherhood in patriarchy. On top of that, many men separate their mothers from women as a group, and even from mothers as a group. This allows them to refuse to transfer to other women any affection, sympathy, or understanding that has grown up in their relations with their mothers. Instead, the transfer goes the other way, given prevailing antiwoman attitudes; men learn to ignore and devalue their mothers as they become more distant from women.

Men learn to become self-absorbed *as men,* and to seek affirmation and confirmation from male peers, who are defined by the values of the masculinity list. All of these values ultimately exclude and deny the possibility of a man's acting out of love and compassion for his mother, or extending good feelings to other women.

Many men say that they are attracted to women like their mothers, that they marry women who remind them of their mothers. But other men say that their female friends, lovers, and wives are nothing like their mothers. Now, we cannot know if these women do or do not actually share distinctive traits with the mothers of their spouses and lovers. But we know that most men, including gay men, do marry, and most men seek women who will maintain for them a domestic arrangement that includes children, security, and familiarity—in keeping with the patriarchal ideal of motherhood and family, if not precisely with the actual experience of any specific man's childhood. The fact that most married men seem to spend less time at home than elsewhere, or even that most married men have extramarital sex,[6] does not deny the fact that they feel the need for "the comforts of home," and that these comforts are symbolized by —are in fact *provided* by—a woman, a mother.[7]

One of the strongest ironies in most men's lives is the fact that they need and desire a woman to make them comfortable, but at the same time feel contempt, anger, and resentment for women—even perhaps for the very women for whom they feel attraction or friendship. Their need must make them even angrier, though they go to great lengths to deny both the need and the anger. Men learn to need women, but they resent the need because they also learn to believe women are unworthy. Men live in this conflict from boyhood, when they learn from the parental imbalance of power to disdain their mothers—at the same time that they get love, comfort, and approval from those mothers.

Young boys learn never to relate to girls as people; instead they ostracize or victimize girls. But men seek out women as nurturers and confidantes, and to do this they have to get past at least part of what they learned and practiced as children. Many men do learn to relate intimately to women, but still ostracize or victimize us. Further, they don't relinquish power, often holding on to ugly, stupid attitudes about women.

The medium for this unlikely transition is most often love; romance. Love and romance, spiced with sex, are at the core of relationships between women and men in this culture; expectations and disappointments between the sexes are created and fostered by the sexually charged romantic definitions of what their relations may be. Almost all straight men consider the possibility of sexual intercourse to be a factor in any relations they have with women.

The idea may be romance, or just sex, but the reality is emotional and economic dependence or exploitation. In fact, gay sons seek mothering from their male lovers; daughters seek mothering from women friends and lovers—and from males as well, especially from lovers and spouses. Everybody wants motherlove.

The mother/child relationship is where we learn what to want—even if we don't get it. It is the first, and perhaps the most long-lasting, relationship in which there is supposed to be loving—touching and caring, admiration and support. Male culture has created the ideal of selfless and all-giving motherhood; sons feel *entitled;* they feel that such mothering is *owed* them. Since no mother can meet that demand, sons grow up seeking more mothering, or the mothering they didn't get. As children grow, because they learn that love *is* romance, and because heterosexual romance is the mode through which both females and males are supposed to seek emotional gratification and satisfaction, the desire for idealized mothering gets hooked in to, or surrounded by, romantic trappings. Notions of *true love* and *love everlasting* have even been tied to the traditionally economic contract of marriage, causing perhaps the greatest disillusionment of all.

The contradictions resulting from this process are not hidden; the culture displays them. Men may publicly cry for their mothers— "Ohhh, mama" is their insistent moan over the radio waves. Because "men manage to acknowledge their emotional need for women without allowing themselves to feel lacking in any important way,"[8] they are not shamed by such blatant pleading.

Early on, in the first years of mainstream rock 'n' roll, the message from the boys to the girls, was: You're gonna do it; do what I say. And the euphemism *love* never did effectively disguise the covert sexual demand.

> *I'm gonna tell you how it's gonna be:*
> *You're gonna give your love to me.*

While there might have been some hesitation to interpret Buddy Holly and the Crickets in this light when they first sang those lines, there could be none in the listener hearing them from the Rolling Stones. The Stones, who understood those lyrics so well that they recorded them too, generally leave no confusion in their audience. The message of male dominance and female sexual capitulation is basic to their music, which has grown more blatant, more threatening and violent over the past dozen years. A particularly sinister combination—bribery and the threat of abandonment, plus a shot at the woman's mother—was an early theme in "Play with Fire":

> *Your old man took her diamonds and tiaras by the score*
> *Now she gets her kicks in Stepney, not in Knightsbridge any more.*
> *So don't play with me, 'cause you're playin' with fire—*
> *Now you've got some diamonds, and you will have some others*
> *But you better watch your step, girl, or start livin' with your mother.*
> *Don't play with me, 'cause you're playin' with fire—*

Maybe it's because they have said all of this—and worse—that these same musicians and vocalists, and hundreds of others, can also indulge in the pleading lyrics of the "I can't make it without you/ Don't ever leave me/You're everything to me" genre. Though they would never tell a male friend that they felt this way, and might not actually say these words to the women who inspire them, men have no compunction about *singing* their need and dependence. Such songs are the direct line to Mama; whereas mockery and threats are addressed to *girls,* the pleading desperation of "love songs" constitute a prayer to the Great Mother. The same men who assault "girls" can sing sweetly to Mama. Elvis Presley wept—

> *I want you, I need you, I love you*
> *with all my heart . . .*

Bob Dylan begged—

> *I am homeless; come and take me . . .*
> *ooh, will you surround me, so I can know if I am really real?*

and admitted—

> *Without your love I'd be nowhere at all,*
> *I'd be lost if not for you. . . .*

Maybe it is *because* so many of their lyrics, so much of their message, is arrogant and blatantly sexist, directed to women as girls—objects of sexual excitement and "love"—that they can be self-indulgently pathetic in their mother worship.

Much of what our sons learn to think and feel about us, about women, is obviously beyond our control at present, and certainly is different from what we would have them think and feel. But we can exercise influence, and make some of the changes that most of us have neglected in the reticence we've learned as women and the guilt we've accepted as mothers. Not only have most of us mothers of sons unavoidably taken into ourselves, like the polluted air and water of our planet, the poison of woman-hating and mother-blaming, but we have learned, and sometimes taught, the sexist definitions of female and male that the patriarchy has dictated; and we have added to the formidable wall between women and men by fostering in our sons a sense of entitlement—the idea that they are special, that they are deserving of the opportunity male supremacy offers them, and that they have the *right* to greater power than women and children.

My mother did give me this: I'm spoiled. She didn't have much energy at the end of the day, but when she did, I'd get her to give it to me. I'd suck my thumb, and sit in the chair, and she'd come and sit beside me, saying, "What's wrong with you, son?" And I'd say "Nothing"—I'm cool, you know. But that feeling of her coming to me, that's some kind of feeling, almost sweet. You feel like you're sitting there with a pocketful of money. I think that's what spoiled me. It seemed like I always wanted to have my own way. I still expect a little more than I'm actually supposed to have.

What did my mother expect of me when I grew up? Oh, to be president of the United States or something like that. Something very high. She's overly prejudiced in my favor; she'll say, "Oh, you're the smartest, you're the cleverest, and blah, blah, blah." For my sister, she just expected her to get married and have children—and definitely not be president, no. She expected me to be real successful.

I never was able, as a kid, to disappoint her very much. She expected me to be an adult. I always had to have responsibilities, even when I was quite young. Those were her expectations. I was meeting them. I was meeting them for a long time. Then I discovered that when I didn't meet the expectations it never flagged her enthusiasm or her respect. So I never bothered anymore. [Laughs.] I didn't have to.

A lot of the messages that I got from my mother as I was growing up were like this: you're smarter than most, you're smarter than usual, and so on. She wanted me to be a doctor—and a gentleman. She would tell me that I resembled her side of the family more, because in her mind they were higher-class.

Oh, yes, there definitely was a lot of expectation, a strong expectation factor, a strong hope for specialness—she always told me I was special—to be sure, to be primary. She didn't want me to be special at someone else's expense, but that's still in there; it's competitive, being special; that's what it means. She understood that, and so she wanted me to do good, to be special in the quality of service, selflessness. That's the redeeming social value coming in. She's perfectly satisfied that I'm a lawyer, that inchoate yearning to have her kid be special is more or less satisfied.

"One of the wrongs suffered by boys is that of being loved before loving. They receive so early and so freely the affection and devotion of their mothers, sisters, and their teachers that they do not learn to love; and so, when they grow up and become lovers and husbands, they avenge themselves upon their wives and sweethearts. Never having had to love, they cannot; they don't know how."[9]

Do not mistake my meaning; I am far from blaming the victim here. It is simply that we can go nowhere different from where we have been if we, in ourselves, remain the same. Women cannot wait until men decide to make changes that they have refused to make for five thousand years. It is we who will change the definition of woman, change the meaning of motherhood, so that Alix Dobkin's words will no longer be true:

> Isn't it just like a woman
> to raise a little boy
> and to train him for the privileges
> she does not enjoy
> when everything is due to him—
> her duty is endless mothering
> It's depressing, but it's just like a woman.

What is the motive of mothers who raise their sons to believe that they are special? That it is somehow significant—"terribly significant," one mother said—to be raising these boys? Is it that the mother's importance is defined by her raising of the son? And is this a replacement for the mother's raising herself—putting herself forward in the world? It seems probable that the primary motive here has been to make our own power and influence felt, thinking, like the royal mothers in chapter two that in rearing the crown prince we touch the crown. But we shouldn't be living on the interest of emotional investments in our sons. Women need to live out of ourselves. We wrong ourselves and our children if we subordinate our lives to theirs.

This motive is no longer acceptable—if ever it was. We can see now that such an upbringing, to whatever degree, allows men to be blind to their use and abuse of us, and to their own bankruptcy of compassion. If we foster feelings of entitlement in our sons, we will further their rapacious use of the earth and rapid despoiling of the cosmos; and we will accept their definition of women as masochistic —desiring and needing to be subjugated, to be used, to be abused.

Mothers resent and fear the current acceptance and popularization of male violence against women. Men—sons of mothers—have invented and practiced suttee, foot binding, and female genital mutilation,[10] instigated and carried out the "official" torture, enslavement, and murder of women,[11] and, simultaneously, have created and idealized an image of perfect motherhood[12]—in their refusal to recognize both the true meaning of these actions and the fact that their mothers are women.

Just as depression is generally anger turned inward, so anger is often fear turned outward. All offense is really defense. Men in sophisticated contemporary patriarchy suffer great fear and anger—which today may be many times removed from primal male envy and awe at the strength and power of women. Woman-hating and violence against women have been ritualized and institutionalized to the point at which pornography, prostitution, wife battery, incest and rape are commonplace and acceptable—though spoken of as rare and shameful. All of these crimes against women come under legal jurisdiction, but the law—as designed and delivered by men—traditionally has provided little or no assistance to women, as in the case of battered wives,[13] or it has actively abused women, as in the case of prostitutes.[14]

The great anger of men in contemporary patriarchy is rarely directly connected—as it was for men many centuries ago—to a conscious fear and envy of women. Many men would deny that they envy women anything, and most would never admit to fearing us. Their violence against us today has multiple sources. Classically, men have viewed with awe women's ability to be pregnant, to give birth, and to nurse infants from the milk of our breasts. But this innocent awe festered into envy and then jealousy, and was transformed into fear, through years of growing male political power, before it emerged into woman-hating.

In their fear, men everywhere told each other stories of the *vagina dentata* (myths of women whose vaginas contained teeth or fangs[15] which cut off the penises of all the men who tried to enter) or the "succubi" (sexually insatiable female demons who drained the soul or essence of men by copulating with them until they collapsed and died). Often, as in nineteenth- and early-twentieth-century U.S. medical practice and among African tribes practicing clitoridectomy, the clitoris was identified as the "tooth"—no doubt because it is the source of women's sexual pleasure and sexual power. Removal of the clitoris in surgery, which renders a woman all but incapable of sexual pleasure and unable to experience orgasm, was considered necessary for the continuation of male domination of heterosexual coitus. Male death fear and its connection to women, especially to women's genitals, is also related to the idea of the *vagina dentata,* along with the notion that men are "consumed" in heterosexual intercourse. Men come from the vagina, and may be taken back into it. And women's sexual passion, long before the

Victorians denied its existence, was thought to be insatiable; men supposedly expired trying to satisfy women.

The fear was less graphically but just as strongly reflected in the tales of the legendary Judith of Bethulia and Delilah of Ashkelon, who seduced and destroyed the most powerful men of their people's enemies. Throughout both testaments, men are warned against the shame and pollution of women, the lewdness and filth of female sexuality. These warnings were specifically and deliberately calculated to destroy the power of women, and to revile the old religion's acceptance and honoring of female sexual pleasure.

In the last two thousand years, christianity has modified the Oresteian definition of mother, creating a split personality commonly known as the madonna-whore. Where Orestes could condemn his mother completely as whore and murderer, the image of Mary makes such wholesale cursing difficult. Mary and Jesus have changed the old form considerably. Because Mary has already lost her powers before her son is born, Jesus doesn't have to blame, defile, or kill her. His father has already taken her essential femaleness from her; she was cleansed of being born of woman (the immaculate conception) and she did not engage in carnal intercourse to produce Jesus (the virgin birth).

Mary has no power, and almost no womanly characteristics. Even her motherhood is only symbolic, so she need fear none of the insults and attacks that her son's followers pour out upon the female sex, because men need not fear her. Though many early christians acknowledged not only her womanhood but also a symbolic sexual/ marital relation between Mary and Jesus (she is not only the mother-in-law, but the foremother of nuns in being the original bride of christ), those aspects are not present in christianity today. Mary has become more than a token goddess, she is an incon set up by the church for women and men to worship, a tool used toward the further weakening and defamation of womankind; she symbolizes purity, chastity, and spiritually perfect motherhood—and none of the aspects of Woman that have been feared or revered by men. She is "the tamed goddess who abjectly adores her son."[16] It is this widespread Marian image that has influenced so many of the sons I interviewed for this book, who displayed love and respect for their mothers—and the usual male disdain, distrust, and distaste for women. The *mothers* have been separated from the *women*. This is a complex process: *mothers* are queenly, pure, and chaste, i.e., Marys;

but *women* are powerfully sexual and dangerous; therefore, mothers are not women. But, as men must know that their mothers are women, they come to fear and distrust us—even while going on to search for mothering in other women.

By the Middle Ages, women were openly persecuted as witches. Priests explained how witches could, by "glamour," magically make penises disappear—so great was their fear and hatred of women, and so desperate was their fear of impotence. Witch burning was a clear manifestation of mother-hating among men; between nine million and eleven million women were killed through man's blatant rejection of the bodies and sexual being of woman, a rejection of the physical source of life—the uterus and vagina—a rejection of *their own birth*. This murderous violence is the logical extension of the denial of sexuality and the degradation of woman's spirit practiced by the christian church.

Once christianity had connected woman and evil with both sexuality and death, man's fearful struggle to deny the nature of woman became a denial of the nature of human life. Men have long expressed their passionate fear of women in the art they make; and male art is more and more fascinated with death, and with the perverse—often pornographic—"romantic" association of women with death. "Men claim, in the voices of the artists, that women represent death, that behind each seductive temptress, behind each virgin daughter of a wealthy father, lies the grinning skull of their own death."[17] But mothers have always known that by making children to live, we make them to die; the seed of death is curled within each sleeping babe. The ancients understood and accepted this;[18] in Egypt they said of the primordial goddess Neit:

> *The earth nestles between her thighs*
> *as daily She gives birth to the sun,*
> *each evening accepting him back into Her body*
> *just as each mortal returns unto Her*
> *when the span of life is over.*[19]

Though men conduct a desperate courtship with death in their art, they fear it. They both love and fear death, and associate their dual passion not only with mother, but all women. It may be that "man's anguish about his own death is . . . somewhat appeased by possessing and impregnating a [woman] in order to possess children . . ."[20]—fatherhood, they believe, giving them a kind of immortality. They fear being devoured by women, consumed and swallowed up into the cave of woman's mystery—and they confuse that sexual and mystical ecstasy with what they call death. Perhaps this is why some men prefer that the women they "love" be dead. Reading fairytales, for instance, we cannot help but notice Prince Charming's "recurring love of corpses,"[21] as in Sleeping Beauty and Snow White, two archetypal stories.

Men have created religion and philosophy that divorce death from life; having first sought physical immortality through their art, creating Olympian banquets and Fountains of Youth, they now seek an immortality of intellect.* They have discarded the immortality symbolized in the natural cycle of the mother and her son, for whom death, like birth, is an element of life. But the mother is more than destroyer: she is destroyer and creator in the same moment, in an instant. Creation and destruction are both simultaneous and constant. There is not one part of her (the good mother) that gives birth and another part of her (the bad mother) that gives death. She —the life force—does all at once, and always. And the son is not only her food, as she consumes him, he is also her mate. That is, he is twiceover a necessary source of energy. He cannot *die* in the conventional western sense, i.e., cease to be. Nor may he, as male artists and philosophers have fantasized, live forever. He is in rotation, in cycle, in flux forever, as is she. The eternal state is change. In the old religion it was understood that there is no goal as a discernible point in time or space. There is only consciousness—being aware of being—the deepening, heightening and intensifying of consciousness. In male culture, both women and men must undertake two processes for such intensification to occur: peeling off the applied layers of accumulated false consciousness, and acknowledging what has been obscured by those layers.

Woman's spirituality and sexuality still inspire dread in men, but the experts have changed from witch-hunting priests to doctors and scientists. Thus, women's minds and emotions have come under scrutiny, and been found dangerous. Mary Daly explains the revulsion expressed by Erich Neumann: "Patriarchal males have always

* The modern form of this desire is well expressed through what I call the Donovan's Brain image, named for a fifties B movie. The idea is that ultimately only (male) brains are really necessary for life. The current update in films is the male-brain-as-computer device, as seen in *2001*, *The Forbin Project*, and especially *The Demon Seed*, in which the computer can even rape.

dreaded and feared the labyrinthine know-ing of women. The Beatific Vision of Hags and Harpies means mortal danger to the fathers, who see [women's creation/vision/quest] as a descent into hell."[22] Andrea Dworkin studies fairytales and sees that it is still true that "grown men are terrified of the wicked witch, internalized in the deepest parts of memory."[23] And Phyllis Chesler discusses male psychology, observing that "most men experience any and all expressions of female emotion as overly intense and threatening, as a form of attack, as an attempt at female control."[24] Chesler goes on to say that "men behave this way because they are guilty . . . for having benefited, as a caste, from the emotional, economic, social, and political castration of women."[25] This benefit is surely most obvious in the case of the mother/son relationship. While sisters, daughters, and wives certainly suffer such castration in relation to the men in their lives, it is as mothers of sons that women are most likely to put the "emotional, economic, social, and political" needs and desires of boys and men before our own.

A second and more recent source of contemporary woman-hating is the popularization and general cultural acceptance of men's degradation and abuse of women. This behavior is *required* of men now, to fit the current definition of manhood. The action varies in extent and style depending on the individual male's class, race, ethnic background, and specific situation, but exists across all those lines. Moreover, men do not degrade and abuse women simply because it is expected of them; there is a payoff beyond the resulting social approval, peer acceptance, and admiration. Their actions serve as scapegoating, and relieve the tension, pressure, and frustration of living as men in this killing society.

A third source is suggested by contemporary research, which points out that, though most men are content to accept traditional patriarchal notions of appropriate sex-role behavior for their own sex, they are angry at women for doing the same thing. Most men resent most women's passivity and dependence—especially economic dependence. But, because they have learned to regard that dependence as "natural," rather than as a political circumstance which can be altered, their resentment results in a hopeless and bitter anger at women, instead of an effort to change the social structures that help keep women weak and dependent. This situation is made more complex by the fact that men have observed their mothers being dominated by their fathers, and have come to believe that men benefit from that same weakness and dependence in women that angers them.[26] Power and dominance cannot be maintained over equals; for men to feel superior, they must believe that women are inferior.

And this suggests yet a fourth cause of men's anger: men are angry because women will no longer serve as mirrors in which men may see themselves reflected "at twice their natural size." Virginia Woolf supposed that when a man "insisted a little too emphatically upon the inferiority of women, he was concerned not with their inferiority, but with his own superiority . . . if [woman] begins to tell the truth, the figure in the looking-glass shrinks." Formerly, men might have been able to "start the day confident, braced. . . ." Everywhere they went, they might "say to themselves . . . I am the superior of half the people here, and it is thus that they speak with that self-confidence, that self-assurance, which have had such a profound consequence in public life. . . ."[27] Certainly European and North American men have been angry for several hundred years on this account: women will no longer readily accept the inferior role.

Underlying all of this is the undeniable fact that, in the culture of male supremacy, men have more power than women. To acknowledge the truth of their mothers' lives, the fact of imposed inferiority, men would have to admit that they do hold power over us, that they are institutionally empowered to dominate women, and that women are oppressed by men. Though we cannot assume that this admission will come from thousands of men at once and be followed by a great outpouring of antisexist sentiment in men, causing an immediate overhaul of the governments of all the countries of the world, we can see that this understanding may be a prerequisite for action on the part of any one man.

People of both sexes resist change, fear upheaval, and avoid pain. In this case, men would not only have to make changes in their behavior and attitudes, accept massive upheaval in the institutions that surround and define their lives, and struggle through the pain that would accompany all of this; they would also have to *give up power*. They would have to step down, to abdicate, and they would have to give up the arrogant assumption that what one *can* take, one *may* take.

Belief in female inferiority is maintained through ignorance; boys and men know little about girls and women. Ignorance is a common enough source of fear and hatred. The separation of the sexes, combined with widespread false representation of the female sex, keeps brothers ignorant of their sisters. This is where mothers can make a profound impact. In a world where the major media never show or speak of true friendship and deep love between women as part of everyday life, or include the physical facts of menstruation or contraception outside of commercial advertisements, where billboards and magazines pretend that women have no hair on our bodies—and suggest that we have no brains in our heads—mothers can provide our boys with the truth.

Our responsibilities as mothers are frequently in conflict with our needs. But here is one of the places where our need for respect and our desire for integrity can serve our children. We can teach our sons the truth of our lives even as we discover it; we can see to it that they understand our value. Then they will view the masculinity list's requirements as contradictions and will reject it. We can press them to be conscious, to take action in their own lives. Let us no longer send them away, giving them the tokens their fathers have left. We will give them our own tokens, teaching them respect for the ways of women, teaching them love for the minds and spirits of women.

Raising our sons this way may appear dangerous—perhaps as dangerous as raising our consciousness. But greater danger, to ourselves and to our sons, comes through keeping them ignorant, and fostering the specialness of their maleness. Though that danger—and damage—is culturewide, Black American mothers and Jewish American mothers can afford us clear examples of the problem.* Both groups of women have long traditions of prodigious strength and competence, of sustaining the economic and social lives of their families under harsh and fearful conditions: racism/slavery and anti-Semitism/genocide.

During the first half of this century, Black mothers were lauded for saving their sons, working incredible hours at the most degrading jobs to keep their children in school, and to help them struggle out of the pit of white male supremacy. The Black mother was respected as the heart of the family, the rock upon which her children could rest, a source of trust and inspiration for her sons. The same was

---

* Black and Jewish *daughters* are another story, of course. I refer the reader to the work of Black and Jewish women poets and writers, suggesting especially *Their Eyes Were Watching God* by Zora Neale Hurston, and *Her Mothers* by Esther Broner, two of my favorites.

true of Jewish mothers. In those days, the apocryphal Jewish mother story was this one: A Jewish youth demands his mother's heart, to give to his lover. The mother lets him cut out her heart, and he races off with the bloody valentine. As he rushes along, he trips and falls full length on the ground, dropping the heart. As he picks it up again, it speaks to him in his mother's voice, saying, "Did you hurt yourself, my son?"

But now, Chicago *Tribune* columnist Bill Raspberry[28] quotes a Black woman psychologist (unnamed) who believes, as he does, that "a good deal of what goes wrong with black men—perhaps with men generally"—goes wrong *because* "Black mothers love their sons; they raise their daughters." He quotes a Black woman community worker (also unnamed) as saying to a group of mothers, "Y'all have got to stop pimping your sons," referring to the practice of allowing sons to do no chores, to have no responsibility for the house and family, and to be waited on by their mothers and sisters. Raspberry feels that "one-parent families, which tend to be female-headed," cause the problem. Since we've learned that live-in, married husband-fathers have little to do with encouraging their sons toward nonpimp attitudes and behavior, we can see that Raspberry is in error, and has moved into mother-blaming. Black mothers are beginning to hear this now; before, it was wives and girlfriends who were blamed; Mama was a comfort. But Black men are moving toward the attitude of the dominant society.[29]

Despite the broad cultural origins of mother-blaming, it is *Jewish men* who have created and popularized the idea of Jewish motherhood as a joke. Dan Greenberg's ubiquitous Jewish mother is a foolish, vain, and meddlesome harridan; Philip Roth's Sophie Portnoy is the source of her son's impotence (you would think that, at the *very* least, they'd take responsibility for their own penises); the mother in Woody Allen films is "castrating," ignorant, and shrill.

Since Wylie coined and defined the term "momism," Jewish men, in their rush to be accepted by christian America, have fallen all over each other to claim the definitive "mom" as a Jew. The *standard* mother joke is now a *Jewish* mother joke—so much so that one man I interviewed said:

I know a lot of people who are Jewish, and we have the classical Jewish-mother syndrome. I've had opportunities to meet and know their mothers; I've heard them lament about their mothers and so forth. But I've realized—what is this? I, too, have a Jewish mother—a *Black* one—who has always told me about doing this and not that, what to eat, and so forth. Also, what about Italian mothers? So what *is* all this about Jewish mothers?

We needn't veer off into mother-blaming to see that cherishing a boy while raising him to expect subordinate behavior from women perpetuates male supremacy—not only preparing yet another man to exploit women, but allowing yet another man to lose himself in masculinity. Both Black and Jewish mothers have acted, often on the conscious level, to *protect* their sons. Their impulses may have been literally to save their sons' lives—to save the race from genocide, as well as to save their children from the oppressive forces fostering hatred of Blacks and Jews. But the results of such personal sacrifice and self-denial, which include such intense mother-blaming as Jewish sons already perpetrate and Black sons have begun, are detrimental both to mothers and to mother/son relations.

These minority mothers, public scapegoats in the white christian west, are not much different from mothers of other races and ethnic groups. Black and Jewish mothers, exaggerated in their stereotypical representation, demonstrate the false position of the mother who is self-martyred for her son; she is used up and destroyed—by her own hand, with her permission and acceptance.[30] Our sons will not become the men we'd have them be, different from "most men," over our dead bodies. In the face of the anger and hatred of most men, self-destruction on behalf of one man is not a reasonable response. By "pimping our sons," we gain their contempt; by martyring ourselves to their aggrandizement, we draw their resentment. But masochism is not our only option.

We might wonder why anyone would choose masochism as a mode—but masochism is not only diagnosed by the experts as *normal* for women, and thus prescribed and required, but is reinforced by rewards and praise—particularly for mothers. (It's a mother's life to live for her child. *Sacrifice!*) It is difficult for women to give up one of the few gifts that might come to the aging mothers of sons: sainthood, pedestalization. Women who've been taught masochism and martyrdom as a way of life can be seduced by institutional motherhood's self-effacement. Some degree of recompense is awarded to mothers with high achievement in this field; a few receive public recognition,* like the mother of Romain Gary, whose son wrote a book about her, as described by New York *Times* columnist John Leonard: ". . . she wanted him to be a great lover, a great warrior, a great writer, and a great statesman. Mr. Gary's greatness is perhaps in doubt, but he was a hero in the Free French air force during World War II, and his mother wrote him every day, and when he came home from the war with his medals, he found that she had been dead for two years. Knowing that she was dying, she had written her letters in advance and arranged for them to be mailed by a friend at appropriate intervals."[31]

John Leonard's own mother, his subject in the above-quoted column, has apparently rejected sainthood, choosing instead respect and affection earned by being as much herself as her son's mother. Mr. Leonard is one of a minority of sons in that he does not count his mother's value as a person only in terms of her role as his mother. "These days, she is to be caught on the wing on her way to Venezuela and South Africa, with expensive cameras to take photographs of coal-gasification plants. She forgets to write. I love it."[32]

Many adult sons who speak well of their mothers explain that they like their mothers and are close to them, saying that the mothers are good listeners, and are understanding. These sons do not speak of the mother's life, her work, her feelings, opinions, or ideas—or her troubles and problems, except insofar as these concern her son. When she talks about herself, and when she wants a two-way relationship, she becomes a problem.

By and large, and just as a friend, someone that I'm really very close to, she's real supportive, you know, she's for real supportive. A couple of weeks ago, I had to make a long drive, so I called up—I hadn't seen her for a while—and said, "You want to drive for a little bit?" So, like, that couple of hours of driving with her, we really talked. I was telling her my life. It was real good. I didn't feel any fear or risk, and I know she's interested and involved, and I'm willing to share it; I was at that point. Professional things, what I'm going to do, and what's important to me, things I'm trying to make happen—whatever. She's a real good audience, and she's a pro. I don't hold back from her about stuff I talk to her about. . . . I don't want to get her involved in any way in personal stuff

* One ironic canonization: "Nobody'll ever write a book, probably, about my mother. Well, I guess all of you would say this about your mother—my mother was a saint."—Richard Nixon in his White House farewell.

between me and Doris. Having her in any way in our lives is a total mistake. That is clear to me.

There are some mothers who have managed to get off the pedestal, who have been willing to dare changing the traditional role of mother, and to risk the resulting displeasure or anger of their sons. The interview mothers who revealed such an attitude did not seem to suffer any more than mothers who completely accept the traditional role; perhaps they suffer less. They seem strong, *though no less harassed*, and more satisfied, though by no means do they always have their way.

These two longer quotations are from a mother of young boys and a mother of an adult man, both holding their own against the demand for sacrifice.

I'm becoming less and less attached to doing things for them. I am less than a doting mother. They get up, fix their lunch and fix their breakfast, and they're getting their clothes at least down into the right place for the laundry; I haven't gotten them to *do* the laundry yet. I mean, they can read; they're eight and ten years old. Like the other day Eddie said to me, "God, Mom, you don't do anything for us anymore." I said, "Right." Then I said, "I'm your mother; that's a lot." I'm trying to do less and less, to get them to be a little more independent. I see them; they have the potential of just laying around and letting someone take care of them. I want them to learn to be responsible for the choices they make, and admit that they're making choices. Eddie will say to me, "You made me do that." He'll say, "Well, you make it so hard on me if I do it my way." I say, "That's it; it is difficult for *me* if you don't do it exactly my way; but I'm telling you, kid: you better do it the way *you're* going to do it. Don't let me make you do anything; have it come from choice." If there's anything I can give them, it's that.

I was in business about twenty years when my daughter-in-law died. And my son came to me and said, "Mother, you know I never wanted you to work anyway. Why don't you give up your place and come and live with us? I will have household help; I don't want you to work in the house. But I want you to raise the children." I said, "Irving, you think it's a good idea now. It sounds good; it sounds like the answer to a lot of problems, but it's gonna create other problems. Number one: I don't want to lose my identity. I want to be Mrs. Cohen or Sophie or Soph, but I do not want to become Irving's mother. Number two: it's not good for you either. You've got a problem; there's no question about it. But this is no answer. This is only a pacifier." He said, "I don't think so, Mother; I would still like you to do it." I said, "Irving, don't ask me again. It will not work. It will create a lot of heartaches unnecessarily. Where it will solve this and this and this, it will create that and that and that." And that ended it. So we didn't do it. When I have to be tough, I am, yeah. Besides, I said, "You know, Irving, you always complain that I'm the best spoiler of kids in the world. And that I spoil your kids. And you're right! That's a grandmother's prerogative, to spoil the kids. She can't spoil her own." So I never did it.

These are mothers who have refused to be used by their sons; their example is valuable. Rejection of the traditional mother role is part of our task. Another part is acceptance—the acceptance of our sons into our daily lives. By now everyone has considered the idea that small boys and grown men should know how to make beds and wash dishes, sweep, dust, and do laundry—and should use these skills regularly. But there is less agreement about bringing men into the rest of our lives—the parts outside, or beside, the role that would make all women into housekeepers. Much effort has been exerted to move women into the world of men, far less to move men into the world of women.

Our sons need, so that they may be different from "most men," to be truly knowledgeable about women. They need to know who we really are, what our lives are made of—our pregnancies, for instance, especially those which produced them. They need to be present at childbirths, and to see women nurse babies. They need to see the bodies and faces of real women in the world as we go about our business. They cannot be allowed to learn that women are invisible.

They have to see us working, see the effect of our work. We have to show them the factories and offices, the desks and the teller's cages; they should be told the meaning and value of a job as a supermarket cashier, as a clerk in a department store. And they need to understand how it is that the work of so many women is paid so little; they'll ask why so many women are clerks and cashiers, while so many managers and directors are men. We'll tell them. We should seek out women when we need services; it can be done with surprisingly little extra effort. My son's pediatrician was a woman; his dentist and naprapath are women; most of his teachers have been women. Daniel and I shop in stores run and owned by women.

When we move, when we need carpentry or painting done, whatever isn't done by us and our friends is done by women workers. We mothers cannot expect our children, of either sex, to take our word, on faith, that a woman can do anything she turns her energy to; we have to show them that it may be so; that even in this culture, it *is* so.

Boys will approach female bodies with wonder and fascination if they can see their mothers examining their cervixes; they can hold mirrors and flashlights, and they can look inside vaginas; maybe if they can see where they came from, they won't forget. My son was born while I was a member of an abortion clinic, and was a toddler when I began to teach bodies and sexuality classes. He was an observer and assistant at many self-help gatherings in those early years, and had a plastic speculum among his toys. I remember him examining me, and reporting that a minor cervical erosion had disappeared, assuring me that my cervix was once again "all shiny pink." Another mother of sons recalls her boys playing a game called "pregnancy test," learned through her clinic job, in which they pretended to test urine in little jars and bottles, and told each other, in the carefully chosen appropriate tone: "I'm so sorry; it's positive/negative."

Every mother doesn't work in a clinic. Unfortunately, every mother hasn't experienced the satisfaction of self-help examination. But every mother of a son can tell her son what it has meant to her to be pregnant or to seek adoption, to cuddle him and to nurse him. We can, as we learn to cast off the fear, shame, and ignorance that has been our portion, tell our sons what we are learning and what we think. The poet and scholar Audre Lorde has said, "The truest direction comes from inside. I give the most strength to my children by being willing to look within myself, and by being honest with them about what I find there."[33]

When I asked mothers if they told their sons about their experience of the boys' birth, many said no—one way or another. When I asked sons the same question, they corroborated this lack of information. Many had been told stories about the weather that day, about where the mother was when labor began, and so on, but nothing about the pregnancy or the birth itself. One reason for this surely is that childbirth is such a bad experience for so many women in this culture. But until that changes, the pain, and the intervention

and manipulation of the medical industry, should be part of what
men know about the lives of women.* Stories of drugs, fear, loneliness, intimidation, and the ever-increasing Caesarean section needn't
be told in detail to a three-year-old; timing remains important. But a
man should know what he cost his mother; and his knowing should
begin with the beginning.

One of the mothers who did speak of childbirth to her son described the ritual she made of that telling:

I wrote a rite of passage for Sam for his eighteenth birthday. And I
asked his father to come, and we had two guides there, a male and a female, both family friends. During the process, which took about four
hours, I described his pregnancy. I explained to Sam that though the
pregnancy was an accident, my choice to have him *was* a choice, and
that he was really wanted. I described the birth. That was a real neat
thing to do; I felt real good about it. He seemed to really be interested in
it.

Truth told in earnest is an antidote to romance and false images.
Growing up with a real woman's body can help men recognize the
sham of airbrushed, made-up, pinned-together, and craftily photo-
graphed "women."

Interview sons told me about their mothers' nervous break-
downs, chronic migraines, alcoholism, hysterectomies, and drug use.
They were often sympathetic, but they had no understanding of the
context into which all these physical disasters fit. They could only
assume that women's bodies were weak and frail, *likely* to suffer, especially as women age. Men must be corrected in that mistaken
point of view, taught by their mothers that these are not natural hap-
penings in the lives of women, but casualties in the great war jokingly called "the battle of the sexes."

To speak of ourselves, to be able to reveal what is inside of
those selves to our sons, we must have established relationships built
upon intimacy and trust. Mothers do want such relations with our
sons. Asked what would be an appropriate and desirable relationship between a grown man and his mother, a few mothers did
respond in terms of the maternal stereotype.

* But from their mothers, not from TV or movies, wherein childbirth is
still a natural disaster, à la *Gone with the Wind.*

Well, I think there should be a certain distance or noninterference as far as their personal lives are concerned. A respect, and I think that would include a nonmeddling or interfering in each other's personal lives. I think a warmth, a sharing of remembered things, and love between the two. If he needed me or if I needed him, I hope that we would be around for each other and I think we will. And that every once in a while he'll call his mother. That he'll every once in a while pick up the phone and call me; I think he will. Somehow I have this feeling that we will stay friends. I would hope it would be more like a normal friendship though. I trust myself not to be a meddling mother or mother-in-law, that I'll keep my nose out of his business unless I'm asked about something. I hope I will get along with his wife. I watched myself; I know how devastating mother-in-law relationships can be. Right now he says he won't marry any girl who doesn't like me; she'll have to.

I think that if I'm still unmarried he's going to feel responsible for me, because he already does, at eleven. I don't like that; I'd like very much to correct and undo that. It's something that comes from his grandparents: "Take care of your mother." And I would like to believe that Lee, when he is a grown adult, will be able to see that I'm capable of taking care of myself, at least temporarily. But when a son becomes a man, whether it's intentional or not, sons generally feel the necessity to protect and care for their mothers, even if their fathers are alive. I would say that you have to be careful what kind of pressures you put on him to begin with, especially if there's another woman involved in the situation. You have to remember that yes, he's part of you and you may consider him your personal property, but he's not. He's an entity unto himself. He may be an extension of you, but you have to defer to whatever his life is. And it would be nice if you could have a friendly relationship; you could turn to your son and say, "This is what I'm planning to do; what do you think I should do? You're out there; you're earning a living." And I don't necessarily think it's wrong to turn to him for advice, because the role is reversed. The older they get, the more responsible they feel for you. But you have to remember that you're not the most important element in his life. As a woman, you have to accept that there's someone else who took your place, who's maybe greater than you'll ever be, if that makes any sense. You have to learn to accept the third party. If you can learn to accept them as two, then you have a good working relationship with your son.

This last woman attributes the traditional attitudes to her son and his grandparents; she does not know that she holds them dear herself. These women, particularly the second, have no inclination to step out of the role of mother, even out of its most negative aspects.

A few mothers were uncertain about what to expect, or ambivalent about what they wanted, some because they would not allow themselves any but modest expectations. But most mothers wanted friendship with their sons, mutuality of affection, and commitment.

The appropriate relationship is friendship. My son was a good kid, but obviously he did do some bad things. I remember standing in the hallway of my old house, looking up at this six-foot person, shaking my finger in his face. I unconsciously stepped up a step on the staircase, and we both actually broke up. We decided then that we'd had enough of this shitty role playing, and from now on we were not going to do this anymore.

If we lived in the same city, we'd see each other, we'd talk on the phone. I hope we could do some things together; I mean have something in common besides the fact that we're related to each other, some interests. Some bond other than blood; that's what makes for good relations between parents and children later on.

Here are two mothers who want real closeness. Though one feels the need to always provide a home for her sons and the other does not, both want an exchange of feeling, a mutual, open love.

Hopefully one where there's communication, one where there's respect, caring, honesty about why they see each other, and about their life. There's something about being the mother and providing yourself, or the place where you are, as a place to come back to, warmth and a sense of returning again to *get* something, so you can go out into the world again. I think that expectation is fair and really okay. But there should be *mutual* support. In the aging process, it's appropriate for a son or a daughter to take some responsibility in the caring, to give *back* some of that which has been given to them.

My thought is that I want to keep working on a relationship with him. Just be in touch and be close. I have enough other things going in my life that have priority; he's not my whole life. I've thought about it, and I want to be close to him, to have an open relationship. I don't feel like I always need to supply a home for him, or a place to come back to—but to be available to him. I would like *him* to work hard in the relationship and be available to *me*.

Other mothers want, or say they have, relations with their sons that transcend the narrow boundaries this culture allows.

The relationship? Venus and Adonis is nice. No can do, these days. Settle for genuine affection and good cheer. I will say—a Freudian is leaning over my shoulder and trying to stop me from saying this—I have lately had a real, though nonsexual, love affair with my older son, who is suddenly an adult person who can go places and do things with me without feeling awkward, and we can joke about stuff better than I ever could with his father. Curiously, there seems to be a possibility for real human equality in this relationship, although I could be fooling myself. Mostly both sons tell me what I need to know.

I have come to disagree with many of my friends who think that relationships between mothers and sons should pretty much disappear, that they should become quite independent of each other as they mature. I don't have to agree with them. My instincts are different, and I think probably it's one of those social concepts that needs to be reexamined. I think that a son should be as much as possible financially independent of his mother. He should have respect for the fact that her experience might be valuable to him. He should like to be around her. He should like his girlfriends to have good relations with her. The mother and son should try and learn as much from each other as they can. It's very important for me to stay in touch with what a younger generation's up to. I'm not only afraid of becoming hidebound in my ideas. I know the world is changing all the time, and it's fascinating and important to me. I really want to know about it and empathize with it as much as possible. That's something I expect my son to give me. I want him to share his world view with me. At the same time I would expect that he could learn a lot from me. He could learn, for example, about things that happened before he was born, as well as what the world looks like from the point of view of someone born long before he was born. I think it's very important for both mother and son to be aware of the fact that they live in a different world, so they don't anticipate that each should be like the other, or share an identical belief system. I think they should remain physically close as much as that feels natural. They should further each other's decisions, support each other. It should grow into an older person–younger person friendship, filled with the depth of years of intimate relationship.

But the reality for most mothers and adult sons is not much like what these women want. What they want requires high consciousness and intimate knowledge of each other, being in relation to each other with mutually responsible love. To do this, both mother and son must become aware of the traditional roles they've played, be willing to drop those roles, change these patterns, and accept the ongoing struggle the process requires.

In asking men to describe their relations with their mothers, I found that many, maybe most, had little experience or understanding of their mothers as whole people. They did have, though, much less anger, resentment, and fear than they have for their fathers, or than daughters have for mothers.

One kind of response was unconscious contradiction. These respondents spoke readily and candidly, apparently with no recognition of what they were disclosing. They deny what they say even as they say it. One man, for instance, defines/explains being "emotionally close" to his mother as a series of holiday phone calls to a rest home.

Well, I only see her once a year. When we first come down here, Mom come down with us and stayed thirty days. I've always wanted her to live with us because she was alone. She had lived with my brothers for years and years, up north. My mother would never—my mother didn't want to live with me because she couldn't run my home. She was on the dominant side; she had raised us all herself. She could pretty much run Tom's home: if she wanted that piece of furniture moved, Tom would grab it and move it. But she just didn't want to live with me because she couldn't tell *me* what to do. Simple as that. Oh, we are definitely still close emotionally. I call her every holiday and talk to her on the phone at the rest home. I have my sister go to the rest home and call me and get Mom on the phone.

I could say the relationship is a good one, but that doesn't say much, does it? It's sort of a responsible one; it's one that's mutually giving. I think she's a very giving person, she's always helpful. She does a lot of things for me and I do things for her. On my part, that tends to be a measure of responsibility. I suppose it's an average, normal, mother-loving-type relationship. It might be closer on her side than mine. I think it's more emotionally important to her. Where there's responsibility on my side, there's dependence on her side. I can exert power over her by just pulling away from her; I could do that to her, but there's no way she could do that to me.

She tells all her friends her son's a salesman; he's successful. But she doesn't like my life-style; she still thinks I spend too much money. (My dad thinks that too. Maybe I do spend too much money.) But she's warm to me, friendly, nonhostile. She's still encouraging. She's still sticking her two cents in, but in the kindest way she possibly can. An example? Okay, okay, sure. I'll get a letter in the mail. It'll be a new diet for me to go on, okay? She wants me to lose weight. Understandably so. I do too, but I'm a weak person, I must admit. So she wants me to lose weight; its understandable, a mother's anxiety. She wants me to lose some weight and look good and keep healthy. Do we really know each other? That's a good question. Maybe I don't let her see who I am, and maybe she neglects to see also—a little bit of both. She does pretty good, she's fulfilled her motherly obligation as far as I can see. She writes letters. And she does things for me; she's very good that way. But as far as knowing what makes me tick, my wants and my needs, I think she may be innocent of both somewhat. About her, I think I know who she is, yeah. She's changed, though. My mother went through a transition; I remember her being sort of prim. Didn't want to hear words like fuck or shit. That wasn't permitted in our house. But after she got over her acute anxiety and began to live a little bit, to read, to become more worldly, then she, as the years went by, got more liberal, and I could talk to her; now I'm not afraid to say anything in front of my mother. She really has changed. She reads so much, and she reads all the best-sellers, so there's nothing that goes on she doesn't know about. I mean, there's *some* things I wouldn't say in front of my mother. I wouldn't say blow job in front of my mother, or anything like that. That would probably upset her. If it was put in the right way, maybe not, but I think so.

Though this next man feels guilty about his mother, he does not choose to change the way he regards or relates to her.

She and my grandmother together supported me all the way through college and she helped me out a lot after that too. And now I am doing the same for her. It's been a real reversal of roles between her and me right now. Sometimes I treat her like a child, rather than my mother. And then she gets madder than hell at me. In terms of being able to talk to one another—absolutely! Absolutely! In terms of sharing things, and anything like that, well, we both love Chinese food. Whenever I go back to San Francisco, I take her out for Chinese food. She doesn't get out. She doesn't have any money to get out and do things, and I feel guilty because I don't give her more money, but I want to be able to do things too. Because during my entire life, she always managed to have enough money for me to do basically what I wanted to do, and I don't give her as much as she gave me. I throw an extra five or ten dollars in, you know, so she can go to a movie, but she doesn't go out much. At the same time, she's not the same person she was before her stroke. She is not as strong-willed at all. She's changed from being a strong intense person, somebody I remember as being able to help me whenever I was down. Occasionally I tell her she's becoming senile (I'm feeling very guilty over these things right now). Sometimes, when I say that, I'm joking. Sometimes I mean it; sometimes I say very seriously, "Mother, I think you're being senile in some ways." She says, "I'm not senile!" [Hearty laugh.] She's just not as strong as she used to be. But then again, I may have idolized her, put her up on a pedestal in some sense, because of all the shit she went through in getting me through college and getting herself through graduate school, and doing all these things. You know, my view of her back then may be far more intense than she really was. I just realized that what I have done is shift completely away from her intelligence. Even though we do have talks sometimes, she's lost part of her intellectual interest. I mean, I think that's because she's quit teaching and moved to selling. She drinks too much. I take after her in that way. But she does it, I think, because she's lonely.

Other men see quite clearly that their relations with their mothers are weak, distant, or poor, and assume that condition will continue. Some of these sons are regretful, though.

There's not a lot to the relationship, maybe a letter every two or three months, a phone call maybe every three weeks. For her part, she wants me to think that she's living a happy and full life. At the same time she wants me to think of her as a person who is sick and might not live too much longer. That is a topic in her conversation, although really she is very healthy as far as I can tell, giving no signs of wearing out. She's said for the past few years that I should see them more often; she wants me to move closer to them. And one of the things she brings up is that she won't be around that much longer. When we talk, she seems to feel strongly that I am about to criticize her. I think she feels very ill at ease with me, and she's always trying to— She's very feisty, very contentious. She's looking for slights. At the same time, she wants my approbation. She wants to feel that I approve of her and her style of life. For my part, I pretty much do. What I'm suggesting is probably I don't express to her as well as I should that I'm not a threat, and I'm long past wanting to judge her—the way one does as an adolescent. I would like to get along better with her. I like her. But she doesn't get along with my wife, so for that reason alone I would keep some distance. My mother is used to fighting; my wife is not. It was not a mode in her house, so she doesn't know how to fight, and certainly doesn't want to walk into someone else's psychodrama. But no, we don't have a very good relationship, and we don't communicate very well. She probably doesn't express what she feels toward me, and I probably don't express what I feel toward her.

At some levels my mother knows who I am. There are times when we are very genuine with each other. They are very rare, and it's an automatic flip back when they're done. It's always painful, after there has been real contact, to go back to standard operating procedures. About a year and a half ago, when my life was going very badly, my mother asked me how I was. I said that I felt lousy. She was too taken up with her own pain to become interested in my problems, so she just said, yeah, it's really hard sometimes. It was just very simple, very honest. Not some memorized speech, just an admission that life is sometimes difficult. Usually, I am more careful than that: if I admit anything is wrong, I have to let her in. Generally, I don't want to let her in. Both of us have many strong images of what we think the other is like, but we misapprehend each other consistently. Some of it has to do with leftover adolescent bitterness on my part, and still seeing her as the mother that gave me a hard time, not as the woman she is. And some of hers is her fantasies of what she wants me to be, what she thinks I should be. I'll tell you a couple of things I've discovered, just by having this interview. One is that I have a much more positive and benevolent view of my mother than I thought I did. Another is that I really think I have had to make the choice to cut my mother out of my life in order to function well. That's a painful choice, but I think it's a realistic one. I only can allow her a certain range in my life. I see her occasionally, I'm pleasant with her, but she's not part of the real functioning of my life. I would like to be able to be friends. In some ways I need my mom. So it's a painful decision.

Some sons express no regret; they explain that the lack of intimacy is acceptable to them, or even welcome. They do not seek to know more of their mothers' lives, or to encourage their mothers to know theirs.

She ain't into my life that much. She don't see but one side of me; that's the side I bring home to her. It's not like I'm young, you know. I'm a grownup too; I'm a parent too. I've been both those things for a long time. You just reach a kind of arrangement. Our relationship has this and not this in it. All this other stuff in her life and my life *ain't* in it. There's probably more of my stuff that she ain't aware of, than of hers that I don't know.

She knows who I am as much as anyone. But I don't really think I do know her. Why? I would say there was a long period of estrangement because I was in athletics; that really separated me from her. And then I also picked up a pretty low estimate of her in high school—not her in particular, but of women in general for a while, and that may have adversely affected my understanding and my intuition about who she really is. If you know a person and you have a finger on their pulse for twenty years, you'll know who they are. Like I think she's had that finger on my pulse, but I've lifted mine off, so I don't really know. I guess I'd describe the relationship now as that of mutually interested people. But not fanatically interested, or dependent. Definitely not dependent.

And a few—far fewer than daughters—have decided that there's just not enough in the relationship to bother with.

I do find that I can only be around my mother for a short time. It's a little bit touchy. She has said to me that of all the kids, I am the one she feels she has to be careful with what she says, because I fly off the handle. And I do. I guess maybe I do. And I don't know why I'm the only one. I think the other ones really do it too. She has said that she cried over me more than any of the rest of the kids. The last time I was down there visiting, we had a row, which is not unusual for us, over something really stupid. That's the kind of thing where I don't give in to her like the rest of the kids. Maybe I am stubborn, whatever, but if I know I'm right, I don't see any point in saying, "Yes, Mama."

She's so preoccupied with herself that she's not available. She has shut herself off from everything else around her. She's just swept up with herself now. She doesn't care about what's going on up here, where her kids live. I mean, she does, but it's probably way back in her mind.

But the following group is conscious—consciously struggling to build something of substance out of the rubble of outworn forms developed in childhood. These sons describe the deliberate work they have entered into to improve the relationship, perhaps to come to affection and respect. These men have given an enormous amount of time and energy to understanding or working through their relations with their mothers.

I remember telling a friend, in an Oscar Wilde-type quip, that my relationship to my mother improves in reverse proportion to the distance I am from her. I do get along with her much better than I used to. My mother is just a pretty strong personality. I have definite ways of wanting to run my apartment and run my life, and she has definite ways of running her house and her life—and they clash sometimes. Aesthetics is the issue lots of times, that sort of thing; we would get annoyed at each other over almost picky kinds of things. But now I put myself in the frame of mind that I'm going to *her* house, and I will do things *her* way, because it *is* her house, and that is her right. It's perfectly all right; it's only for a week or so. That works pretty well. The relationship is distant; I would like it to be closer—except that if we were closer, it might not be so close. That's the problem. But how much can you communicate with a person who is not used to communicating? If she lived here, it would be even more difficult. She's never come to visit me, though she knows she's got an open invitation. I think she's afraid, one, that she might bore me and bother me—which is part of her pattern, to think she's such an imposition; and, two, that she might find out some things that she doesn't want to find out—possibly.

Where that man decided to accept his mother as she has been, this next man demanded change, and feels that his mother responded in a good way.

In the past, she would suggest things to me about my life that just drove me up the wall—like, "Why don't you go to work for your brother-in-law? That will solve all your problems." Simplistic thinking, immediate answers. But she hardly ever does that anymore, and our relationship is pretty good. I think she knows me pretty well; she might even admit to herself the part about the sexual preference, but to state it would just be trauma for her. Sometimes I wonder if she really does know. I think it's just something she doesn't think about. I think I know her pretty well— about 80 percent of her, anyway. Or maybe more. She has never really talked about her feelings about her husbands, about her own sexuality, so there's that whole thing. I would love to know the real reasons she married my father—ultimately. She had real doubts about it down to the wire, kept saying this was going to give her daughter a father, give his son a mother, and all that. But that was when she believed that marriage meant endless security. She would always tell me, "You can't do it alone, you have to get married, and your children will take care of you, and blah, blah, blah." Now I say to her, "Where are all these people who are married? You see, among your own friends, their children never come to visit them, or they farm them out somewhere, their mates have died or they've been divorced six times; none of these things are certainties. Marriage does not assure you that you are going to have companionship and care in your old age." And she really agrees now. I'll tell you, once she came at me and said, "Look, why are you always yelling at me about things?" I don't know if she said yelling—maybe contradicting. And I said, "Look, do you want me to be a middle-aged son that just says 'Yes, Mama' to everything you say, or do you want a grown-up person you can trust, an intelligent friend in this world? I am willing to be your friend. And I think that you can be a real good one, but I say you've got to meet me at that level." She didn't say anything at that time, just looked real hurt, but the relationship has gotten better and better because more and more of the time she does treat me like an adult.

Here is a man whose mother has begun to relate to him in new ways on her own—and he sees and appreciates that.

I don't really think she actually knows me, but I think she's discovering me more. I don't know if I know her. Not entirely. I feel as if I'm going through a process of discovery. Trying to find out more and more about her, searching, I'd call it. Trying to see. I do see. She never did for me when I was a child, but now I find my bed turned back, or she made the bed for me. She ain't *never* made up my bed when I was a child. And I'll find my clothes in the closet, hanging; I really appreciate that. But I understand what it's about. I say, "Mama, thanks a lot." I understand what's taking place here.

And here is a mother/son pair who have worked together on their changes, reciprocally.

Maybe a year ago, I had done some acid and I was sitting around with people. We had been smoking some reefer too, and everything was real nice. There was this sense of warmth for me, and feeling good, feeling high, feeling comfortable, just enjoying what's happening. Kind of spontaneously the thought of Mother came to mind, and my body and my consciousness were heightened, so I was aware that I went through *such* a metamorphosis. I slowly became cold and my visual experience just became gray and misty. My sense of that was that there's a veil of sadness around the concept of my mother. But I think that we have a good relationship. I have reverted to calling her Mother, instead of Carla. She is my *mother*, and I need to be clear on that. I sense a very genuine affectional relationship now, whereas previously it was a surrogate relationship for both of us. We've managed to get rid of a lot of that. We both feel that there's nothing to hide at this point. We might as well be honest about what's happening. She still, literally, depends on me for strength. There's an awful story by Dorothy Parker that has a refrain of saying "I live on your phone calls." There is a sense in which she lives on my phone calls. I'll call her, and she'll be real depressed, and she'll build up and carry that feeling for a while. I'm really wiling to give her that, and I don't feel any discomfort about it. No, it doesn't take anything away from me. It's genuine. I can deal with being a strong person for her. There were times when I needed a strong person and she was that for me. Now that our relationship is somewhat cleared out and is again a mother/son relationship, it's really okay for me to be the kind of support that she needs. I think we like each other now, and that's really important.

And these men, the youngest still living with his mother at twenty-two, the oldest in his mid-fifties and a thousand miles away from his mother, describe relations with women they like, love, admire, respect, and enjoy. Some have accepted—or insisted upon— the traditional role of mother; others have been able to relate to their mothers as friends.

We do talk about intellectual things, but we also talk about movies. The things I can talk about with my mom is I can talk about, see, like who Hugh Herbert was. Hugh Herbert was a comedian who would always put his hands together like this. I can talk to her about Olsen and Johnson, the comedians who I really like. And with the girls I go out with, who are my own age, they have no interest in that kind of stuff. But it's one of my key interests, it's one of my *loves,* to talk about these old films and the actors in them.

I think we have a deep love and a close understanding of each other's circumstances. We explain situations to each other, try to help each other out. Like if she feels there's something going on that shouldn't be, she'll ask for advice, and I ask her for advice at times. If it's a trustworthy problem, or something involving someone else, then I'd like to talk to my mother. Also, if it's about work, I give her good coaching and she coaches me. Coaching—I mean like saying "Just keep on hitting, don't let up. Do your thing."

I feel she's more dependent on me now than I am on her. And I can understand that, because she can't work as much as she used to work, and of course the Social Security benefits are not the greatest. I consider that her spending money, because I pay all the bills. We can sit down and talk much better today than we could before, when I was dependent on her; it was different then. I was so young. I call her every week, twice a week, especially if I know she's not feeling well. Mom will lie when she's not well. Then I get to my sister, and she'll tell me. That's when I start to worry, and I call three, four times a week. I hope to be a good son to her; I appreciate her a lot for all that she's done for me. When you're young, you don't appreciate too much. She went out to work to keep me in school; she gave me money she wouldn't spend on herself. This is something I didn't realize until after the fact.

She is the most extraordinary woman I've ever known, personally known. I've read about other women that I've equally admired—Isadora Duncan and George Sand and some of those others—but I've had my own Isadora, my mother.

Even here there are problems. We no more need to be idolized than we need to be degraded. We want our sons to see us as *women, human beings who have needs and passions and ideas.* We must make the maternal task of raising sons include the (now paternal) task of making men. We want to make men who will see who we really are, so they can live among us in ways befitting that vision.

Yes, I recognize that danger here. I see the risk. What if we expose ourselves to men, show them our truth, making ourselves yet more vulnerable to them—and then they use this knowledge to hurt us, to further manipulate or oppress women? What about the lesson of our mythic history here? All those stories of how women gave the magic, the secret tools and the sacred words, to men—only to have men seize power, killing or enslaving the women? What about the fact that as soon as men were allowed to be present and assist at childbirth, they took it over, and excluded midwives, inventing gynecology and obstetrics for themselves, abusing women as servants and subjects?[34]

I have these fears myself. But those men were separate from women. Those grown men came to the wisdom and expertise of women as outsiders; they were jealous, and eager to tear the web, to break open the labyrinth; they were ignorantly resentful of their secondary role in the creation and maintenance of human life. But if we raise our boys as sons of the Mother, if we keep them with us from the beginning, accepting them as equals, neither worshiping them nor expecting their worship, we will be doing a different thing altogether. We can learn from history, especially if it is our own history we study.

7

Here and Now

*The strongest lesson I can teach my son is the same les-
son I teach my daughter, how to be who he wishes to
be for himself. And the best way I can do this is to be
who I am, and hope that he will learn from this not how
to be me, which is not possible, but how to be himself.
And this means how to move to that voice from within
himself, rather than to those raucous and persuasive or
threatening voices from outside himself, pressuring him
to be what the world wants him to be.*

—AUDRE LORDE[1]

Despite the facts that between one third and one half of American
marriages end in divorce, that nearly 60 percent of married women
now work full time outside of their homes, and that increasing numbers of women live in nontraditional family circumstances, i.e.,
alone, with their children only, with other women, with a group of
women, children, and men, or with men who are not spouses,
women still bear and raise children in the shadow of the patriarchal
nuclear family. This kind of family is so widely believed to *be* the
family that many people have no idea that it is a relatively recent arrival in human culture, or that the form we recognize today has been
narrowed down from the extended family, and from the clan.

Thus, no matter how we live, or with whom, we all have learned
that Dick and Jane's family, including Father, Mother, Son, and
Daughter, *is* the family. We know that we are still judged, by ourselves and others, against that pattern. The people in the pattern are
white, christian, and middle-class. They live in a house with a front
yard and a back yard, a garage and a driveway, on a block and in a
neighborhood filled with other such houses, yards, and families. Father goes to work in the morning carrying a briefcase; Mother
spends most of her time in the house; she wears dresses and aprons.

It will do no good to object that these images are out of date, that even children's readers no longer promote such pictures. Maybe they've changed their clothes, that family, but they are still with us. Not only do middle-class mothers by the millions work outside their homes, but working-class mothers have done so all along; nonetheless, the ideal dies hard. In the mid-seventies, my son and his nursery-school peers, only one third of them living with a married parental pair, already knew that the separated, divorced, or never-married mothers were the irregulars—and the children were not yet six years old. Prevailing cultural images overcame their daily experience.

No, I don't think my sons know who I really am; they still think of me as something that goes with the apartment. Listen, I've been going to school; they've seen me come and go; I'm a full-time student, *full-time*. I come home and do my homework though the house is dirty; I tell them to fix their own supper. I do oil painting, I do needlework. I make quilts. I play tennis three times a week. I ride horses. I just graduated from college last month, okay? Well, my youngest son's teacher asked the class to draw a picture of their mothers—and he drew me with a bucket and mop! I mean, I do mop the floor, but—buckets and mops! I do all those other things, but the kid draws a picture of me with a bucket and mop. It just wiped me out.

The assumption is that the nuclear-family form is the right form, the natural form. There must be a mommy and a daddy, they should live together with the children, and they should play the appropriate roles. The purpose of these requirements is something else again. As with most widespread cultural assumptions, people rarely ask, "What's it *for?*" The prevalence of the form and the roles makes their purpose unquestionable for most of us, most of the time. But when we do question traditional patterns, the answers are always interesting.

I asked mothers these questions: Do you feel that your son needs a father? That most boys do? What for? If he has had no father present, have you sought male role models for him? Why? Why not? A minority of the mothers asserted that their sons did not need fathers.

I think he did great without one. I think everybody needs a loving parent, or a loving somebody to center them. But not necessarily male; no, I can't buy that. I've seen too much to the contrary.

Oh, no. *I* need their father. They don't need a father any more than they need a mother. They need people to care about them.

No, I don't feel that he needs a father. I know he does fantasize about having a father. He talks to friends of mine, friends of his, and says, every so often, "I pretend that you're my father," and usually that's okay with that person. He's done that with my dad, in fact. I don't know what I am depriving him of; there'll always be doubts about something like that. Sometimes I feel that I would like the father, but I like our family just the way it is now. Feels real good to me. And he feels pretty much the same way. Given the state of fathering in America today, I wouldn't say that most boys need a father, no.

I can't answer that. Maybe I'm just being evasive about this. I think that I am sufficient as a role model in all the different jobs I have done, all the different things they have seen me do. Kids need somebody to take care of them for a certain amount of time. A mother or a father could do that. I don't think they need either if there is somebody who really loves them and takes care of them.

Do they need a mother? It's the same thing, isn't it? That's a very difficult question. I think children need adults. They need people.

Some mothers held out for the traditional patriarchal ideal of the live-in, married father, despite their own experience. They ignored the facts of current social practice. Many of these women spoke as if their sons' fathers were actually *doing* the fathering the mothers were saying was necessary or good; they spoke as if fathers in real life were not severe, absent, distant, and so on. And mothers sometimes slid off into the idea of a "male image," rather than a father.

I think they need their father—for just a plain father image. I'm afraid I couldn't fill my husband's shoes if he wasn't there. Taking them to the ballpark, playing with them. At one time I thought I could do very well without him. But I didn't, because I was really insecure. But I have a lot of friends who are dynamite mothers who don't have a husband. Their boy children are well adjusted. This is just how I feel about *myself*, and about *my* boys—what *we* need.

Oh, yes—my son needed a father. My husband was a marvelous influence on the children. He liked to do things, play baseball and go fishing, picnicking, and canoeing—no violence there, like in some of the rest of their relationship. It was a friendly, teaching, protective relationship. Boys do indeed need a father. Having a father gives a purpose; the boy is stronger, and more able to face the world. Women have been homebodies, homemakers, and mothers, and have tended not to face the world in its reality. Fathers are more practical. Of course, this role is changing, but you still need a strong person around.

Interesting question. In other words, could we have done without him? Good grief. We could have done without him. But I think there's something going on; between the boys and their father less is said, but there is *something* going on there. Yes, a younger boy needs some criteria by which to judge the outside world and his position in it. And as far as the boys are concerned, Mother is not successful. But I think they just use the father. He's out there. Outside and inside is two different things and without that person leaving the home and coming back with a paycheck and great stories—I don't know, I think they'd be less prepared without having a father—to meet those challenges.

Oh, yes, they need a father, because the biggest thing, I think—though I may not be right—the biggest thing they need a father for is when they've been out to play with other kids, they hear them say, "My dad this and that." They need that. That's number one. They need a male image in the house. What do I mean? Well, somehow a man has a complete different personality than a woman. And we are all a product of our environment. So if there is no male personality in the household, then the sons take on the female personalities. When I say male image, I don't mean that I was afraid that any boy who would grow up without a father would become a homo of any kind. No, that's a different subject altogether. I wasn't afraid of *that*. But I feel that children, that a boy should have a father. Even a *daughter* should have a father.

I think it's good. I think it helps. It usually does create a balance. I can only equate it to the way that I feel about having a daughter. That there is something special, quite special, about a relationship—I think there should be, I hope there is—with someone who is essentially the same sex as you are, and who's going through the same major life stages. You recognize it. A man looks at his son and he remembers what he was like at that age. Having these two tall young men who are both taller than I—it's different for me.

Gabriel does need a father now, yes. But the baby, Gideon—he could probably go off with me into the hinterlands somewhere and never know the difference. But there's a point that you cross, and now there's no way that Gabe could be without his father. Had he never known him, why, there'd be no difference, just like with the baby. I think he needs him because he's a boy [sigh], eight years old, and he's trying to figure out what that means in the world. One of the ways that he finds that out is by being close to a male adult, living with him. He's really struggling with the issue of going out into the world, learning what it is to be a male adult in the world. But the whole thing depends on the context, on what has happened all along. I mean a male child could be raised by an all-female household and go to an all-female day-care center, in school and everything else, and be all right. I don't see that they'd suffer terrible consequences. It's when they have a relationship, a significant relationship with an adult male, and then that ceases, that's where something happens —with the interruption.

A fatherly presence, rather than a biological live-in father, was what this next group felt that their sons needed—men in their lives.[2] They generally spoke in terms of traditional masculine roles.

I always thought it was very important that they have good male influences. It was a very short period of time that I thought there had to be a father. We all need to have heroes and heroines, to give us goals to strive for, some sense of what we're to become. My boys needed men who were not their mother's lovers. They needed men who were doing things, who were involved. For me the criteria was political things in the Black community, models for them in terms of what I expect as their responsibility in the community. And men who were involved with good relationships with other women, so that could be seen.

I don't think he needs his real father to turn out all right, to feel good about himself. He needs men in his life, but I don't think he needs one in particular. I would like to have him grow up feeling real close to some good man. On the other hand, I wouldn't want him to be desperate for a man's attention. It's really fortunate that I have a couple of really good men friends. They mean a lot to him; they're real special. I think both boys and girls need to be close to men.

This mother's struggle to enforce the culture's sex-role requirements really stunned me. She has worked as hard as I have—in the opposite direction!

I think most boys need to have a male image, at least some kind of male image, constant in their life. It isn't absolutely necessary, but I do think it is helpful to them. Women can't be masculine no matter how hard you try. Even if you believe you're equal to them. You're feminine and he's masculine, and there's a difference right then and there. I went to a lot of trouble to send Lee to summer camp for one purpose: to put him in a situation where he would be with young boys, males, for a long enough period of time that their behavior could be reinforced on him. Because he can't spend that much time with his father. And from what I've seen so far, it worked—to the point that he's come back very much aware of the fact that he is a man and I am a woman. He's much more aware of his own body and the differences between us—something that he never paid much attention to before.

The next woman takes the distinction between biological fathers and male role models even further.

I think that what any boy needs is a positive male image. After all, my son lives in a real woman household, two adult women and two younger women. He's not a woman; he's not going to cut it as a woman. There's no way he can completely fit into that picture. So he gets positive male identification when his stepfather is present in the house. He gets to see a man who comes and fits himself into a woman's world. Which means he might possibly do that himself, and feel comfortable. Whether it's a mystique or not, there's this sense that a man can understand men and these broads never will. So he has these adolescent problems with his girl-friends—Dad can understand better than Mom. . . . I guess that as children we really do have some need for a role model that seems within our grasp: "I could become like that person." It must be frightening to have role models all be women if you're a boy or all men if you're a girl. There's some way you're never going to make it. You're never going to be like that role model, because of your gender. I mean, I can fantasize a society that's androgynous, that would be perfectly reasonable; you might not even know people's sexes. But it does seem that in a world where the sexes are real separate and where sexism is prevalent, that it is important to have role models. I think gay fathers are terrific in this time for just that reason. That's what I think are best for boys. I guess I mean *conscious* gay fathers. Gay men who have dealt with the issue of sexism on some level, because of the woman in themselves, deeply, become terrific role models for the boys. They don't go out using girls, exploiting girls, which is the fear of any feminist mother—that I'm going to raise a macho kid. Society's going to win. I do think that gay fathers open up to boys the possibility of being men who don't exploit women. Of course, there are gay men, gay fathers, who hate and exploit women—more than straight men. So the best role model for boys in this society, at this time, where sexism is such an issue, is a conscious gay man. A feminist gay man.

And both of these last two women, despite their choice not to pair up with men, say that men are good, or necessary, for their sons.

I think they need a male; I don't know if they need a father. They need him so they know what they're supposed to do. I don't think I'm supposed to have a relationship with some man to provide him for my son, but I would encourage Paco to deal with men other than his father. I don't feel like dealing with men for a while myself.

If I could do it over again, I would have found a good, decent, warm, loving man and had a relationship that lasted, so my son could observe and be a part of it, having a strong male role model right there that he could bounce things off and look at, take the best from. I think he should have had a male role model, with all the good and bad. Maybe just the opportunity to watch a male go through different changes. Something he could cast off from; he could say, "This is an admirable trait," or "I don't want to be like this when I grow up." I would like for him to have seen a man in relation to me, too. It didn't work out that way. Too late now. I'm devoting my energy to other things.

It is striking that so many mothers are willing to accept men as models for our sons. Despite woman-hating and mother-blaming, despite man's creation and development of this murderous culture, mothers say that boys should be around men so they can learn what to be. What can they be thinking of, to say in one breath that most men are regrettably lacking, and in another that our sons need to spend time with them, to learn "what they're supposed to do"?

The comments of this next group of mothers are characterized by the ambivalence resulting from this contradiction. Knowing most men, living in this less-than-perfect world they've made, and having to contend with the forms and patterns superimposed on our lives by the nuclear family ideal, ambivalence becomes a kind of balance; confusion becomes a position.

Yes, I do feel a father is needed; it's probably my own problem. What for? I have firmly believed that a child should have both a male and a female influence during their formative years. As my son got older there were things that I thought he didn't necessarily want to talk to me about, or subjects he wouldn't bring up with me, and it would be good if there were a male there. I had always thought that he sought out that kind of conversation with his father, but it turns out his father is not especially conversational. You know, relationships with women, approaches to women, biological changes, oh, probably masturbation, if men even talk about that. Then I discovered that men don't especially talk about that. They don't really have those conversations with their fathers—so it was all a misconception in my own head.

Freud says there is no substitute for the strong father. . . . How much truth to that? Some. . . . The males with strong fathers inherit the earth. Power is handed down from father to son. There are severe limits on what a mother can give a son. I believe, however, that what she has to offer if she has any brains at all is infinitely more valuable over the long run. As far as older male friends are concerned, my sons have always found lots and have tended to hang around the more humorous, nonauthoritarian types, so I am well pleased with their choices.

I used to say I'd rather have him dead than be like his father. But my son has a lot of trouble surviving in the world, because you have to be rotten to survive—and who better can you learn it from than men? The other side is, you see, that having his father as a greater influence would have given him survival skills.

It's a big concern of mine, and I change my mind a lot about it. I thought Frank would be a good father, and good guidance into what I perceived to be necessary masculine traits and skills. Like I've never made more money than just enough to live on; I assumed it was a male thing to make *good* money. So I was very careful, both before and after the divorce and all the carrying on, to keep up Harvey's respect for his father. I never spoke of him disrespectfully, always admiringly. It was our plan that when Harvey was in high school, he would go to live with Frank. He spent occasional months with him in the intervening years. I learned that Frank was great at a *gesture*, like he would cook an elegant dinner from the Larousse encyclopedia, but he couldn't keep it up. He made really fine moves like that, but he couldn't sustain it. He got into the habit of making incredible promises to his son, all of which revolved around money, or a career. Like he promised him a new suit for graduation, but the women—his mother, his second ex-wife, and I—wound up buying it and presenting it *as if* it came from Frank. I have come to believe that my son's life would have been a lot better if he had never expected to have a father. He didn't really need a father. I mean, he *felt* a great need for a father, but a lot of that I contributed to, encouraging him to wait for his father, till his father would come through for him. So he still feels the need for a father, but in reality it would have been a lot better if he had never been encouraged to wait for his father. There are lots of men in the world he could relate to, if he hadn't been waiting for Frank. I think it would be very neat, even in this changing world, if a man were available, to be going through the changes that men have to go through, learning how to let go of their privileges, their unfair prerogatives. It would have helped my son a lot if an older, presumably wiser, more experienced, man were in his life. It would be great guidance. It would be a great interchange, that would be ideal. In terms of absolute need, I guess boys don't need fathers.

In an extended interview with Alan Howell, who taught children aged five to twelve in Chicago's Parents' School, I asked him to talk about whether boys needed fathers or not, and whether boys need to be around men.

Alan: I don't know that it's absolutely necessary. It's advantageous if the men have positive relationships with the boys, but I don't think it's a matter of having to find men to be around a boy just for the sake of having men, in spite of flaws or whatever negative influence those people might bring. No men at all is better than a real negative person. If, for example, the kid has a father like I did, an older male with whom he has a horrible relationship, then no father is likely to be better than the real bad one.

Judith: Let's say there's a little boy with no men in his life. And there are grown women in his life who are, of course, not all the same, and some of them relate to men and some of them don't, but basically there are only women in his life. What do you think that'll mean for him as he grows up?

Alan: For little boys, one of the most important things is their ability to relate to other little boys. To be with them, to know how to be with them, and to do the kinds of things the other little boys characteristically like to do. So if this hypothetical child were reared with only women, but had access to play groups, playmates, he would have the basis for all those male interactions that are going to be so important ten and fifteen years later in school situations. If he feels

*good about himself and the other boys, he's going to be fine.
I don't think he needs to have a male person over twenty
around him to get what he needs.*

Judith: *What is the responsibility of adult males who have sons, or
who teach little boys, like you do, or who just happen to
know little boys? What, if anything, is their responsibility to
those little boys?*

Alan: *In our society we have this image whenever we think of men
and boys doing things together; it always comes back to the
same kind of thing: they play sports together, they camp,
they join Boy Scouts— It's always physical activity. Right?
I mean, always sports or something like that. That image is
so ingrained, and it's exclusive; there are no images of men
and boys doing or being anything else together. So everybody
thinks in those terms, that if you're going to have a relationship with a boy, you're going to take him fishing or hunting,
you know? There are a whole lot of boys and a whole lot
of men that aren't interested in those things, and even those
who are, are interested in other things too. We are really bad
at recognizing that, and at finding alternatives, because the
models just aren't there for us. Men and boys sharing books,
for instance; you never see that anywhere. So I would say
that the most important thing to do, if you're going to have
a relationship with a kid, is to find out what his real interests
are, what his talents are, what he wants to do, and then be
supportive of those. Not to say that you couldn't encourage
other things too; let's say he's not interested in sports, you
could try to awaken some interest there, and so on. But not
to insist on this, on this traditional kind of relationship.
Fathers and sons go through so much strife about this. If
the father supports who the son really is, what he feels, and
lets him know that he's okay, the rest of society could all be
taken, could be felt in other ways by the boy. Here's where
the thing comes in about your first question. If a father, or
a teacher, or any man, can do that for a boy, then of course
it's just fine to be around that man, and the boy might come
to need him, to need that kind of fatherly thing. But with
most boys and most men, nothing like this ever happens. Just
the opposite happens, and I don't think boys need that.*

Like Alan, the interview mothers were concerned with the actual influence of men on our boys, and with the possible influence of *no* men on our boys. We want them to be around men, but the men who are available are almost always inadequate. They are models of the roles we reject; they cannot provide our sons with positive male images. Moreover, we struggle with this issue in a vacuum, for we know that despite *Kramer vs. Kramer* and *Ordinary People,* despite judges' punishment of women in disputed custody cases, very few men have anything to do with caring for (even their own) children. Those men who do have custody of their children are almost always moneyed enough to hire a woman as a "housekeeper," and she raises the children for them.[3]

The presumed need for a father is addressed by the experts, of course, and we can well predict that they find fathers indispensable, especially in their traditional patriarchal role—despite the fact that that role does not include child-raising. Generally they hold views of women and sexuality that lead them to believe, as one male professor of psychiatry has suggested, that boys may be better off with their fathers because their mothers constitute a "danger" to them. This man accepts the common belief among psychiatrists that women may become "unconsciously sexually provocative" to their sons, or make "excessive demands" on them, because of the mother's "grief" over the "lost husband." Even though this seems to suggest that the father is unable to find his way home, the professor further states, "The father helps the son to know what is important in life."[4] Presumably, mothers do not know what is important in life, or do know, but refuse to share this information with sons.

Essentially, because men do not raise children, all mothers are raising children "alone." But a single mother leads a different life from a married one, and a family with no grown men in the house is more different yet. The position of divorced, widowed, or never-married mothers is made more difficult than that of women who remain married by the socioeconomic structures of patriarchy and the continuing presence and influence of the idealized nuclear family —that still-lively notion that we all live on the set of "Father Knows Best."

While all women who raise our sons without live-in men must address the issue of the missing father, lesbian mothers of sons have to consider it from more angles than are visible to most straight women. Lesbian mothers experience an added measure of fear and greater danger in their motherhood than straight women do. Where straight mothers may worry whether sons will move into the patriarchy without a backward glance, taking a view of women that is distasteful at best, most lesbian mothers live with the fear that, because of their lesbianism, they will be declared unfit mothers. Painful enough for a lesbian mother to agonize over her son in terms of male sexuality, poor role models, and the oppression and discrimination of patriarchal culture—but she also knows that through the efforts of the boy's father, grandparents, teachers, or neighbors—or the intervention of social service agencies acting "on the boy's behalf"—her son might be taken from her. Should that battle not have to be fought, lesbian mothers of sons must still concern themselves, in their double jeopardy, with the fact that their sons are encouraged not only to abuse and despise women, but to treat lesbians specifically with contempt and disgust.

Well, my sister also became a lesbian. So my son's thing was to make up a story that Betty really has invisible boyfriends. He does that because he's really scared there's no place for him. Not only that, but he understands that if women really put it out there, we'd control the destiny of the race. Little boys know that. They know that when they're a year old. But my parents—they're really tortured. They called me up about my sister and said, "You set a trend." I'm afraid as my children get older, they'll put more pressure on them, especially on the boy. Like they wanted to send him to this all-boy macho camp; I put my foot down on that one. One doesn't worry about a four- or five-year-old boy living with gay women, but one does worry about a twelve-year-old boy, or a sixteen-year-old boy. So it may go that way. We'll see.

I just came out to my sons last year. And, you know, I'd been living with somebody for four years at that time. Right, she was in the house with us, but I never talked about it. She would say to them, "I love your mother and that's why I'm here. We sleep together." Sandy would always insist that I kiss Charlene good-bye in the morning when I went off to work. They had a real understanding of it without its being explicit. The way it finally came out was that this straight woman who was doing an article about this gay parents group that I'm a coordinator of, she called up, and left a message with Barry. So when I got home, Barry said to me, "Someone called about the gay parents group. She said *gay* parents. That group you belong to, is that a *gay* parents group?" And I said yeah. He had met all the parents; we had had picnics together with all the kids. He said, "Well, is everybody in it gay?" I said yeah. So he asked, is this one gay, and that one, and this person, and so on. Finally he said, after a long pause, "Well, do you mean gay like happy?" I said no, gay like *gay*. And he said, "Well, are *you* gay?" I said yes, and he said, "Oh. Does that mean you and Charlene fool around?" You know, he got real flip about it. So we talked about it a little bit, and he wanted to know who knew. You know, who he was safe with. Then we started talking about it in terms of human rights, and could I lose my job, and so forth. My younger boy, Sandy, he was immediately into what does this mean to *me?*—I don't know if I like my mom being gay. "Can you like me 'cause I'm a boy?" and "Maybe you ought to get out of that parents group," and all that kind of thing. . . . Now a lot of lesbians want nothing to do with my sons—which really pisses me off. But I met a woman recently, to whom I was very attracted—and I think the biggest thing I liked about her was that when she talked to Barry she actually liked him. You know, he's the hardest one to like; he's the oldest, and he's more like a man. It's very interesting. The sexiest thing about her is that she got along with Barry.

This is the kind of oppression that kids can look at and define. We're standing outside of the society, and they know it. When I left my kids' father, the boys were three and five. All my friends were women. I was deeply involved with women, with helping women, working for women, and all my time and energy that didn't go to them and their school went to women. I also had a woman lover, and they knew that. They knew her and loved her too. We were very open; the word lesbian was used all the time. I mean, they certainly had questions and those questions were answered; we talked. My only problem with being open and out was that I was really terrified of a custody fight. I did not want my husband to know anything about my life. One reason was that I didn't want to share anything with him, any part of myself; and another was that he was angry that I wanted to leave, and I thought he might suspect, and use my lesbianism against me to take the boys away. Now he never *talked* about my being a lesbian, but he would kind of hint around, like when I would push him for child support, he would say, "You know, if you start pushing we could have some real trouble"—that kind of thing. So while I wanted to be real open with my kids, I did have some fears about giving them words they would naturally use in other places. I didn't come out to my parents until three years ago, and I was really afraid they'd tell their father, and all of those things. But they were always good about it, and they have really struggled with their own feelings a lot. Like when May and I broke up, after five years, I told them how heavy it was for me, and they were wonderfully supportive. But one day after she left, one of them said to me, "Well, do you think you could ever fall in love with a man?" And I said no, and he said why. By then they were both sitting there, and I said, "Well, because I'm a lesbian, and there are men I admire, and that I'm friends with and feel good about, but I identify very strongly with women, and I choose to be lovers with women; that's where I choose to put my energy, and to have my intense relationships, my primary relationships, except for you two." My sons hear a lot of bad things about men, from my friends and from me. I work at the rape crisis center, and I am constantly dealing with men at their worst. Also, I have lived with separatist women, who could not deal with my sons at all. But I am very conscious of that problem, and now I choose my friends, actually, on the basis of who can deal well with my boys. I go out of my way to say things positive about men when I can, and to point out male beauty and good men. And while that helps in one way, it sometimes puzzles them in another, because they say to me, "If you think a man is beautiful-looking, and you feel good about him, then could you fall in love with him?" So we go over it again. And sometimes I know that they're embarrassed in front of their friends; they don't want their friends to see me touching or kissing a lover—though of course if I had a male lover no one would even notice. It's not easy.

Audre Lorde has said, "The sons of lesbians are trailblazers, having to make their own definitions of self as men. . . . sons of lesbians have the advantage of our blueprint for survival, but they must take what we know and transpose it into maleness."[5] Most mothers of sons are not lesbians—but all of us can heed these words. We all have to make blueprints for survival, and all our sons must take what we know—if they would make new men of themselves.

These tasks are not easily done, nor even readily understood. For women are denied full humanity; and mothers especially bear the brunt of the degradation and exploitation that comprise this denial. Where men are constrained, women are oppressed. That is why the imbalance of power is the important focus in relations between women and men, mothers and sons. Though both sexes are constricted and suppressed, twisted out of shape, men hold more power than women, and wield power over women. As Black people have understood that even the weakest, meanest low-rent white can subordinate the wisest, strongest Black through the racist system of white supremacy, so women have come to see that any man may literally overpower any woman, in the sexist system of male supremacy.

Is there a difference between being a good man and being a good woman? There certainly shouldn't be. I really hate the ways in which good men and good women are different. But the way it works is that men take control, men do the defining, men do the leading. A good woman is one who can maneuver for herself within that context. And I just hate that, okay? A bad woman is one who just gives up completely and just lets them run the show. A good woman is one who learns to run and dodge—but that's horrible too. We've got no real space.

Understanding this, I am wary of taking a fault-finding or blame-casting stance in examining the position of mothers of sons. Analysis, however, is not enough. Now that we see how mothers have aided and promoted the making of men by men, now that we understand the way we have been used against our own interests and those of our sons, we have to take responsibility for making change. Not only would it remain futile to wait for men to initiate the necessary social and political changes, it is foolish to expect that such change will come from the next generation—from the children. That is an excuse for inaction, an excuse for remaining as we are. Children cannot change the world; they have no power. In the spirit, then, of nineteenth-century women's-rights activist Lucy Stone, let us face our disappointment: "In education, in marriage, in religion, in everything, disappointment is the lot of woman. It shall be the business of my life to deepen this disappointment in every woman's heart until she bows down to it no longer."[6]

We mothers have bowed to the education of our sons in male culture. We've raised sons and given them over to the fathers, who've made men of them. We have accepted our assigned roles, putting our dearest hopes into our sons and other men—so that they might live for us; we've raised them to believe they are special enough to carry out those hopes. We have allowed men to treat us disrespectfully in the presence of our sons, so that they've learned to see us as victims. We've accepted their childish mother-blaming with no challenge, and accepted their use of us, letting what should pass with childhood remain to fit the pattern of male domination. We've neglected to tell them the truth of our lives—so that they don't know who women are. We've believed that masculinity is natural to men—despite the evidence of our own senses, the evidence of our sons' lives. We have encouraged in them a sense of entitlement, urged them to go off and conquer the world. We've put others before us, especially their fathers, demonstrating that we have little value and less self-esteem. We've assumed that our sons are inherently very different from us, and we have helped to strengthen and lengthen the list of those differences, while feeding the notion that what is different about them is *better*.

He's very different from me. He is reserved in his feelings. It took me twenty-five years to learn to keep my tongue. You know, I would just come out with whatever I thought, irregardless of whether it hurt anybody or not. But that's not Lee. He thinks constantly about all kinds of things; I really think he's far more intelligent than I am. Anybody who can make almost straight A's when you study a little bit and make B's and C's when you don't study at all has to be a whole lot smarter than I ever was in school. I don't really think he's much like me, somehow he's *more*.

He's so gypsy; he'll go anywhere with anyone. My mother said that I did that, but he's like that even more. He's more adventurous than myself. He's going to go out there and he's going to see things that I sit back and just wouldn't do. He rides bicycles and roller skates. I don't ride a bike today. He'll bike, skate; I imagine that he'll even go on to motorcycles. I imagine that before he's twenty-five or thirty he'll probably be to Europe twice, and just do all sorts of things that I've never done, travelwise. He's much more of what I would like to be; he's the same, but he's got more of it than me.

I had been very able academically. Lucas was clearly more able than I. So I really did expect him to produce all kinds of things. Probably for me. I would love to say that he's like me since I admire him so much. But he is like me, and then he's so much better in all of these areas. He really is, ah, what's the word; it seems to me that he's very like me but he's a little more adventuresome. He's reached out in more directions. I've accepted too many limitations and he's accepted fewer than I. I am very pleased with me. I am more pleased with him.

They're all very different from me. Hugh is more tolerant than I am. And, goodness knows, he's smarter. He has a much wider vision than I have. I'm much narrower; my experience is much more limited than his. With Henry, I think he just has a good sense of humor, better than mine. And of course, he has talent, which I don't have. I am not creative. All my kids were creative in one way or another. And I am totally uncreative. The youngest is perhaps more like me, but he, too, like Hugh, is tougher than I am. And he's critical of people in a way that's less judgmental than my way. Henry, too, is very soft about people, more than I am—but they're all more tolerant than I am. I think they are kinder in a way. Their world is wider, in a sense, than mine. So I have been more rigid than they will ever be.

This last woman, without making a feminist analysis of the culture that allows her sons greater freedom, has clearly shown that the differences between her life and her sons' lives are *made of* the political reality of male privilege.

And those of us who are feminists—whose anger at men and rage at the institutions of male supremacy have pushed us through many of the cultural constraints on women—have often allowed ourselves to be swept past our sons.[7] We have come to consciousness when and while raising male children, but many of us have not made the connection between our male children and the problem of male supremacy. Some women who consider themselves feminists are content to let their sons grow into oppressive patriarchal power. We are afraid. We are ignorant of the history of mothers and sons so that, like men, we fear to face the fact that out of our bodies, out of the core of the female—vulva, vagina, and uterus— has come the male. And we are slow to acknowledge the daily corruption of these sweet small boys—though we are the earth from which they sprang, the ground in which they are rooted.

We must take care. As we grow into our power, becoming more and more conscious, we embrace the image of the Great Mother in ourselves. But we cannot use our reclaimed power as a weapon against our sons. In their young maleness and relative helplessness, they would be easy victims to our rediscovered strength, especially when they experimentally flex the muscles of masculinity. We can't fall into the pattern of most men, striking out at the available smaller folk when we are made small by those with power over us. Ironically, through the centuries of patriarchy, we mothers have been accused of doing this very thing. But how many of us had the power, or the active sense of self, to *begin* to be the Medusa who could turn men to stone, or the Circe who would reduce them to swine? In the tradition of mother-blaming, we've been accused unjustly. Is this because the male collective unconscious memory is stronger than the female? Men have kept alive their fears of us, stoking that fire with their insistent suppression of our memory, which lay in cold ashes on the domestic hearth, gray and pale approximation of our once-bright altar.

The patriarchal seduction of our sons is blatant; the lure is power. If we are to combat the process that makes our children into "most men," we have to understand the terms of the struggle—and so must they. Raising girls in a male culture, mothers are made into the instruments of daughters' oppression; mothers train daughters to fill woman's traditional roles. Daughters rebel against those roles, blaming mothers for our pain. But, like the Furies, most daughters learn to subside and accept domestic safety like our mothers before us.[8] Contrarily, in raising sons, mothers are the primary source of praise, encouragement, and selfless service. Sons learn that they are to be the beneficiaries of male culture: they will grow up to power, status, and the admiration and support of women. If a mother wants to change the pattern with her daughter, they can struggle together for liberation. But when she moves to change that pattern with her son, he understands that she wants him to give up power, and to draw the disapproval and anger of other male power-holders. Whatever her fears, a girl can see that she will *gain* by being strong, brave, and smart. A boy has to begin by *losing*. In overturning sex-role stereotypes, young boys will be labeled weak and cowardly.

Because we mothers have, in ignorance or weakness, colluded in the cultural conditioning of our sons, we have to reverse our position. We must seize every opportunity—and they arise daily—to challenge the assumptions of male culture. In Daniel's first reading workbook, right out of kindergarten, there was this typical instruction: "Draw a line from the picture on the left to the matching picture on the right." The picture on the left was a small boy. The correct answer was a line drawn to a picture of a large striped ball. Not a truck or a train, mind you, but a brightly colored ball. The second picture, of a small girl, had as its correct answer a line drawn to the inevitable doll. Should that little girl reach for that ball, should that boy try to pick up that doll, they'd be worse than tomboy and sissy; they'd be wrong answers. This book, purportedly among the best of the new school texts, had obviously been designed by progressive educators. The children pictured were of two or three colors; the mommies and daddies lived in city apartments as well as houses; old people were in the illustrations, and the occupations of the adults were both blue-collar and professional, i.e., letter carriers and doctors. But the basic sexist bias was intact.

For this one we needn't write to our congressional representatives, but a thorough job, done by the perfect mother, would include a letter to the publisher and to the school board, a talk with the teacher, and the attempt to whip up enthusiasm among other mothers to do the same. In a busy year, I'd settle for talking to the teacher, but the most important thing is to show it to your son. Make a little scene. Make sure that boy sees what's wrong, though it may only get you what it got me: "I *know* that, Mom. But they think that's the right answer, and I wanted to get it right."

If all we do is establish ourselves as watchdogs, critics, cranks, and overseers, we will have opened the subject. Then we can maintain an ongoing conversation with our boys about the injustice and foolishness of the mindset that promotes such definitions and constraints. And we will have shaken up the order a bit; so what if we get reputations, if the principal learns to dread the sound of our names? Did that stop Elizabeth Cady Stanton? Worse things can happen to us than to be known as "women's libbers." In decades to come, we may be made into cartoons, into flimsy caricatures like that of Carry Nation, whose notorious reputation singlehandedly brought about the return of the matriarchal battleax. We could do worse. We could be cowards; we could be ignorant; we could let our children see us sit silent in the face of our own oppression—learning that we accept "woman's place."

Much of this work is as simple as pointing out such obvious sexism as that in the reading workbook. Only the tediousness, the dailiness, of that constant assault will be a problem. The tougher stuff is more personal. We have to fight back, fight for ourselves. We have to challenge, in front of our sons, the domination of men who demonstrate their lack of respect in the way they treat us and the way they speak to us. We have to learn to argue and not give up, to be aware of our own desires and preferences and to make them known. We have to take power for ourselves, and use it.

We have to take it because, of course, men will not give it up. We have only to study the history of the women's movement, or read a biography of Susan B. Anthony, to know that. Men do not give power away readily, for in giving up male power, they will suffer.

Well, I am happy that I am male. I don't think I could go through what
the women go through. Well, the women are always thought of as—not
inferior, but second-class—and they're expected to cater to the male.
And I don't think I could live a life like that, catering to people. I don't
cater to anybody now, and I don't intend to. Call me chauvinist or whatever they want, that's how it is. Yes, that's a masculine trait, my attitude.
I think a lot of these men are hypocrites who agree with the women's
movement. I strictly don't. Free—yes, fine, they should be free, but still
they have a place in this world, and it's to cater to the male.

Women often speak of the "glaze" that comes over men's eyes
when we try to speak to them seriously or tell them what we actually
think; this is part of the defense of their power, and the denial that
they have it. It is not only greed that prompts the glaze and the refusal to relinquish power; it is fear of the consequences of that act.
If a man gives up his rank in the hierarchy, he will be treated like a
woman, despised, ostracized, and abused by other men. For a man
to become a true friend of women is rare because it is hazardous.
For men to say of another man that he is "henpecked" or "pussy-
whipped" may be worse than to say that he is gay. Secretly, the
straightest and most masculine of men might envy those who find it
in and among themselves to ignore women, to have nothing to do
with the despised sex, to never *need* a woman. But those men who
appear to be dominated by women (and what other reason could
there be for giving up male power?), who agree with women, ally
themselves with women, or identify with women's needs and tasks,
and who do all this out of love or admiration, simple affection or
approval, real sympathy or understanding—such men are to be
mocked and shunned, if not beaten or killed.[9]

The male bond is deeply grounded in fear and distrust. The
brothers will turn on a man who bonds with a sister; an alliance
with a woman is a break in the brotherhood. That is why so many
"antisexist" men, men of goodwill who admire women and try to
change the way they are with women, do *not* try to change the way
they are with men. They talk to women about their male colleagues
and comrades, or about the phenomenon of men in groups; they tell
us what they see and hear. But they say and do little or nothing
among men. They are afraid, and they keep quiet in their fear. They
often claim that no other man would understand or respond in kind.
So they rest on a laurel wreath bestowed by grateful women, never

interrupting or challenging sexism, never pushing other men to see what they see, or to act on what they see. They have it both ways: they keep their position in the male hierarchy, and they have the good opinion of women. This is not enough. We want our sons to go beyond that fear as they mature—to take responsibility for themselves as men, and for their relations with other men.

There are men who try to be different. They struggle in isolation, or in the tiny groups that a few men have formed, such as the Berkeley Men's Center, Minneapolis Men Against Rape, the Men's Resource Center in Portland, the Chicago Men's Gathering, and the Denver Area Men's Network. Though these groups generally begin as a response to the women's movement, if they stay together they come to focus on their identity and definition as men, not solely in relation to women. When such groups break up, they often break up at the point at which they would have to stop talking about their reactions to women and start talking about their relations with each other and themselves. As one man points out, "for many men, simply to admit need is a new behavior." Men in this culture are not allowed to respond to or work together on their "rage or psychological pain over destroyed relationships, dehumanizing work or personal crises."[10] Even the struggle to acknowledge this is intense.

We have to raise our sons to be conscious of sexual power dynamics from the beginning of their lives—or the beginning of our own understanding. We have to help them recognize the bribes and the pressure for what they are, and urge them not to take destructive power—to refuse it, to be too decent to wield it. Instead, as part of our mothering, we must help them to live in the power of their own spirits—that power which cannot exploit others. As mothers, we will be overturning male power when we resist the patriarchal demand to give up our sons.

As we struggle to be strong and brave, while our boys watch us being what we've told them women are, we'll have to support them against the list. We'll have to go out of our way, way out of our way, for this. Women who want to break out of women's roles have a community of women to turn to; we have resources. The women's movement has created interlocking networks across the country and around the world. These resources are still slim, but they are *there* —at every level of society. Women have a history and a tradition of such conspiracy behind us: like all oppressed groups, we've understood how to be ourselves and take care of our own when the man's gone out, when he's looking the other way. Men! What do *they* know? ask the women working in the kitchen, drinking tea around the table, sitting toweled in the hot room on ladies' day at the Turkish baths. We always feel the difference, and *flex,* in the absence of men.

But our sons have no such tradition, no support system. The "men's movement" remains a tiny unseen minority, unknown by and unavailable to most men. Most important, our sons are not, when they seek such connection, rejecting the position of the oppressed like their mothers, but the whiphand, the position of the oppressor.

There are not enough men who would congratulate a boy for quitting the wrestling team because the coach made unreasonable demands and consistently treated him badly; rather, that boy would face mockery, disdain, and banishment for abdicating, for refusing to "take the heat." Our boys have to be taught what is wrong with that assessment, that view of life. We have to help them understand what is actually happening, by supporting their struggle against the masculine comprehension of human events.

With our encouragement and the information we can supply about sex roles and cultural expectations, our sons might be able to seek other boys with whom to share their feelings and thoughts. They will move very cautiously, very slowly, taking great care—for this is dangerous and difficult. Before they reach the age of six, boys have learned not to tell other boys what their fears and fancies are —and their caution is well advised, for the sad truth is that men very rarely find full trust and friendship with other men. We can help them relate to their friends in nonmasculine ways, showing them that friendship includes mutual confidence and support, rather than constant challenge and competition.

Because Daniel is now of an age, and at a school, where boys and girls work and play in separate, often hostile, worlds, I am more conscious of, and will be deliberate about, our spending time among women and girls. Such family friendships make a place where Daniel can be with girls without suffering the scrutiny of his male peers.

It is that scrutiny, especially from older boys, that keeps young boys in line. Though the rules and roles come down from the fathers, other boys are quick to point out and punish those who stray from the prescribed path. Teachers and counselors sometimes are aware of this, and the more sensitive among them will make their judgments accordingly. Speaking of the seven boys among sixty-eight girls taking a child-care class at a suburban high school, one teacher said, "A fellow has to be pretty mature in his own sexuality to submit himself to teasing by other guys. That's why the boys we *do* get are pretty neat people."[11] The younger they are, the more readily boys can accept and enjoy the presence of girls as companions, and the idea of doing the tasks and activities assigned to girls in male culture.

The creator of the course popularly called Babies at the Collegiate School in Manhattan discovered that offering the class to ten- and eleven-year-olds rather than high school students was what made the class a success. Meeting two days a week, assigning a pair of boys to each real live baby, the course taught students to bathe, diaper, soothe, and feed infants of both sexes. The boys' delight and fascination with the babies may seem incredible in a culture where boys are actively encouraged to shun both the task of childcare and small children—but "for a male gender acculturated to compete without sharing, to hide feelings without seeming hurt, and to make love without loving, Collegiate's class on infant care is a good step in another direction."[12] One boy who has completed the course says, "I'm going to beg and beg them to let me take the class again. I'm going to sign up again even if I have to get down on my knees. I just love babies. I mean I'm going to get down on my knees and beg them."[13] That determined young boy has learned that he can nurture, despite what the patriarchy would have him believe. This kind of experience is exactly what our sons need to give them evidence, to give them support, to help them believe that they can be what their feelings tell them they are.

Though the raising of male consciousness is certainly not women's responsibility, those of us who choose to be committed to relationships with individual boys and men have to be willing to expend a great deal of energy in making ourselves competent to deal with them. We have to understand their lives, to know that masculinity is a barrier against their search for spiritual and emotional connections to us, to each other, and within themselves. Male socialization is not secret, or difficult to understand. We do not live as our distant ancestors did, when the men took the boys away from the clan, out of the village, into a lodge or temple that housed their secret rituals. We can watch it happen; we can see them being made into men, even in the smallest ways.

It's very interesting. I never deliberately (unless they would ask) taught my children how to sew, cook, whatever. Melanie picked it up; I don't know how. She just picked it up. When I realized that Tom had grown up *not* knowing these things, I was outraged. He'd come and spend summers with me, and I would then teach him, as an adult, every year, how to cook, how to sew. I thought it was outrageous for a man not to know that. And every year he would forget it, and I'd have to start all over again. Why did Melanie pick it up and Tom not? Tom is so brilliant, it's not like he *couldn't*. I mean, he's not real coordinated, but how coordinated do you have to be to cook? It must be that he did internalize some of the stuff from the society.

Frank and I were walking to this meeting together, and all of a sudden, when we got within two blocks of the place, he did something really funny to his shoulders, and started walking real different. I said, "Honey, what's the matter with you?" He said, "What are you talking about?" I said, "What's this Frankenstein number?" It had to be uncomfortable; it was weird. He kept denying there was any change, but I just said, "Bullshit—what is this crap? You've rearranged your body!" He didn't feel *too* threatened or defensive—just enough to deny it, but not enough to refuse to talk about it. We started struggling back and forth, arguing as we walked. We passed this construction site, and I had to walk behind him on a narrow path. He called back, "I have to do it, because my shoulders are broad." And I said, "Honey, from the back your shoulders are not necessarily the broadest thing about your body. You ain't but twelve years old!" With him, I see all the isms making their play, to get at him. If people are allowed to appreciate fully the kind of human being they are, it's a lot more difficult for them to slip into an oppressive pattern.

At a backyard Fourth of July party the summer before Daniel was ten, I watched him relate to various men—most of them strangers to him. There were several men, several women, and several children, but Daniel was the only boy there. One man spent a considerable amount of time and energy urging Daniel to move closer to the concrete driveway where the firecrackers were being set off—mostly lit by two or three men. He wanted Daniel to "get in on it." Daniel disliked the noise, may have been fearful of the danger, and hung back. But this man never stopped taunting and cajoling him. Obviously, it was important to him that Daniel, a boy, act a certain way; he said nothing to the girls, two of whom grabbed the matches whenever they could.

Later, when the noisy crackers were all gone, and only the visible fireworks—sparkling little light shows—were left, all the men but one had gone inside. A twelve-year-old girl now superintended the show. All the women and children, and the one man, waited on the lawn to see the pretty ones. Suddenly the man jerked his head up, looked around the yard, and said, "How come I'm the only guy out here?" I told him, "You must be the only one with the sense to know that this is the best part of the show." But he just couldn't handle it. He went into the house and missed the grand finale—a four-color fountain—unable to cope with being "the only guy out here." Now these two men were ordinary, and a Fourth of July lawn party is ordinary too.

We surely cannot miss the larger, louder signs of man-making, as in a "commercial . . . for a game called Tank Command, described as the strategic military game from Ideal. The two men playing it make a lot of faces to show you that it is an exciting, tough game. The man who has just been outsmarted looks up and says: 'War is hell!' "[14] The curriculum in both public and private schools continues to present "the history of the world" and the evolution of the human species as if all women have ever done is a sort of constant KP duty, while men—"armies"—waged war across the lands and seas of the earth. We can't pretend that we don't see this process, that we can't catch it happening. We have only to pay attention.

That attention includes seeing not only what happens to our sons but what doesn't happen. For more than fifteen years, the contemporary women's movement has set about educating girls and women—providing alternatives to male culture's pattern. There are now thousands of books, movies, conferences, and workshops, all designed to help women see, and to further our vision. But with few exceptions, there are still almost no resources for boys and mothers of boys. It makes sense that providing for male children was not the first item on our list, but we're long past the first item now. For those of us who have male children and choose to raise them, there has to be more action.

We have asked ourselves if we are trying to do the impossible in raising our sons to be refugees from patriarchy, if men might be genetically bound to aggression, violence, and woman-hating.[15] But those of us who are satisfied that males do have the capacity to be human and humane can begin to seek assistance from other mothers of sons, from men of goodwill, and from books—research about male behavior and attitudes, men's fiction, and their letters, memoirs, and autobiographies. We must begin to look at male culture from our perspective as mothers of sons—to see magazines, movies, and TV, as well as clothing, architecture, and foreign policy, as products of male culture which potentiate the conditioning of boys and men.

We have to make things happen that will help us mother our sons. We have to acknowledge that, like the mother/daughter relationship, the raising of male children by mothers is an *issue*. Those of us who have already begun to make issues—if not federal cases—out of what we've learned about the social and political history and lives of women can welcome the women who've just begun to recognize and talk about their uncomfortable, puzzling feelings. We can use our organizing experience here; we needn't reinvent the wheel every time we want to take a ride. Feminist consciousness is basic to this struggle; we have to know who we are before we can tell our sons.

In the interest of this information exchange, here are some of the things I have done in the past several years, trying to combat the effects of male culture and patriarchy's claim on my son: I've kept journals and notes, recording incidents, conversations, and dreams. Reading these over, and aloud to Daniel, I can see patterns; we can compare his memory and sensibility to mine, enriching our understanding. I have taken him with me to concerts, museums, movies, plays, lectures, and discussion groups where (male) children were welcome. I have consciously included him in my life as a *person*, not only as my son or as a child-care responsibility—especially after I realized that I had been separating him, thinking I had to, from the nonmother part of my life.

I took up the task of reading male authors, reintroducing them to myself, seeking men I could approve of and appreciate. I started with Shakespeare, Melville, Hawthorne, and Twain; I knew I could find something there to keep me going. (I wound up reading long parts of *Hamlet* and all of *Twelfth Night* aloud to Daniel; that was great fun.) In the years when I chose all his playthings, I chose very few, and these were not sex-typed; they were usually old-fashioned, like bubbles, balloons, dominoes, and blocks. I made a rule never to buy, or allow in the house, toys that represented war or police action as play. Originally, I tried to outlaw all guns—but found that he became obsessed with them, and fashioned make-believe guns out of everything. So I bought a dayglo pink plastic squirt gun, and restricted its use to bathroom and porch; I know how to compromise.[16]

I found a great equalizer in books. I brought him mostly books that are *not* considered to be for boys—like *Mary Poppins, Heidi,* classic fairytale collections, and radical feminist stories, such as *Selene.* I selected woman-centered books like *Amelia Bedelia,* the *Ramona* books, *Charlotte's Web,* and *Harriet the Spy,* even if they do contain unfortunate plot turns or attitudes. I wanted books that had little girls or women as heroes and main characters, such as *The Wizard of Oz.* Or I chose the *Frog and Toad* series, wherein gender is irrelevant beyond the pronouns. I introduced all of these by reading aloud to him, long before he could have read them himself, because I knew that when he was older he might reject them out of hand. There was a deliberate imbalance, though we also read *White Fang, The Jungle Book,* and *Sherlock Holmes.* That imbalance is meant to correct, as much as possible, the overwhelming masculine influence in the world outside our home. TV alone has the power to wipe out any and all positive female images.

When he was very small, I edited as I read, changing pronouns and leaving out lines and paragraphs that were racist, sexist, and otherwise offensive. (I remember the first time I deliberately censored a book. My action was a shocking departure from a life of respect and love for literature. I had bought him a book I remembered from my own childhood. *Tootle* is the story of a young train who is a free spirit, who is made to learn to stay on the tracks. I didn't read it in the bookstore, because I bought it out of nostalgia, and when I got it home I discovered that at the end Tootle is subjected to a form of behavior modification which subdues him, and resigns him to keeping on the tracks forever. It was so awful that I literally ripped out the final pages, making the book end with Tootle's escape into the meadow, where he played among wildflowers and green grass.)

As Daniel grew older, I read all the words that were there, with my commentary. Later, his own criticism supplanted mine. In the beginning, he often repeated what he thought I'd say, but he has become rather independent of my views in the last year or so—and subject to the views of many others, adolescents especially. For instance, a preference for folk-style music has been submerged beneath a passion for the sound of the Ramones and the Police. But this is to be expected, even welcomed—though it remains disconcerting to be subject to such teenage-style condescension as "Jazz is old people's music."

In choosing his clothes, I've sought bright colors, frequently finding them on the girls' side of the store. One of my greatest finds there was a white cotton terry robe with a hood trimmed in rainbow cord. Too small now, it's in the costume collection, to be worn with zany hats, baggy pants, and face makeup. He loves bright colors, but I'm afraid the boys' departments' unending racks of brown, blue, and dark green are having their effect. Boys are trained like the Gammas in Huxley's *Brave New World:* they learn to reject flowers, music, and sunlit color.

I spend time with other mothers of sons, sharing our feelings and thoughts—and we urge women who aren't raising male children to consider our situation. I talk to such men as *will* talk, about their sense of the struggle, their memories of boyhood and growing up to masculinity. I collaborated with two other mothers to rent a film about adolescent male sexuality which we viewed with our sons. Though the film was disappointing, and only a few people came, we had a fine time. It was a good idea; we'll try another film. I organized a series of mother-and-son theater workshops. Again, only a few people came—but the program was a success. Though we came together because of our relationship as mothers and sons, we worked as peers, individuals in the group. This gave us another opportunity to see who we are and what we do outside of the family's roles. It was exciting and satisfying for all of us; Daniel and I both want to do it again.

We both go on trying to find out who we really are, as Daniel says, and trying to live as we really want to live. When and while we raise male children, mothers must take to ourselves the making of men. When and while our sons live out their lives, they must take upon themselves the responsibility of their manhood.

We have been trapped with our sons, imprisoned in false ways of being, blocked into "feminine" and "masculine" by a culture whose very language turns *mother* into mocking profanity, *son* into demeaning insult. But if sons can recognize that there is no danger to them inherent in the mother, discarding the layers of masculinity that cover their humanity, and if mothers will undertake the painful struggle to restore our integrity as women, then mothers and sons can begin to break the constraints of fear and anger between us.

We cannot live the lives the great-grandmothers lived, long times ago; women know this. And we know that men have gone far away from us; they have replaced their ancient respect for the mother with a desperate and abusive need of women. They have become aliens, strangers to their past and to our present. But when we learn that it has not always been so, we know that it need not always be so.

We can begin to speak a different word: We say that the sons may be wild and beautiful, exciting and tender, wise and loving. We say that the son of the mother is the young god—and that he can move through the world in harmony with her music.

Notes

British editions of the books quoted in these notes are listed in the Bibliography on page 303.

Chapter 1

1. Ruth Fainlight, from "Sleep-Learning," in *To See the Matter Clearly and Other Poems* (Chester Springs, Pa.: Dufour Editions, 1969).

2. Excerpt of letter from MOM (Mothers of Males), *New Women's Times*, Aug. 31–Sept. 13, 1979, p. 3.

3. Adrienne Rich, *Of Woman Born: Motherhood as Experience and Institution* (New York: W. W. Norton, 1976), p. 31.

4. Virginia Woolf, *The Waves* (New York: Harcourt Brace, 1959), pp. 206–7.

5. Violet Oaklander, *Windows to Our Children* (Moab, Utah: Real People Press, 1978).

Chapter 2

1. Linda Pastan, from "Fresco," in *The Five Stages of Grief: Poems* (New York: W. W. Norton, 1978), p. 27.

2. Jennifer Stone, correspondence with the writer, 1980.

3. Linda Wildmare, "Raising a Male Child," in *Women*, 7:1, 1980.

4. All of these citations are found in Judy Chicago, *The Dinner Party* (Garden City, N.Y., Anchor Press/Doubleday, 1980).

5. Louisa May Alcott, *Little Men* (1871; New York: Collier/Macmillan, 1962), p. 37.

6. Dorothy Dinnerstein, *The Mermaid and the Minotaur: Sexual Arrangements and Human Malaise* (New York: Harper & Row, 1977), p. 276.

7. See Margaret Mead, esp. *Sex and Temperament in Three Primitive Societies* (New York: William Morrow, 1963). Also Anne M. Seiden, "Research on the Psychology of Women," in *The American Journal of Psychiatry*, 133:10 (Oct. 1976), p. 997: "Despite the theoretical importance of intrinsic biological differences and the considerable belief in them . . . it is easier to demonstrate *belief* in these differences than the differences themselves." She cites findings that "fathers described their newborn daughters as 'delicate' and their

sons as 'strong' before they had seen the children," and that "mothers played differently with and observed different attributes in a strange child, depending on whether the child had been introduced as 'Beth' or 'Adam' . . . the plasticity of human behavior is such that many biological differences can be overcome by learning. And the variability of human behavior is such that there is considerably more variation within than between the sexes."

8. Carrie Carmichael and Lindsey Van Gelder, "But What About Our Sons?," *Ms.*, Oct. 1975, p. 52.

9. Sherry B. Ortner, "Is Female to Male as Nature Is to Culture?" in *Woman, Culture, and Society,* Michelle Zimbalist Rosaldo and Louise Lamphere, eds., (Stanford, Calif.: Stanford University Press, 1974), p. 67.

10. Philip Wylie, *Generation of Vipers* (New York: Rinehart, 1955).

11. Read Betty Friedan's *The Feminine Mystique,* Barbara Ehrenreich and Deirdre English's *For Her Own Good,* and Joe L. Dubbert's *A Man's Place.*

12. Wolfgang Lederer, *The Fear of Women* (New York: Harcourt Brace Jovanovich, 1968), p. 6.

13. Joe L. Dubbert, *A Man's Place* (Englewood Cliffs, N.J.: Prentice-Hall, 1979), Chapters 6, 7, 8.

14. Carmichael and Van Gelder, op. cit., p. 56.

15. Letty Cottin Pogrebin, in the New York *Times*, Aug. 27, 1979, "How Feminists Bring Up Their Sons," by Judy Klemesrud, p. C-15.

16. Jerry Kramer, *Instant Replay* (New York: New American Library, 1968), p. 2.

17. People of both sexes are happier and healthier when they can and do cry. Weeping helps us handle stress; men have a higher incidence of stress-related disorders than women. See research presented by William Gottlieb in "Have a Good Cry," *Prevention,* Aug. 1980, pp. 126–30.

18. Maxine Hong Kingston, *China Men* (New York: Ballantine Books, 1980), p. 251.

19. Adrienne Rich, *Of Woman Born* (New York: W. W. Norton, 1976).

20. But not everywhere and always. See Margaret Mead's work for the germinal studies; also Seiden, op. cit., "II, Women in Families, Work, and Psychotherapy," p. 1111. Dr. Seiden says: "For primary child care, contemporary American society is distinctly unusual in relying far more heavily than most cultures on mothers alone, with variable but relatively little participation by older children, husbands, and other kin."

21. Selma Greenburg, *Right from the Start* (Boston: Houghton Mifflin, 1979), p. 5.

22. From the traditional ballad "The Sweetest Gift: A Mother's Smile."

23. Evelyn Reed, *Woman's Evolution* (New York and London: Pathfinder Press, 1975).

24. Ibid., p. 14.

25. Rich, op. cit., p. 186.

26. Ibid.

Chapter 3

1. Susan B. Anthony, quoted in Ida Harper, *The Life and Work of Susan B. Anthony* (Indianapolis: Bowen-Merrill, 1898), vol. II, Appendix.

2. Kingston, op. cit., p. 268.

3. Michelle Zimbalist Rosaldo, "Woman, Culture, and Society: A Theoretical Overview," in Michelle Zimbalist Rosaldo and Louise Lamphere, eds., *Woman, Culture, and Society* (Stanford, Calif.: Stanford University Press, 1974), p. 28.

4. Evelyn Reed, *Woman's Evolution* (New York and London: Pathfinder Press, 1975), pp. 280–98.

5. Elizabeth Fisher, *Woman's Creation: Sexual Evolution and the Shaping of Society* (New York: McGraw-Hill, 1979), p. 156.

6. See Reed, Fisher, Rosaldo, Reiter, et al., and most traditional (patriarchal) anthropologists as well.

7. Fisher, op. cit.

8. Reed, op. cit., pp. 294–96.

9. Joseph Pleck and Jack Sawyer, eds., *Men and Masculinity* (Englewood Cliffs, N.J.: Prentice-Hall, 1974). Also see *Unbecoming Men*—Ewing, Rubin, Dubbert, et al.—in bibliography.

10. Ruth Hartley, "Sex-Role Pressures and the Socialization of the Male Child," pp. 7–13 of Pleck and Sawyer, op. cit.

11. Margaret Mead, *Sex and Temperament in Three Primitive Societies*, op. cit.

12. Susan Griffin, *Woman and Nature: The Roaring Inside Her* (New York: Harper & Row, 1978), p. 150.

13. Roger Ebert, Chicago *Sun-Times*, June 12, 1979, p. 4.

14. Gary Wills, Chicago *Sun-Times*, June 16, 1979, p. 26.

15. Marc Feigen-Fasteau, quoting Nancy Gager Clinch in *The Male Machine* (New York: Delta/Dell, 1975), p. 101.

16. Feigen-Fasteau, op. cit., p. 102.

17. Feigen-Fasteau, op. cit., p. 111.

18. Joe L. Dubbert, quoting Jonathan Daniels, advisor to Franklin Roosevelt, in *A Man's Place* (Englewood Cliffs, N.J.: Prentice-Hall, 1979), p. 230.

19. Feigen-Fasteau, op. cit., p. 114.

20. Jerry Kramer, op. cit.

21. Study by William Griffen, J. Marciano, and R. Knowles of twenty-eight textbooks used in the United States for history and civics classes, cited in *Winners and Losers* (see note 24, below; also specifically the books entitled *Promise of America: Sidewalks, Gunboats, and Ballyhoo; American History for Today;* and *The Free and the Brave*).

22. Traditional Scots-Irish ballad.

23. *Hearts and Minds,* directed by Peter Davis (Columbia Pictures, 1974).

24. Tran Thi Bich's story is from Gloria Emerson's book *Winners and Losers* (New York: Harvest/Harcourt, 1978), pp. 108–9.

25. Emerson, op. cit., pp. 364–68.

Chapter 4

1. Alta, in an interview by Jennifer Stone in *City Miner,* San Francisco.

2. Andrea Dworkin, *The New Woman's Broken Heart* (Palo Alto, Calif.: Frog in the Well, 1980), p. 46.

3. Urie Bronfenbrenner, "American Families: Trends and Pressures," in Urie Bronfenbrenner and J. C. Condrey, *Two Worlds of Childhood: U.S. and U.S.S.R.* (New York, Russell Sage Foundation, 1973).

4. Sherry B. Ortner, "Is Female to Male as Nature Is to Culture?" in Rosaldo and Lamphere, eds., *Woman, Culture, and Society* (Stanford, Calif.: Stanford University Press, 1974), p. 82. "Since father is almost always more remote than mother . . . building an identification with father involves a 'positional identification,' i.e., identification with father's male role as a collection of abstract elements, rather than a personal identification with father as a real individual."

5. David Steinberg, *Fatherjournal: Five Years of Awakening to Fatherhood* (Albion, Calif.: Times Change Press, 1977).

6. Linda Pastan, from "In the Old Guerrilla War," in *The Five Stages of Grief: Poems* (New York: W. W. Norton, 1978), p. 15.

7. The same process occurs in *daughters* as they regard their *mothers*, especially when the daughters become mothers themselves. See Arcana, *Our Mothers' Daughters*, esp. Chapter 7.

8. Again, the excusing of fathers *by daughters* in these same terms is a common theme in patriarchal families; see *Our Mothers' Daughters*, as above, esp. Chapter 5.

9. Chicago *Sun-Times*, May 5, 1981, p. 45, excerpted from Kathy Cronkite's book *On the Edge of the Spotlight* (New York: William Morrow, 1981).

Chapter 5

1. Merlin Stone, *Ancient Mirrors of Womanhood, II* (New York: New Sibylline Books, 1980), p. 25.

2. Starhawk, *The Spiral Dance* (New York: Harper & Row, 1979), p. 96.

3. Stone, op. cit., p. 64.

4. Ibid., p. 16.

5. Ibid., p. 37.

6. Ibid., p. 167.

7. Ibid., p. 92.

8. Ibid., p. 48, vol. I.

9. Ibid., p. 104.

10. Ibid., p. 27.

11. Starhawk, op. cit., pp. 2–3.

12. Stone, op. cit., p. 78, vol. I.

13. Ibid., p. 150.

14. Ibid., p. 173.

15. Ibid., p. 90.

16. Ibid., p. 168, vol. II.

17. Sir James Frazer, *The Golden Bough* (New York: Macmillan, 1963), p. 415.

18. Phyllis Chesler, *About Men* (New York: Simon & Schuster, 1978), pp. 42–43; see also Mary Daly, *Gyn/Ecology* (Boston: Beacon Press, 1978), p. 68, on transsexual counseling.

19. Frazer, op. cit., p. 404.

20. Ibid., p. 416.

21. Ibid., p. 437.

22. Ibid., p. 407.

23. Ibid., pp. 408–9.

24. See *The Golden Bough*, pp. 416, 418, 419, including Frazer's consideration that the rise of Buddhism followed the same order, displacing by encompassing the old Mother worship.

25. See Andrea Dworkin, *Take Back the Night;* Phyllis Chesler, *About Men*, and Martha Boesing's play *The Gelding* in *Journeys Along the Matrix*.

26. For contemporary images of the Primordial Goddess, see Judy Chicago's *The Dinner Party* and *Embroidering Our Heritage* and read Susan Griffin's *Woman and Nature*.

27. Stone, op. cit., pp. 101–2.

28. Frazer, op. cit., p. 379.

29. Stone, op. cit., I, p. 210.

30. See Evelyn Reed, *Woman's Evolution*, Chapters 6, 7, 10, 11, 12, 13, 16. This clash of kinship and power systems also necessitated the creation of tales about the killings of fathers, some of which went unpunished or were not considered crimes at all.

31. Aeschylus' Oresteian trilogy and Euripides' *Orestes*.

32. Aeschylus, *The Oresteian Trilogy*, translated by Philip Vellacott (New York: Penguin, 1956–79), all quotations from dialogue.

33. Reed, op. cit., p. 361.

34. Euripides, *Orestes and Other Plays*, translated by Philip Vellacott (New York: Penguin, 1972).

35. See *When God Was a Woman, The Golden Bough, Ancient Mirrors of Womanhood* (both vols.).

36. Reed, op. cit., p. 319.

37. See Reed, op. cit., p. 304: "In the earliest stage of matrimony the husband was little more than a visitor to his wife's community"; p. 321, "a man . . . had few rights as a husband and none as a father to his wife's children"; p. 341, "Paternity [later] began as a social relationship between a woman's husband and her child"; and so on. Also see Chapter 3 of Arcana, *Our Mothers' Daughters*.

38. Bronislaw Malinowski, *Sex and Repression in Savage Society* (New York: Meridian, 1927, 1960), pp. 101–3.

39. See Frazer, op. cit., esp. Chapter 26, and Reed, op. cit., esp. pp. 398–407.

40. Wolfgang Lederer, *The Fear of Women* (New York: Harcourt Brace Jovanovich, 1968), p. 273.

41. Whose quoted work is called *The Fear of Being a Woman* (!).

42. Erich Neumann, *Origins and History of Consciousness* (New York: Pantheon Books, 1964), p. 168.

43. Ibid., pp. 157–58.

44. Ibid., p. 63.

45. Lederer, op. cit., p. 41.

46. Ibid., p. 249.

47. Muriel Rukeyser, "Myth," *Breaking Open* (New York: Random House, 1973), p. 20.

48. See Chesler, op. cit., Epilogue.

49. Felix Salten, *Bambi* (New York: Grossett & Dunlap, 1929), pp. 60–62.

50. Ibid., p. 81.

51. Ibid., p. 250.

52. Ibid., pp. 286–87.

Chapter 6

1. Susan Griffin, op. cit., p. 150.

2. Iris Andreski, *Old Wives' Tales* (New York: Schocken Books, 1970), p. 57.

3. Viewed January 5, 1980, *Julia Warhola, 1974* (New York: Whitney Museum).

4. One of the most recent studies showing men's views of women and feelings about women is Shere Hite, *The Hite Report on Male Sexuality* (New York: Knopf, 1981).

5. These are men who responded affirmatively to my request to interview them, with a tape recorder, for two or more hours, about their lives with their mothers and their feelings about their mothers. Several were men I knew slightly; a few were men I knew well. Most were strangers to me. In any interview group, "scientifically" structured or informal like this one, the subjects are self-selected—through sometimes, as in prisons or colleges, under great pressure. Perhaps those men who said no to me, or the men I never asked, would have given very different answers, revealed feelings markedly different from these. Given the correlation between these interviews and literature, I doubt it. (See Bibliography.)

6. See Hite, op. cit.

7. "Most men liked marriage for the domestic warmth and security, and the stability and regularity of home life, having someone there to help and care for them . . ." (*Hite Report*, p. 208).

8. Dinnerstein, op. cit., p. 217.

9. Lincoln Steffens, *The Autobiography of Lincoln Steffens*, Vol. I (New York: Harcourt, Brace, 1931), as printed in *A Book of Men*, ed. Ross Firestone (New York: Stonehill, 1978), p. 120.

10. See Daly's *Gyn/Ecology* and Dworkin's *Woman Hating*.

11. See Daly, Dworkin, Barry, Griffin, Chesler, Brownmiller, Rich, et al.

12. See Rich, and, in *The Lost Tradition*, see Cathy Davidson's essay, "Mothers and Daughters in the Fiction of the New Republic."

13. See Del Martin, *Battered Wives;* Leonore E. Walker, *The Battered Woman;* and Jennifer Baker Fleming, *Stopping Wife Abuse*.

14. See Barry, *Female Sexual Slavery*.

15. See contemporary men's fear of teeth in *The Hite Report*, pp. 532, 534, and this, on p. 542: "To have the penis in the control of another person may be appealing and pleasurable in many ways, but it can also be inhibiting—particularly to the kind of man with a profound distrust of his own potential passivity"—from one of Hite's male respondents.

16. Daly, op. cit., p. 317.

17. Chesler, op. cit., p. 76.

18. The other kind of acceptance is reflected in writer Ernest Hemingway's comment in a letter to Scott Fitzgerald: "Summer's a discouraging time to work—You don't feel death coming on the way it does in the fall when the boys really put pen to paper." New York *Times Magazine*, Feb. 15, 1981.

19. Stone, op. cit., II, p. 76.

20. Chesler, op. cit., p. 221 note.

21. Andrea Dworkin, *Woman Hating* (New York: E. P. Dutton, 1974), p. 44.

22. Daly, op. cit., p. 413.

23. Dworkin, op. cit., p. 35.

24. Chesler, op. cit., p. 212.

25. Ibid.

26. *Hite Report, Males*.

27. Virginia Woolf, *A Room of One's Own* (New York: Harcourt, Brace and World, 1963), pp. 34–37.

28. Bill Raspberry, Chicago *Tribune*, March 8, 1979, "American Moms and Their Sons."

29. Michele Wallace, *Black Macho and the Myth of the Superwoman* (New York: Warner Books, 1979).

30. The level of public acceptance of this stereotype, and the belief that the situation constitutes a *joke*, is the basis for the syndicated comic

strip "Momma," by Mel Lazarus. The typical strip depicts Momma as scheming, manipulative, selfish, and self-pitying—while her son is eternally her guilty victim.

31. John Leonard, "Private Lives," New York *Times*, March 5, 1980.

32. Ibid.

33. Audre Lorde, "Manchild: A Black Lesbian Feminist's Response," in *Conditions*, 4, 1979.

34. Adrienne Rich, *Of Woman Born*, Chapters 6 and 7; also Suzanne Arms, *Immaculate Deception*.

Chapter 7

1. Lorde, op. cit.

2. Their need for mothers, who raised them, does seem to be different, though. Discussing children's need for frequent and regular visits from absent parents, one psychologist said, "Little boys, ages six to eight, are . . . most vulnerable. . . . They experience longing for their fathers with almost physical intensity. . . . But, where the missing parent was the *mother*, we found the same intense longing and unhappiness—*except even more so*—in the child if he didn't receive frequent visits." (My italics.) Judith Wallerstein, quoted by Bella Stumbo of the Los Angeles *Times*, reprinted in the Chicago *Sun-Times*, "Visiting Kids Called Vital in Divorce," Oct. 9, 1978.

3. See, for instance, Phil Donahue, "When a Father Gets Custody," *The Ann Landers Encyclopedia* (Garden City, N.Y.: Doubleday, 1978).

4. Aaron Esman, quoted in *New Women's Times*, 6:12, June 6–20, 1980.

5. Lorde, op. cit.

6. Lucy Stone, speaking at a National Women's Rights Convention in Cincinnati, in 1855.

7. See Van Gelder and Carmichael in *Ms.*, Judy Klemesrud in the New York *Times*, Linda Wildmare in *Women*.

8. See Arcana, *Our Mothers' Daughters*, Chapters 1 and 2.

9. As in the Middle Ages, when men *accused* of homosexuality were burned at the feet of women being burned as witches; hence "faggots"; see Robin Morgan's notes on *Double-F, A Magazine of Effeminism*, in *Going Too Far* (New York: Random House, 1978), p. 235.

10. Wayne Ewing, *Changing Men: Mission Impossible?* (Denver: The Research Center on Women, 1978).

11. Julie Ellinger, quoted by Richard Phillips in "Oh Boy, Babies!", the Chicago *Tribune*, Feb. 22, 1981.

12. Richard Phillips in "Oh Boy, Babies!", the Chicago *Tribune*, Feb. 22, 1981.

13. Student in Babies class, quoted by Richard Phillips, ibid.

14. Gloria Emerson, *Winners and Losers* (New York: Harvest/Harcourt, 1978), p. 195.

15. See Laurel Holliday, *The Violent Sex*.

16. There is much, as my son grows older, beyond even compromise. He frequents electronic games with his buddies, all of them being trained to seek out and destroy enemies by machine, in zip-zap cartoon fashion. These boys will be even more removed than the Vietnam bomber pilots, when they are asked to kill by pushing buttons and pulling levers.

Bibliography

Entries marked with an asterisk (*) are those which were especially useful to me in the writing of this book, either for their content or for their inspirational value.

Aeschylus. *The Oresteian Trilogy.* New York and Harmondsworth: Penguin, 1956-1979.

Alcott, Louisa May. *Little Men.* New York: Collier Books, 1962; London: Octopus Books, 1978.

―――――. *Jo's Boys.* Garden City, N.Y.: Doubleday, 1957.

Anderson, Sherwood. *Winesburg, Ohio.* New York: Viking, 1968; Harmondsworth: Penguin, 1977.

*Andreski, Iris. *Old Wives' Tales.* New York: Schocken Books, 1970.

Arcana, Judith. *Our Mothers' Daughters.* Berkeley, Calif.: Shameless Hussy Press, 1979; London: The Women's Press, 1981.

Arnow, Harriette. *The Dollmaker.* New York: Avon Books, 1972; London: Heinemann, 1955.

Bambara, Toni Cade. *The Black Woman.* New York: New American Library, 1970.

Bart, Pauline B. "Depression in Middle Aged Women (a.k.a. Portnoy's Mother's Complaint," in *Woman in Sexist Society*, ed. Vivian Gornick and B.K. Moran. New York: Basic Books, 1971, pp. 99-117.

Bible: The Old and New Testaments and the Apocrypha.

*Boesing, Martha. *The Gelding*, in *Journeys Along the Matrix: Three Plays.* Minneapolis: Vanilla Press, 1978.

*Bouton, Jim. *Ball Four Plus Ball Five.* Briarcliff Manor, N.Y.: Stein & Day, 1981.

Bradley, Marion Zimmer. "The Wind People," in *Women of Wonder.* Edited by Pamela Sargent. New York: Vintage Books/Random House, 1975; Harmondsworth: Penguin, 1978.

Bradley, Mike; Danchik, Lonnie; Fager, Mart; and Wodetzki, Tom. *Unbecoming Men: A Men's Consciousness Raising Group Writes on Oppression and Themselves.* New York: Times Change Press, 1971.

Brindel, June Rachuy. *Ariadne: A Novel of Ancient Crete.* New York: St. Martin's Press, 1980.

Brownmiller, Susan. *Against Our Will: Men, Women, and Rape.* New York: Simon & Schuster, 1975; Harmondsworth: Penguin, 1977.

Budapest, Z. "The Sacred Sons," "The Spell to the Force," "Acceptance of Manhood," and "Acceptance of Matriarchal Manhood," in *The Holy Book of Women's Mysteries: Part II.* Los Angeles: Susan B. Anthony Coven Number 1, 1980.

*Chesler, Phyllis. *About Men.* New York: Simon & Schuster, 1978; London: The Women's Press, 1979.

_____ *Women and Madness.* Garden City, N.Y.: Doubleday, 1972.

Chicago, Judy. *The Dinner Party.* Garden City, N.Y.: Anchor Press/Doubleday, 1980.

Colette. *"Chéri" and "The Last of Chéri."* New York and Baltimore: Penguin, 1974; Harmondsworth: Penguin, 1968, 1969.

Daly, Mary. *Gyn/Ecology: The Metaethics of Radical Feminism.* Boston: Beacon Press, 1978; London: The Women's Press, 1979.

*Demeter, Anna. *Legal Kidnaping.* Boston: Beacon Press, 1977.

Dinnerstein, Dorothy. *The Mermaid and the Minotaur: Sexual Arrangements and Human Malaise.* New York: Harper & Row, 1977; as *The Rocking of the Cradle,* London: Souvenir Press, 1978.

*Dubbert, Joe L. *A Man's Place.* Englewood Cliffs, N.J.: Prentice-Hall, 1979.

Dworkin, Andrea. *Woman Hating.* New York: Dutton, 1974.

Ehrenreich, Barbara, and English, Deirdre. *For Her Own Good: 150 Years of the Experts' Advice to Women.* Garden City, N.Y.: Anchor Press/Doubleday, 1979; London: Pluto Press, 1979.

*Emerson, Gloria. *Winners and Losers: Battles, Retreats, Gains, Losses and Ruins from a Long War.* New York: Random House, 1976.

Euripides. *Orestes,* in *Orestes and Other Plays.* Baltimore: Penguin, 1972;   Harmondsworth: Penguin, 1972.

_____ *Medea* and *Hippolytus,* in *Three Great Plays of Euripides,* New York: Mentor Books, 1958. *Medea,* London: Oxford University Press, 1977; *Hippolytus,* London: Heinemann, 1980.

Ewing, Wayne A. *Changing Men: Mission Impossible?* Denver: The Research Center on Women, 1978.

*Feigen-Fasteau, Marc. *The Male Machine*. New York: Delta Books/-Dell, 1975.

*Firestone, Ross, ed. *A Book of Men: Visions of the Male Experience*. New York: Stonehill, 1978; Edinburgh: Mainstream Publishing Co., 1979.

*Fisher, Elizabeth. *Woman's Creation: Sexual Evolution and the Shaping of Society*. Garden City, N.Y.: Anchor Press/Doubleday, 1979; New York: McGraw-Hill, 1979.

*Frazer, Sir James George. *The Golden Bough: A Study in Magic and Religion*. New York: Macmillan, 1963; London: Macmillan, 1980.

Greenberg, Selma. *Right from the Start*. Boston: Houghton Mifflin, 1979.

Griffin, Susan. *Woman and Nature: The Roaring Inside Her*. New York: Harper & Row, 1978.

Guest, Judith. *Ordinary People*. New York: Ballantine Books, 1976; London: Collins, 1977; Fontana, 1978.

Hamilton, Edith. *Mythology*. New York: Mentor Books, 1969.

Hapgood, Fred. *Why Males Exist. An Inquiry into the Evolution of Sex*. New York: Mentor Books, 1979.

Hite, Shere. *The Hite Report on Male Sexuality*. New York: Knopf, 1981; London: MacDonald, 1981.

Holliday, Laurel. *The Violent Sex: Male Psychobiology and the Evolution of Consciousness*. Guernville, Calif.: Bluestocking Books, 1978.

*Hurston, Zora Neale. *Their Eyes Were Watching God*. Urbana: University of Illinois Press, 1978; London: Dent, 1938.

_____*Mules and Men*. Bloomington: Indiana University Press, 1963, 1978.

Ibsen, Henrik. *Ghosts*, in *Ghosts and Other Plays*. New York: Penguin, 1978; London: Eyre Methuen, 1973.

*Kingston, Maxine Hong. *China Men*. New York: Alfred A. Knopf, 1980; London: Pan Books, 1981.

_____ *The Woman Warrior*. New York: Vintage Books/Random House, 1976; London: Allen Lane, 1977.

Klemesrud, Judy. "How Feminists Bring Up Their Sons," *New York Times*, Aug. 27, 1979.

Kramer, Jerry. *Instant Replay*. New York: New American Library, 1968.

*Lang, Andrew, ed. *The Blue Fairy Book*. New York: Dover Publications, 1965; Harmondsworth: Kestrel, 1975.

_____ *The Red Fairy Book*. New York: Dover Publications, 1965;

Harmondsworth: Kestrel, 1976.

————— *The Grey Fairy Book*. New York: Dover Publications, 1965; London: Longman, 1900.

————— *The Lilac Fairy Book*. New York: Dover Publications, 1965; London: Longman, 1910.

————— *The Green Fairy Book*. New York: Dover Publication, 1965; Harmondsworth: Kestrel, 1978.

Lawrence, D.H. *Sons and Lovers*. New York: Signet Books, 1960; Harmondsworth: Penguin, 1976.

————— "The Rocking Horse Winner," in *The Short Story Reader*. Edited by R.A. Kimball. New York: Odyssey Press, 1961; and in *The Ghost Book* compiled by Lady Cynthia Asquith, London: Hutchinson, 1926.

Lederer, Laura, ed. *Take Back the Night*. New York: Morrow, 1980.

*Lederer, Wolfgang. *The Fear of Women*. New York and London: Grune & Stratton, 1968.

Lerner, Gerda. *Black Women in White America*. New York: Vintage Books/Random House, 1973.

Lessing, Doris. *The Four-Gated City*. New York: Knopf, 1969; London: Michael Joseph, 1974.

————— *The Golden Notebook*. New York: Ballantine Books, 1972; London: Michael Joseph, 1972.

*Lorde, Audre. "Manchild: A Black Lesbian Feminist's Response," in *Conditions*, 4, 1979.

*Mead, Margaret. *Sex and Temperament in Three Primitive Societies*. New York: Morrow, 1963; London: Routledge Kegan Paul, 1977.

*Meggyesy, David. *Out of Their League*. Berkeley: Ramparts Press, 1970.

*Miller, Arthur. *Death of a Salesman*. New York: Penguin, 1980; Harmondsworth: Penguin, 1976.

————— *All My Sons*, in *Arthur Miller's Collected Plays*. New York: Viking, 1957; Harmondsworth: Penguin, 1961.

Montagu, Ashley, ed. *Sociobiology Examined*. Oxford: Oxford University Press, 1980.

*Moraga, Cherríe, and Anzaldúa, Gloria. *This Bridge Called My Back: Writings by Radical Women of Color*. Watertown, Mass.: Persephone Press, 1981.

Morgan, Robin. *Going Too Far*. New York: Vintage Books/Random House, 1978.

Paley, Grace. *Enormous Changes at the Last Minute*. New York: Dell, 1974; London: Virago, 1979.

*Pleck, Joseph H., and Sawyer, Jack, eds. *Men and Masculinity*. Englewood Cliffs, N.J.: Prentice-Hall, 1974.

Raspberry, Bill. "American Moms and Their Sons," Chicago *Tribune*, Mar 8, 1979.

Rawlings, Marjorie Kinnan. "A Mother in Mannville," in *The Short Story Reader*. Edited by R.A. Kimball. New York: Odyssey Press, 1961.

———— *The Yearling*. New York: Scribner's, 1938; London: Pan Books, 1976.

*Reed, Evelyn. *Woman's Evolution*. New York and London: Pathfinder Press, 1975.

Reiter, Rayna R. *Toward an Anthropology of Women*. New York and London: Monthly Review Press, 1975.

Renault, Mary. *Return to Night*. New York: Morrow, 1947; London: Longmans Green & Co., 1947.

———— *The Bull from the Sea*. New York: Vintage Books/Random House, 1975; Harmondsworth: Penguin, 1973.

———— *The King Must Die*. New York: Bantam Books, 1978; London: New English Library, 1966.

———— *Fire from Heaven*. New York: Pantheon Books, 1969; Harlow: Longmans, 1977.

Rich, Adrienne. *Of Woman Born: Motherhood as Experience and Institution*. New York: Norton, 1976; London: Virago, 1977.

———— *On Lies, Secrets and Silence*. New York: Norton, 1979.

Rosaldo, Michelle Zimbalist, and Lamphere, Louise, eds. *Women, Culture, and Society*. Stanford: Stanford University Press, 1974.

Roth, Philip. *Portnoy's Complaint*. New York: Bantam Books, 1970; London: Jonathan Cape, 1969.

*Rubin, Michael. *Men Without Masks: Writing from the Journals of Modern Men*. Reading, Mass.: Addison-Wesley, 1980.

*Salten, Felix. *Bambi*. New York: Grosset & Dunlap, 1929; Leicester: Knight Books, 1976.

Saperstein, Alan. *Mom Kills Kids and Self*. New York: Ballantine Books, 1979.

Shakespeare, William. *Hamlet*, in *Shakespeare: The Complete Works*. Edited by G. B. Harrison. New York: Harcourt, Brace and World, 1952.

*Shange, Ntozake. *For Colored Girls Who Have Considered Suicide When the Rainbow Is Enuf: A Choreopoem*. New York: Macmillan, 1977; London: Eyre Methuen, 1978.

Sloan, Bernard. *The Best Friend You'll Ever Have*. New York: Crown, 1980.

Sophocles. *Oedipus*, in *The Theban Plays*. New York: Penguin, 1978 and in *The Three Theban Plays*, London: Allen Lane, 1982.

Sprenger, James, and Kramer, Heinrich. *The Malleus Maleficarum*. London: Arrow Books, 1971.

*Starhawk. *The Spiral Dance*. New York: Harper & Row, 1979.

Steinbeck, John. *East of Eden*. London and New York: Penguin, 1979; London: Heinemann, 1970; Pan, 1963.

Stone, Jennifer. *Over by the Caves*. Berkeley, Calif.: Berkeley Poets Workshop and Press, 1977.

*Stone, Merlin. *When God Was a Woman*. New York: Harvest Books, 1976; as *The Paradise Papers*, London: Virago, 1979.

————— *Ancient Mirrors of Womanhood: Our Goddess and Heroine Heritage*. Vols. I and II. New York: New Sibylline Books, 1979 and 1980.

Turgenev, Ivan. *Fathers and Sons*. Geneva: Heron Books, 1962; London: Bantam, 1959, 1981.

Twain, Mark. *Huckleberry Finn*. New York: Signet Classics, 1959; Harmondsworth: Penguin, 1977.

————— *Tom Sawyer*. New York: Rainbow Classics, 1947; London: Hamlyn, 1977.

*Van Gelder, Lindsey, and Carmichael, Carrie. "But What About Our Sons?", *Ms.*, Oct. 1975.

Walker, Alice. *In Love and Trouble: Stories of Black Women*. New York: Harcourt Brace Jovanovich, 1973.

————— *Meridian*. New York: Harcourt Brace Jovanovich, 1970; London: The Women's Press, 1982.

Wallace, Michele. *Black Macho and the Myth of the Superwoman*. New York: Warner Books, 1979; London: John Calder, 1979.

Washington, Mary Helen. *Black-Eyed Susans: Classic Stories By and About Black Women*. Garden City, N.Y.: Anchor Press/Doubleday, 1975.

White, T.H. *The Once and Future King* (esp. "The Queen of Air and Darkness"). New York: Putman, 1958; London: Collins, 1978.

*Wildmare, Linda. "Raising a Male Child," *Women*, Vol. 7:1 ("Survival With and Without Men"), 1980.

*Williams, Juanita H., ed. *Psychology of Women: Selected Readings* (esp. Freud's essay on Femininity, and Mead's criticism of Freud's essay). New York: Norton, 1979.

Williams, Tennessee. *The Glass Menagerie*. New York: New Directions, 1970; Harmondsworth: Penguin, 1962.

*Wolfe, Tom. *The Right Stuff*. New York: Farrar, Straus and Giroux, 1979; London: Cape, 1979.

Woolf, Virginia. *Roger Fry: A Biography*. New York: Harvest Books, 1976; Harmondsworth: Penguin, 1979.

_____ *To the Lighthouse*. New York: Harcourt, Brace and World, 1955; London: Hogarth Press, 1977.

_____ *Three Guineas*. New York: Harcourt, Brace and World, 1966; Harmondsworth: Penguin, 1977.

_____ *A Room of One's Own*. New York: Harcourt, Brace and World, 1963; St. Albans: Triad, 1977.

_____ *Jacob's Room and The Waves*. New York: Harcourt, Brace and World, 1959; St. Albans: Triad, 1976 and 1977.

Yamada, Mitsuye. *Camp Notes*. Berkeley, Calif.: Shameless Hussy Press, 1975.

Zyda, Joan. "Women Behind 'Mama's Boys,' " Chicago *Tribune*, Aug. 13, 1978.

Index